TAMING CANNIBALS

TAMING CANNIBALS

Race and the Victorians

Patrick Brantlinger

Cornell University Press
Ithaca and London

First published 2011 by Cornell University Press
First paperback printing 2019
Printed in the United States of America

Library of Congress Cataloging-in-Publication Data

Brantlinger, Patrick, 1941–
    Taming cannibals : race and the Victorians / Patrick Brantlinger.
        p. cm.
    Includes bibliographical references and index.
    ISBN 978-0-8014-5019-8 (cloth : alk. paper)
    ISBN 978-1-5017-3089-4 (pbk. : alk. paper)
    1. English literature—19th century—History and criticism.
2. Cannibalism in literature.   3. Race in literature.   4. Racism in
literature.   5. Cannibalism—History—19th century.   6. Race
relations—Great Britain—History—19th century.   I. Title.
    PR468.C28B73   2011
    305.800941—dc22   2011009588

To the Memory of Edward Said

Contents

Part IV. Ancient and Future Races

Acknowledgments

I am grateful to many friends, colleagues, students, librarians, and editors who have given me ideas and information over the years in regard to my Victorian and postcolonial studies projects. These include Nancy Armstrong, Todd Avery, Sarah Bilston, Daniel Bivona, Florence Boos, Howard Booth, Eva Cherniavsky, Laura Chrisman, Mary Jean Corbett, L. Perry Curtis, Martin Danahay, Deirdre David, Gaurav Desai, Jonathan Elmer, Rob Fulk, Regenia Gagnier, Helen Gilbert, Pamela Gilbert, John Glendening, Shane Graham, Maurice Hewitt, David Higgins, Richard Higgins, Josephine Ho, George Hutchinson, Pranav Jani, Martin Jay, David Johnson, Anna Johnston, Chris Keep, Hussein Khadim, Peggy Knapp, Paula Krebs, Ivan Kreilkamp, Todd Kuchta, John Kucich, Bob Langenfeld, Jil Larson, Andrew Libby, Ania Loomba, Teresa Mangum, Joss Marsh, Sara Maurer, Brook Miller, Jim Naremore, Bikhu Parekh, Sang-ki Park, Linda Peterson, Jan Nederveen Pieterse, Tom Prasch, Don Randall, Brian Rasmussen, John Reed, Henry Reynolds, Suk-koo Rhee, Lee Ann Richardson, Ranu Samantrai, Cannon Schmitt, Joanne Shattuck, Janet Sorensen, Bill Thesing, Chris Tiffin, Yung-hsing Wu, Dan Wylie, and Tania Zulli.

I also thank the editors of *English Literature in Transition* and *History and Anthropology* for permission to include revised portions of articles from those journals in *Taming Cannibals.* Thanks as well to Aracne, the publisher of Tania Zulli's anthology of essays on H. Rider Haggard's *She,* and Quintus, the publisher of Anna Johnston and Mitchell Rolls's anthology *Reading Robinson,* for permission to include revised portions of essays from those works.

I am especially grateful to Purnima Bose for encouraging me to become more fully engaged in postcolonial studies, and also to Martha Vicinus. When Martha turned over the editorship of *Victorian Studies* to me in 1980, she had commissioned most of the essays for a special issue on the British Empire. As I finished editing that issue, I began teaching the graduate seminars that became the basis for *Rule of Darkness: British Literature and Imperialism* (1988). And as always, Ellen Brantlinger has helped in countless ways.

Introduction

Race and the Victorians

For nothing more glorious...can be handed down to the future than to tame
the barbarian, to bring back the savage...to the fellowship of civil existence.

RICHARD HAKLUYT

Four hundred years of conquest and looting, four centuries of being told that
you are superior to the Fuzzy-Wuzzies and the wogs, leave their stain. This
stain has seeped into every part of [British] culture, the language and daily
life; and nothing much has been done to wash it out.

SALMAN RUSHDIE

Taming Cannibals is the third in a trilogy of studies that I have published
dealing with race and imperialism in British culture from about 1800 into
the modern era. *Rule of Darkness* (1988) explored the relations between
imperialism and literature with reference to different territories and issues (the exploration of central Africa, the Indian "Mutiny," emigration
to Australia, and so forth). It investigated some of the intricate and often
contradictory connections between abolitionism and liberalism on the one
hand, and imperialism and racism on the other. It also dealt with a wide
range of literary forms such as maritime novels, "imperial Gothic" fiction,
and Joseph Conrad's impressionism. *Dark Vanishings* (2003) analyzed the
pervasive discourse of blaming the victim that treated many indigenous
populations as causing their own extinction. Savagery was supposedly
a principal cause; besides warfare, savages practiced infanticide, widow

strangling, and cannibalism, all held to be self-exterminating customs. It was frequently also asserted that many or perhaps all "primitive races" were doomed by the forward march of "the white man" and "civilization." In literature, proleptic elegies—mourning dying races before they had actually expired—became common. Scientific racism, as in Charles Darwin's *Descent of Man* (1871), sought to explain why some primitive races such as the Aborigines of Tasmania were in fact perishing.

In contrast to these earlier studies, *Taming Cannibals* focuses on various contradictions inherent in racist and imperialist ideology. For many Victorians, the idea of taming cannibals or civilizing savages was oxymoronic: civilization was a goal that the nonwhite peoples of the world could not attain or, at best, could only approximate as "mimic men." And yet the "civilizing mission" was viewed as the ultimate justification for imperialism. Another contradiction is evident in the widely shared opinion that race provided the main explanatory key to history; this opinion was ordinarily coupled with white supremacism or Anglo-Saxonism. But many commentators recognized that modern races had resulted from centuries of intermixing; as Daniel Defoe insisted in "The True-Born Englishman" (1701), the English are "a Mongrel half-bred Race." Furthermore, with the widespread acceptance of evolutionary theory, it was often asserted that today's Anglo-Saxons might be superseded by something superior—an even "fitter" or "higher" race or species. But the Anglo-Saxons might also be superseded by some degenerate caricature of themselves, perhaps an apish avatar like the "white chimpanzees" Charles Kingsley claimed he saw in Ireland. If Count Dracula had his way, humans might even be superseded by the diabolical race of the living dead. In the period from about 1860 to 1914, white supremacism was contradicted and undermined by fears about white, or more specifically English, racial degeneration.

Against Colorblind History

In Defoe's *Robinson Crusoe* (1719), the white hero saves black Friday from the cannibals. Friday himself is a cannibal, but after his rescue he grows tame and slavishly loyal to his savior. Several features of Friday's story are frequently repeated in later colonial discourse: cannibalism is the absolute nadir of human behavior; it is practiced by black or brown savages but not by white Christians, who are horrified by it; cannibals need to be saved from themselves (they are self-exterminating, with or without warring against Europeans); if they can't all be tamed, it is still worth taming just one, both because a soul will be saved and because a tame cannibal will be a thoroughly grateful servant to his white master.

Before his shipwreck and island exile, Crusoe engages in the slave trade—a trade that Defoe invested in—and is himself enslaved by a "Moor" after Barbary Coast pirates capture him. Robinson escapes and later purchases a "plantation" in Brazil, which he farms with the help of an African slave.[1] Defoe's novel is not the first text to express white racist assumptions about dark others in relation to cannibalism, slavery, and colonialism. Such assumptions are both expressed and contested in Aphra Behn's *Oroonoko; or, The Royal Slave* (1688). Her black hero is not a cannibal but is instead a version of the antithetical stereotype, "the noble savage," a phrase John Dryden coined in 1672.[2] In any event, the popularity of Defoe's novel suggests that by the early 1700s, racist assumptions, including the belief that savages are likely to be cannibals, were widespread among the British public. As numerous scholars have shown, moreover, scientific racism did not emerge with the "new imperialism" in the 1880s or even with controversies over slavery in the West Indies and the American South. It emerged instead during the Enlightenment (Hannaford; Poliakov; Valls).

In common with social class and gender distinctions, racial distinctions have affected all aspects of modern, Western cultures. (Britain is hardly alone in this regard.) Although historians used to downplay or ignore racism as a factor in domestic British culture and even in the colonies, the advent of the "new imperial history" and of postcolonial studies in the late 1970s has altered the picture. Still, many recent historians take a gingerly approach to the subject of racism. In the introduction to *The Nineteenth Century* (volume three of the 1999 *Oxford History of the British Empire*), Andrew Porter writes: "At the levels both of Empire and colony, the definition of races...held *enormous potential* for justifying rule, generating unity, and for establishing practices of political or administrative exclusion" (22; my emphasis). The phrase "enormous potential" is puzzling, because "justifying rule" was a major function of the racist "definition of races." Porter also makes the standard claim that racism in the colonies, and presumably in the metropole, was strongest between the 1890s and World War I, which is probably true, but can be taken to imply that it was not much of a factor before then. Moreover, he expresses this late-century strengthening of racism as "concern about racialism," writing, "Late-nineteenth-century British concern about racialism was prompted by dislike of its crudity and accompanying violence" (23). One wonders who exactly expressed this "concern," when "racialism" was supposedly at its most virulent? Also, "racialism" is a dodgy term, though perhaps Porter believes that it is more neutral or objective than "racism."

Porter states as well that the British only "gradually abandoned the late-eighteenth-century consensus that the hierarchy of human societies rested on *cultural* not racial differences" (24). Or was the "consensus" closer to David Hume's belief that "there never was a civilized nation of any other complexion than white" and that "negroes" have no "ingenuity" and are at best "parrots" (86)? Enlightenment thinkers did not have a clear biological explanation for race, but in attempting to explain racial differences, they did not stress "cultural" over "natural" factors.[3] As Henry Pye put it in his poem "The Progress of Refinement" (1783), "The African no culture boasts" (quoted in Young 34), which is exactly what Hume and Kant believed and what Hegel would assert in his lectures on the philosophy of history. In the 1700s, natural historians such as J. F. Blumenbach began to place human varieties and races in hierarchies along with other organisms; the white race always came out on top. These hierarchies, moreover, adumbrated evolutionary theory. Linnaeus included apes in his version of *Homo sapiens,* and Lord Monboddo speculated that orangutans could mate with humans (Banton, *Racial Theories* 4–5). But the relationship of present-day races to the biblical story of Creation was debatable, as were also the effects of climate, location, and culture on racial variation.

Like Defoe, John Locke invested in the slave trade, and he served as a colonial administrator. He helped to forge the racial justification for slavery by coauthoring a document declaring the "absolute power and Authority" of every "freeman of Carolina" over his "Negro Slaves" (quoted in Bernasconi and Mann 92). In his *Two Treatises of Government* (1689), the restrictions Locke places on the practice of slavery seem to pertain only to prisoners of war and not to African slaves (Bernasconi and Mann 96). Also germane is Locke's convenient argument about "the Indians." If later Enlightenment thinkers did not make clear distinctions between cultural and natural or biological factors in causing racial variation, neither did Locke. He argued, however, that because they don't use money and do not cultivate the land, the Indians do not have any conception of property; they do not own anything. They also do not need all of the vast tracts they roam over. Those tracts are, says Locke, mere "waste lands"; they will lie fallow until colonizers arrive to cultivate them and thus turn them into property. Locke's argument was useful not just to the colonizers of North America but in Australia, where the legal doctrine of *terra nullius*—meaning that the Aborigines did not possess any of that continent—was in force until the High Court overturned it in the 1992 Eddie Mabo Land Rights case (Reynolds, *Law* 185–202).

In his *Essay on the History of Civil Society* (1767), Adam Ferguson agreed with Locke when he declared that "the savage" is "not yet acquainted with property," while "the barbarian," though property is "not yet ascertained by law," knows what it is to be poor or rich (149). Quite simply, "property is a matter of progress," or rather, as later in Adam Smith, desire for it is the chief cause of progress (149). At the same time, for Ferguson savagery "is not any permanent station, but a mere stage through which [all societies are] destined to pass" (14). While Ferguson's stadial theory of progress may be interpreted as cultural, much depends on climate and its effects on "the human frame." He suggests that it is no accident that the savages and barbarians of the world are located in intemperate regions, the tropics or the Arctic. Furthermore, although savages and barbarians may eventually leave behind their "rude" condition and join the "respectable" nations of Europe, that they have not progressed on their own and may very well need the assistance of Europeans to achieve civilization implies their natural inferiority, just as it would later do after Darwin's theory of evolution was well established and when the phrase "backward races" became familiar. It may be humbling to acknowledge, with Ferguson, that "the inhabitants of Britain, at the time of the first Roman invasions, resembled...the present natives of North America" (137), but it is also a matter of self-congratulation that the British have progressed from rudeness to respectability.

During the Romantic period (ca. 1790–1830), the idea that racial differences were determined by natural causes became further entrenched among British intellectuals. Samuel Taylor Coleridge, for example, who in the late 1790s had studied under Blumenbach at Göttingen University, combined the biblical account of Creation with natural or physical causation to explain what he viewed as the "degeneration" of all existing races from the perfect human specimens God had originally made (Kitson

38–44). The "Caucasian" race remained closest to perfection but had still degenerated. "The Boschesman in the wilds of Caffari or the New Hollanders" of Australia had degenerated the most (Coleridge quoted in Kitson 42). Theories of racial degeneration were contrary to theories of social progress like Ferguson's, but degeneration seemed logical to those who believed that all of the races of the world had sprung from Adam and Eve.

As have many other critics, in his study of race and Romantic literature, Peter Kitson stresses the racial otherness of Victor Frankenstein's monster. When the mad scientist begins to construct a female monster, he fears that the two of them will produce a "race of devils" who will make "the very existence of the species of man a condition precarious and full of terror." The "race" of these twin monsters seems to be a combination of various "lower" races. Thus, the male has "yellow skin" and "straight black lips." Abandoned by his creator, the monster resembles wild men and savages in many familiar accounts. He threatens cannibalism: when he confronts William Frankenstein before strangling him, the boy fears the monster will eat him. He also behaves like a rebellious slave, and if Victor were to create his "bride," their hellish propagation might fulfill Thomas De Quincey's opium-induced dread of "the yellow peril" (Kitson 75–87; Mellor; Barrell, *Infection*).

Kitson does not think that race "was the most significant discouse of difference in the Romantic period." He contends, however, that after mid-century "there is a much stronger case for regarding race as the primary and crucial category that Europeans used to understand their relationships with other people" (2). With the caveat that race did not supplant class or gender as also "primary" categories of distinction in Victorian culture, I agree with Kitson's assessment. It is perhaps worth stressing, moreover, that the purpose of studying race in Victorian, Romantic, or Enlightenment culture is not to cast retrospective blame on those eras or on the writers who expressed views that we now identify as racist. Rather, like Kitson's, Edward Said's, Robert Young's, John Barrell's, and many other examinations of race in cultural history, *Taming Cannibals* is an exploration of how various attitudes and ideas pertaining to race infused many aspects of British literature and culture between the 1830s and World War I. Above all, the ideologies of racism and imperialism were powerfully symbiotic and often indistinguishable from each other. That the discursive roots of modern racism lie in British, European, and colonial writing that deals with the slave trade and imperialist expansion is now widely acknowledged. What is less often acknowledged is the extent to which racism informed virtually all aspects of Romantic and Victorian culture.

Colonial Modernity and the Modernity of Racism

In her classic study of totalitarianism, Hannah Arendt declared, "Imperialism would have necessitated the invention of racism as the only possible 'explanation' and excuse for its deeds, even if no race-thinking had ever existed in the civilized world" (63–64). So, too, in *Modernity and the Holocaust,* Zygmunt Bauman argues that racism is not antithetical to modernity but has been a fundamental aspect of it. Imperialism brought the benefits along with the drawbacks of modernization to many parts of the world. One of those drawbacks has been racism. Another way to put it is to say that imperialism and modernization—capitalist globalization at first under the aegis of newly formed European nation-states—have been inseparable since the Renaissance. With the exception of Antarctica, European explorers, conquistadors, and colonizers invaded every part of the world, where they discovered indigenous peoples who were not able to withstand their onslaught. Guns and germs everywhere led to the victory of the Europeans. What Marx called "primitive accumulation," including slavery, brought prosperity to many of the colonists and to the nation-states they came from. The Europeans understood the superiority of their ships and weapons, and they also realized that disease was a major factor working in their favor. They translated their successes into racial terms: supposedly because of the innate superiority of the white race, it has been almost universally victorious; the nonwhite races of the world show their inferiority by being defeated and by falling prey to diseases imported from Europe.

Yet with the conquistadors came the missionaries and the so-called civilizing mission. Perhaps most nineteenth-century imperialists and racists believed in that mission. Certainly the missionaries believed in it. And even as the European empires devastated indigenous peoples and exploited the land and resources in what had once been their territories, some aspects of "colonial modernity," as Frederick Cooper calls it, began to benefit the colonized. In many places, Cooper notes, colonizers launched "campaigns against indigenous forms of slavery, widow-burning, or child marriage" (145). To this list can be added cannibalism and infanticide. The missionaries saw their main task as abolishing superstition, fetishism, or devil worship and replacing it with Christianity. Many "heathens" may have found the new religion irrational, but the missionaries typically introduced literacy to indigenous societies and often opened the path for trade goods from abroad. Two European imports that indigenous societies eagerly accepted were guns and Western medicine. Missionaries frequently found converting the heathens very difficult or impossible, but in some circumstances, as Gauri Viswanathan demonstrates, conversion offered the converts an escape from social or political entrapment—the caste system in India, for example. As I show in the next chapter, the Wesleyan missionaries in Fiji offered access to Western goods, including both medicine and guns, but also, through conversion, a path beyond traditional warfare and its customary accompaniment, cannibalism.

Britons in India may have viewed Hinduism as mere superstition or even devil worship, and they typically believed that Indians of all religions and races were both culturally and biologically inferior to themselves. But in the subcontinent the British designed and oversaw the construction of the most extensive railway system outside Europe, and they also oversaw the construction of telegraph lines, irrigation systems, schools, hospitals, and many other public works. Despite the patronizing condescension of Macaulay, the legal system he helped develop was, K. M. Panikkar declares, "a great improvement on the previous systems" (497). And "in causing a social revolution in Hindustan," wrote Marx, Britain "was actuated only by the vilest interests, and was stupid in her manner of enforcing them. But...the question is, can mankind fulfill its destiny without a fundamental revolution in the social state of Asia? If not, whatever may have been the crimes of England she was the unconscious tool of history in bringing about that revolution" (Marx and Engels, *Colonialism* 41). Many of the modernizing efforts under the Raj helped stitch the various polities, cultures, and religions of the subcontinent into today's independent nation-state.

Nevertheless, as an aspect of colonial modernity, racism in its supposedly scientific forms was basic to the colonizers' mapping, census taking, legal and taxation systems, anthropology, and general understanding of the colonized. The "government of subject races," Lord Cromer asserted in 1908, was what the British did better than any other European power. Of course that "government" could not be left to the "subject races" themselves. "It cannot be too clearly understood that whether we deal with the roots, or the trunk, or the branches, or the leaves," Cromer claimed, "free institutions in the full sense of the term must for generations to come be wholly unsuitable to countries such as India and Egypt" (25). Indeed, he continues, they might not be practicable at all: "If the use of a metaphor...be allowed, it may be said that it will probably never be possible to make a Western silk purse out of an Eastern sow's ear" (25). This racist point of view was widely shared among British politicians and the British public.

Throughout the history of the European empires, taming cannibals, or in the words of Catherine Hall, "civilizing subjects"—the "civilizing mission" or the general project of cultural modernization—was at best a mixed blessing, in large measure because it was everywhere underwritten and undermined by racism. If they attend to it at all, many past and present historians of Britain and the British Empire have viewed racism as an unfortunate excrescence mainly affecting activities overseas, on imperial frontiers or in the colonies. The gist is usually that racism may have been a colonial problem, but in Britain it was not very important. It might crop up in British public opinion during a war or a crisis in imperial affairs. Most historians acknowledge that the Indian Rebellion or "Mutiny" of 1857–58 strengthened British and Anglo-Indian racism (Metcalf; Chakravarty; Chatterjee 19–24). The 1865 Jamaica uprising and Governor Edward Eyre's brutal suppression of it caused Charles Dickens, John Ruskin, Thomas Carlyle, and other defenders of Eyre to fulminate about what Carlyle called "the Nigger Question" (Semmel; Evans). Various moments in the history of Irish resistance to British rule—Young Ireland in 1848, Fenianism starting in the late 1860s, the Land War of the late 1870s and 1880s—increased the virulence and frequency of anti-Irish stereotyping in the British press (Curtis). Emphasizing such critical moments still allows some historians to suggest that racism in Victorian culture was a minor affair.[4]

There is the further habit of attributing racism to the prejudices of individuals, ignoring its lengthy history, its relationship to slavery and empire, and the many ways it has been structured into institutions, laws, language, behavior, and culture. Writing in 1982, Salman Rushdie noted that "racism is not a side-issue in contemporary Britain" (129), and it certainly was not a side issue during the Victorian period, at the height of the British

Empire's power and glory. Noting the "darker side" of imperialism in his popular account of British conquests and colonies, Dennis Judd writes: "Centuries of supremacy have left many British people ensnared in a mesh of prejudice and shallow assertiveness. Imperialism rested on, indeed was sustained by, assumptions of superiority, where one white person was thought to be worth literally any number of blacks and browns. This deeply engrained tendency towards racial prejudice was lent greater strength by mass migration to the United Kingdom" in the twentieth century (16). Judd's account is accurate as far as it goes, but the tepid phrase "tendency towards racial prejudice" does not fully reflect the cultural and institutional effects of racism. Nevertheless, Judd is right that "centuries of supremacy" has meant centuries of white supremacism.

As Edward Said argued in *Orientalism* (1978) and *Culture and Imperialism* (1993), racism and empire have been two sides of the same coin for the European nation-states as they explored, expanded, and established colonies. Racism is always comparative and, hence, two-sided: members of a superior race believe themselves to be superior because the peoples they conquer, colonize, exterminate, enslave, exploit, and rule have demonstrated their inferiority by being conquered et cetera. Over time, moreover, racism becomes inscribed in laws, institutions, languages, and cultures in ways that make it far more than a matter of individuals' "prejudices." For "racism is a social relation," writes Étienne Balibar, "not the mere ravings of racist subjects" (41). It is only since World War II that hierarchical distinctions based on race have been widely regarded as irrational and stereotypic. Nor has racism disappeared from any modern Western society, but is instead deeply embedded in many of the institutional structures enforcing inequalities: immigration quotas, school and neighborhood segregation, job discrimination, and the like. Efforts to counteract racism often themselves reinforce it, as Rushdie notes concerning "multiculturalism" in 1980s Britain:

> In our schools, [multiculturalism] means little more than teaching the kids a few bongo rhythms, how to tie a sari and so forth. In the police training programme, it means telling cadets that black people are so "culturally different" that they can't help making trouble. Multiculturalism is the latest token gesture towards Britain's blacks, and it ought to be exposed, like "integration" and "racial harmony," for the sham it is. (137)

To understand how racism has operated in nineteenth-century British culture and still operates today, it is necessary to move beyond the ideas that it is merely the outcome of poor race relations, faulty understanding, or individual inclinations to stereotype others. According to Balibar, racism is a necessary, inevitable "supplement" of nationalism, and both are distinctly modern developments. Or is nationalism the supplement of racism? In the 1700s and earlier, the terms "race" and "nation" were used interchangeably; both entailed the idea of a group or community that shares descent from the same ancestors. Furthermore, nationalism is rooted in positive but inherently stereotypic perceptions of collective identity ("we" Americans or Norwegians or Chinese are a successful, superior, or even chosen people because…). In *The Island Race* Kathleen Wilson writes, "Englishness itself…emerged by the 1760s and 1770s as a nascent ethnicity that, although defined through government" and other cultural and historical categories, "still had within it what we would recognize as racialized assumptions" (13). And what was true of Englishness was true of other European nationalities.

Under the pressure of capitalist expansion, moreover, modern nation-states strive to exceed their original boundaries, most obviously by forging empires and establishing colonies. The modern empires, from the Renaissance forward, have themselves been "supplements" or extensions of modern nation-states, from the early Spanish, Portuguese, Dutch, and British empires to current versions, among which America's domination of much of the world is the most obvious one.[5] From the outset of the modern era in the 1400s, racism has been the discursive or ideological supplement of both nationalism and imperialism. "The colonial castes of the various nationalities (British, French, Dutch, Portuguese and so on) *worked together* to forge the idea of 'White' superiority," writes Balibar, and "of civilization as an interest that has to be defended against the savages" (43). Here is the initial, fundamental dichotomy and racist stereotype stemming from imperialist expansion, often expressed as "the white man's" aversion to black savagery and cannibalism. Further elaborations of this dichotomy tend to be repetitions of it, or in other words, stereotypes breeding more stereotypes.

That racism has also often masked or distracted from class conflict has made it invaluable as an ideological support for capitalism and its imperial expansiveness. Kenan Malik argues that over the last five hundred years, the "concept of race emerged…as a means of reconciling the conflict between the ideology of equality and the reality of the persistence of inequality. Race accounted for social inequalities by attributing them to nature" (6). And Arendt declares that colonization enabled capitalist societies to relieve themselves of "superfluous men" (criminals, the poor, the unemployed), who in their new homes asserted their racial superiority versus the indigenous peoples they pushed aside and often exterminated (30–37).

Racist Stereotypes

The chapters that follow deal with racial stereotypes mainly in Victorian literature and culture—stereotypes that helped consolidate and justify British imperial authority.[6] But many theories of stereotyping are ahistorical, viewing "racial prejudice" and its units of discourse in terms of individual psyches. In *Public Opinion* (1922), the work that put stereotypes on the map of modern ideas, Walter Lippmann claimed that they are "axiomatic elements of human perception" (Ewen and Ewen 52). They are therefore hard to distinguish from representation in general (Pickering, *Stereotyping* 2). "The abandonment of all stereotypes...would impoverish human life," Lippmann opined—well, yes, if they are defined as the atomic particles of thought (Lippmann 60). He argued that stereotypes are mental shortcuts necessary to make sense of modernity and also "defenses" supporting our identities (64).[7]

Four major theoretical approaches lead to the impasse whereby stereotyping equals all representation. First, the liberal approach—Lippmann's—identifies stereotyping with "public opinion" and the necessary but simplifying "pictures in our heads." Second, psychoanalysis views at least some stereotyping as "pathological," while also viewing it as fundamental to both unconscious and conscious mental processes.[8] Third, some versions of Marxism treat the stereotype as the basic unit of ideology or false consciousness, while also contending that ideology affects everyone or nearly everyone.[9] And fourth, Derridean poststructuralism views all language as misrepresentational—hence, stereotypic. Strands from all of these theories are evident in postcolonial studies, notably in "The Other Question," Homi Bhabha's influential essay on "the stereotype." Bhabha focuses on what takes place in the mind of an individual stereotyper ("the colonizer"). He emphasizes "ambivalence": "the stereotype" "vacillates between what is always 'in place,' already known, and something that must be anxiously repeated" (66). And "the stereotype" strives for "fixity," but also undoes that fixity—or else fears that it is coming undone. Like the fixity of "the fetish," that of "the stereotype" connotes "rigidity and an unchanging order as well as disorder, degeneracy and daemonic repetition" (66). A stereotype attempts to "fix," typically through simplification into anti-thetical binaries (good/evil, male/female, white/black), what is unfixed, messy, diverse.

From this opening gambit, Bhabha complicates commonsense notions of stereotypes as merely negative and always false "images" of "the other," generated to rationalize imperialism, or the "subjectification" of "the colonized" by "the colonizer" (67). He invariably refers to "the stereotype" in the singular, however, implying that there is only one process or pattern of misrepresentation that needs to be analyzed, rather than various processes. Bhabha thus weakens the poststructuralist aspect of his argument, even as he contends that stereotypes always differ from themselves: they are always more "ambivalent" and contradictory than they seem. Hence, they are always relational and plural rather than singular; no concept, including "the stereotype," is an island. For example, Bhabha notes that, according to "the stereotype" of "the Negro," he is "both savage (cannibal) and yet the most obedient and dignified of servants (the bearer of food); he is the embodiment of rampant sexuality and yet innocent as a child," and so forth (82).

Bhabha himself generates two stereotypes, moreover, "the colonizer" and "the colonized." This standard pairing in postcolonial theory evokes Hegel's master-slave dialectic. Despite supposedly being dialectical, however, Hegel's and Bhabha's binarism suggests that domination and subordination come in only two flavors, vanilla and chocolate. But throughout history there have been many kinds of slavery (indentured servitude, child labor, convict workers, "wage slavery" in sweatshops, and so forth), just as there have been many kinds of imperialism and colonialism (a territory of white settlement such as Canada versus a slave colony such as Jamaica before 1833, for example).[10] In the British Empire, "colonizers" ranged from Queen Victoria to "Pakeha" or white Maoris. The "colonized" included both Australian Aborigines and Indian maharajahs.[11]

Although Bhabha occasionally utilizes sociological terms such as "governmentality" (83), he does not explain how stereotypes are collectively generated.[12] Like most analysts of stereotyping, he psychologizes the problem.

"The larger society has withdrawn from view," writes Jan Nederveen Pieterse; most theorists fail to "address forms of institutional or structural racism" and cannot account historically for how these arise (*Empire* 224). In *Images of Savages,* Gustav Jahoda agrees: "Most social psychological approaches [to the stereotype] either ignore history altogether, or at best pay lip-service to it" (xv).[13] Jahoda cites Hegel on African cannibalism: "For Hegel the values of humans lay in their connection with 'the Absolute,' and, since Africans do not recognize that entity, he inferred…that they attach no value to human life. Hence they slaughter their fellows, drink their blood and eat them" (114).

Jahoda adds that Hegel did not dream up the "fearsome image" of African cannibalism "in his armchair"; it instead "originated from a stream of colourful reports by travellers and explorers, a stream which barely abated in the course of the 19th century" (114). Out of this collective "stream of colourful reports" sprang the European belief in the widespread practice of cannibalism by Africans and other non-Europeans. Needless to say, this "stream" helped rationalize the slave trade and the carving up of most of Africa into European colonies, starting with the Portuguese in West Africa and the Dutch at the Cape. By Hegel's time, so-called natural historians as well as philosophers were transforming old stereotypes into new, apparently scientific categories. And in regard to cannibalism, as *Robinson Crusoe* suggests, by 1800 few Europeans doubted that it was widely practiced by "savages" in Africa and other parts of the world. After all, a century before Rousseau produced his versions of primitivism and noble savagery, Montaigne turned the fearsome ideas of savagery and cannibalism upside down, presenting "the cannibals" of South America as morally if not technologically advanced over his "civilized" readers.

Stereotypes are not accurate depictions of reality, but they have many, often unpredictable and profound effects on the real world. In *White on Black,* Pieterse contends that stereotypes can and often do act as "self-fulfilling prophecies." He writes:

> Though they may have no basis in reality, stereotypes are real in their social consequences, notably with regard to the allocation of roles. They tend to function as self-fulfilling prophecies. The targets of stereotyping are manoeuvred into certain roles, so that a vicious circle develops, in which social reality seems to endorse the stereotype. Social representation echoes social

realities which are in turn modelled upon social representation. A kind of societal typecasting is set up from which it is difficult to escape. (11)

As Frantz Fanon puts it in *Black Skin, White Masks,* Richard Wright's Bigger Thomas "responds to the world's anticipation" (139). The thesis that stereotypes are often "self-fulfilling prophecies" perhaps helps to explain the murders committed in 1990 by Howmore Ngcobo and four other Zulus. In his account of European perceptions of Shaka and the Zulus, Dan Wylie writes that Ngcobo and his friends "stabbed five whites at random on Durban's tourist-thronged beachfront." During Ngcobo's trial, "one of his possessions presented in evidence was a 'photograph...of Shaka,' across which was written the word 'Renaissance'" (3). It seems that Ngcobo considered himself a Zulu nationalist. In cases like these, the collective, institutional nature of "the world's anticipation" needs to be stressed, rather than the psychic aberrations either of individual stereotypers or of the stereotyped.

Ironically, nineteenth-century observers like H. Rider Haggard often viewed the Zulus as noble savages while shying away from calling them cannibals. According to Wylie, the eyewitness accounts by white observers of Shaka's rise to power were few and far between. Even these accounts fabricated details with little or no empirical evidence. They obviously exaggerated aspects of the story. Thus, one writer declared that the great Zulu conqueror "has been called the 'Black Napoleon' but, compared with Tshaka [*sic*], Bonaparte was an amiable and benevolent country squire" (quoted in Wylie 195). Though often admiring Shaka's organizing, ruling, and military abilities, the accounts of him and of later Zulu leaders (as well as of the Zulus in general) portray them as savage killing machines, which is how Haggard depicts them, even while he praised their manly bloodthirstiness. During the *mfecane,* or Zulu rise to power, the Zulus killed hundreds of members of other "tribes," causing many to flee and perhaps even to practice survival cannibalism (eating the corpses of the slain to avoid starvation). Although the eyewitnesses frequently call Shaka and the Zulus "bloodthirsty," however, they do not call them cannibals. In this case, perhaps the stereotyping of the Zulus gave way slightly to empiricism.

Fanon notes that, in stereotypes of "the Negro," cannibalism is often invoked, or lurks in the background: "In the first chapter of the history that the others have compiled for me, the foundation of cannibalism has been made eminently plain in order that I may not lose sight of it" (120). He says he was once asked to respond "to an article that made jazz music literally an irruption of cannibalism into the modern world" (225). And he imagines a "little white boy" throwing himself "into his mother's arms" in terror: "Mama, the nigger's going to eat me up" (114). Fanon does not dispute the notion that at least some "savages," including some Africans, once practiced cannibalism. But an interesting attempt to counteract this aspect of stereotyping "savages" has been the controversy, conducted mainly by anthropologists, about whether customary cannibalism has ever been practiced anywhere and at any time in history. That is the controversy that I take up in the next chapter, on missionaries in Fiji starting in the 1830s.

Like Bhabha, Fanon approached racism and the colonizer-colonized relationship by way of psychoanalysis. Nevertheless, he recognized that any psychological explanation of stereotyping must encompass history and the "racist structure" of modern social formations. Fanon criticized Octave Mannoni's *Prospero and Caliban: The Psychology of Colonization* for positing a "Prospero complex" and a "dependency complex," apparently uninfluenced by history. For Mannoni, these "complexes" explained why Europeans want to dominate and "the colonized" want to be dominated. According to Fanon, "Mannoni believes that the contempt of the poor whites of South Africa for the Negro has nothing to do with economic factors" (86). But, Fanon asks, "What is South Africa?" It is

a boiler into which thirteen million blacks are clubbed and penned in by two and a half million whites. If the poor whites hate the Negroes, it is not, as M. Mannoni would have us believe, because "racialism is the work of petty officials, small traders, and colonials who have toiled much without great success." No; it is because the structure of South Africa is a racist structure. (87)

Mannoni identifies racism and stereotyping with "poor whites," but that is a social class position, determined by historical and economic factors, which also determine "racist structures." Under South African apartheid, the "poor whites"—indeed, all whites—were divided against themselves, between the descendants of the Dutch colonizers (the Afrikaners) and the descendants of the British colonizers. And "the Negroes" (Fanon's term) were themselves divided into multiple "tribes," "races," languages, and cultures, which is a key reason why "two and a half million whites" were able to colonize and exploit "thirteen million blacks." Control of land, gold mines, and diamond mines consolidated white rule, internally divided though it was. In part because of its many internal divisions, South Africa spawned an extremely "racist structure," sutured for decades into a pathological but collective polity by racist paranoia, stereotyping, and violence (Keegan). It doesn't make sense to attribute apartheid to the racism of individual white South Africans; rather, racism was the ideological cement that held the laws and institutions of the apartheid regime together.

Like Bhabha and Mannoni, however, Fanon treats colonial histories in terms of the colonized/colonizer binary without much shading or attention to degrees and kinds of oppression.[14] Though itself a stereotypic simplification unless qualified by context, that binary fits many aspects of world history, and also helps to explain the production of racist stereotypes via racist structures. "The colonial world is a Manichaean world," as Fanon famously writes in *Wretched of the Earth* (41). In *Black Skin, White Masks,* however, Fanon examines a number of exceptions to what might be called the rule of the stereotype. He doesn't just address the racism that "the black man" or "the Negro" finds imposed on him by the white man; he is also concerned with "the man of color" and, indeed, "the woman of color." Fanon's second chapter, for example, is titled "The Woman of Color and the White Man," and examines Mayotte Capécia's autobiography *Je suis Matiniquaise* (1948). A mulatta, Capécia longed to enter the white world, had an affair with a white man, and rejected the black world. Several factors make her situation, by Fanon's account, less or more than Manichaean: she is of mixed race; she has an affair with a white man; she is from Martinique, not Senegal and not France; she writes in French; and she is, like other Martinicans, at least quasi-French. (France adopted an assimilationist policy toward its colonies.)

"The stereotype" may be the basic unit of racist and colonial discourse, as Bhabha claims. He also believes, however, that discourse as well as the colonizer-colonized relationship are in some sense always "hybrid," like Mayotte Capécia or like Defoe's "True-born Englishman." If "the stereotype" is essentialist, fixated, and single-minded (or, rather, binary-minded), "hybridity," according to Bhabha, undoes essentialism, fixation, and binaries. So is colonialist discourse always stereotypic, always hybrid, or both?[15] In *Colonial Desire,* Robert Young criticizes Bhabha in part by demonstrating just how thoroughly imbued with hybridity nineteenth-century imperialist discourse was. As I show in chapter 3, on "going native," British colonizers were far more hybrid than is usually acknowledged. Always lurking in colonial cultures is the threat that the colonizers may degenerate into their opposites; in some instances, the fear was that people with white complexions and aptitudes might turn into blacks. In a few actual cases, moreover, white colonizers joined "savage" tribes and became cannibals. Although colonialist discourse was often Manichaean and hence obviously stereotypic, its emphasis on hybridity, even when it evoked anxiety and revulsion, was also both more and less than Manichaean.

As Young points out, there was widespread if often only covert recognition that racial miscegenation was common throughout the European empires. Capécia, after all, was a mulatta who had an affair with a white man. Everywhere sexual relations between colonizers and the colonized produced mixed-race populations. This was evident in India, for example, where over several centuries a sizable "Eurasian" population sprang up, which, by the Victorian era, had been largely disowned by white "Anglo-Indians" like Rudyard Kipling. Especially after the trans-Atlantic slave trade was halted, miscegenation was one way for slaveholders to produce more slaves. In Australia, too, in the first decades of the 1900s, the "half-caste" Aboriginal population, which was increasing, posed a more worrisome problem to many white observers than the question of what to do about the "full-blooded" population, which appeared to be dying out, as many whites hoped it would do (it didn't).

Victorian Crusoes and Cannibals

Queen Victoria presided over Britain's imperial climax, the culmination of geographical exploration, the final end of slavery in the Western world, and the beginnings of unrest and nascent nationalism in many British territories, foreshadowing decolonization. Instead of a lone Robinson Crusoe confronting a tribe of cannibals, from the 1830s to World War I and beyond, there were thousands of British Crusoes throughout the empire confronting those they saw as savages or barbarians but also as potential Fridays. In countless boys' adventure novels, sometimes in explorers' journals, and sometimes as well in missionary narratives, the white heroes encounter dark-skinned people they allege to be cannibals. Whether or not the heroes defeat the cannibals, they almost always escape being killed and eaten. They sometimes also tame if not exactly civilize the cannibals and convert them to Christianity. "To tame the barbarian," as Richard Hakluyt put it, emerges as the ultimate justification for white intrusions into non-white, supposedly savage or barbarian territory. Thus for centuries Africa, "the Dark Continent," was tarred with "the most negative stereotypes... of barbaric practices, bloody human sacrifice, cannibalism, slavery and fetishism, that it was the duty" of European colonizers to extinguish, even if that meant enslaving or exterminating Africans (MacMaster 75). The stereotyping of Africa and Africans did not diminish, but was instead intensified by white explorers such as Richard Burton and Henry Morton Stanley as they "penetrated" central Africa and presumably unraveled its mysteries.

Efforts to tame savages or barbarians undertaken by British missionaries and many others in the colonies and on imperial frontiers often failed. The failures reinforced the colonizers' belief in the racial inferiority of the savages and barbarians. But civilizing and assimilating indigenous peoples was frequently seen as the only way to preserve them from total annihilation by disease and violence. Yet in many cases, civilizing and assimilation can now be interpreted as cultural genocide—for example, in instances of the removal of children from indigenous families and societies. Writing about the situations in both Cape Colony and Tasmania, Elizabeth Elbourne asks: "Is genocide best seen as a linked policy of assimilation and destruction...? Or can these processes be disaggregated?" (91). Among other instances, she has in mind the attempt by George Augustus Robinson in the 1830s to save the remnants of the Aborigines in Tasmania. Robinson, whose writings I discuss in chapter 2, rounded up the final Aborigines and placed them on a reservation on Flinders Island, where he tried to civilize and Christianize them. But they rapidly died out. In his own time, Robinson was accused of hastening the extermination of the Tasmanians by trying to tame them.

The chapters that follow, focused on widely different aspects of nineteenth-century British culture, all demonstrate that conceptions of race helped the Victorians interpret and categorize all humans everywhere and throughout history, including themselves—"the imperial race," the conquering, colonizing, but supposedly humane "Anglo-Saxons." The British past consisted of multiple invasions: Picts, Britons, Celts, Romans, Danes,

Angles, Jutes, Saxons, Normans. History was a record of races in collision with one another, and that history was visible in the present, as colonial frontiers and the empire expanded. The Victorians also continued old humanitarian struggles (abolition, missionary work, the protection of indigenous peoples from colonizers) and engaged in new ones that also foregrounded race. And the British future, especially after publication of Darwin's *Origin of Species* in 1859, was understood in terms of racial progress or degeneration. If the Anglo-Saxon race had so far been superior to all other races, would it forever evolve along a progressive track? Or would it be succeeded by another, even greater or more powerful race? Would Britain and, indeed, all of Europe be overwhelmed by "the yellow peril"? Or would the Martians invade, as H. G. Wells imagined in his end-of-century science fiction classic *The War of the Worlds* (1898)?

The next chapter examines the debate about cannibalism through the writings of the first missionaries to Fiji. Although most accounts of cannibalism throughout history have been fabricated or at least exaggerated, the Wesleyan missionaries in Fiji before 1874 provide some of the best eyewitness testimony about its practice from anywhere in the world. Most Fijians grew tame and converted to Christianity because many of them saw conversion as a way out of their internecine wars that typically ended in cannibal feasts. Furthermore, the Fijians were never directly threatened by British or European conquest, slavery, or exploitation; their most powerful "king," Thakombau, wound up pleading with the British to turn Fiji into a colony. I match this missionary success story in Fiji with the story, in chapter 2, of missionary, humanitarian, and anthropological failure in Tasmania—a pair of contrasting island stories.

The demise of the Tasmanian Aborigines involved a failure to protect and tame them which has sometimes mistakenly been cited as the only genocide in British imperial history. I compare Robinson's journals and James Bonwick's writings on the final Tasmanians, a race that supposedly completely disappeared by 1876. The contrast illustrates the differences between missionary and early anthropological discourse in producing colonial knowledge, although neither approach would have saved the Tasmanian Aborigines from annihilation. Missionaries, of course, aimed to save the souls if not the bodies of savages and barbarians; Victorian anthropology developed as a way of preserving information about cultures that were widely understood to be doomed no matter how Europeans behaved.

The next two chapters examine various examples imitating and advocating savage or barbarian behaviors and cultures. Chapter 3 surveys some of the many forms of "going native." The standard image of "the imperial race," evident in countless texts in many genres, is of the unflinching British hero, braving the attacks and temptations of savages and barbarians. The "natives" are supposed to mimic their betters, not the other way around. But whatever views of other races and cultures the colonizers harbored, they often blurred or transgressed the boundaries of their own culture by imitating and even joining the natives. This was just as true of the British in the 1800s as it was of all the other European conquerors and colonizers. In the early 1800s, for example, "Pakeha" or white Maoris often participated fully as members of the "tribes" that adopted them, even to the point of becoming warriors and engaging in cannibalism (Bentley).

Paired with the topic of going native is Benjamin Disraeli's racist interpretation of history and politics, the subject of chapter 4. By his opponents Disraeli was viewed as racially distinct, dangerous, and alien. His father made sure that he converted to Christianity, but he was still perceived as a Jew, and therefore viewed by his detractors as an out-of-place and potentially traitorous "native." Yet he became Victorian Britain's greatest imperialist statesman. As both a writer and a politician, Disraeli sought to counteract anti-Semitism with a positive version— philo-Semitism—based on the idea, expressed by the wise Sidonia in Disraeli's Young England novel *Tancred* (1847), that "all is race." As much as any other British politician, Disraeli shaped Middle Eastern policy and influenced British attitudes toward the Ottoman Empire. The Ottoman Turks weren't cannibals, of course, but they were viewed as barbarians; Romantic and Victorian authors often characterized them as bloodthirsty, lascivious monsters, even vampires. Yet through most of the 1800s, British foreign policy, including Disraeli's when he was prime minister, supported the tottering Ottoman Empire as protection against Russian meddling in Afghanistan and India.

Chapters 5 and 6 focus on some of the ways ideas about race affected social and political controversies in the 1860s. Causes for the emphasis on race in accounts of the urban slums and "the residuum" include Darwin's *Origin* (1859), reactions to the Indian "Mutiny" or Rebellion of 1857–58, the American Civil War, the 1865 Jamaican uprising and its repression by Governor Eyre, Fenianism, and agitation over the Second Reform Bill of

1867. The temptation to view "the lower orders" as a lower race—savages or barbarians if not cannibals—is an old one. But the 1860s witnessed the emergence of social Darwinism and of Francis Galton's eugenics, along with anxiety about the weakening or degeneration of "the imperial race" which would become much more pervasive in the 1880s and 1890s. Savages and savage races confronted British colonists in Australia or southern Africa; they supposedly also confronted upper-class Britons in the slums of London and Manchester. Like Robert Louis Stevenson's Mr. Hyde somewhat later, the residuum emerged in the 1860s as the homegrown antithesis of the stalwart members of "the imperial race."

Matthew Arnold's "On the Study of Celtic Literature" and the stereotype of the Irish as both intellectually and physically lightweight take center stage in chapter 6. The Irish may have been poetical, musical, and imaginative, but they were often perceived as feathery, frivolous, and full of blarney compared to the solid, beef-eating English. In starving mode, the Irish were sometimes also accused of cannibalism. Historical revisionism in regard to the Famine and to other aspects of the British domination of Ireland has sought to downplay or eliminate racism from its portrait of English-Irish relations. But from the time of Edmund Spenser's "wild Irish" through the Victorian period, English perceptions of the Irish were usually racialized ones. Even an apparent sympathizer like Arnold sees "the Celts" as both a lower and a dying race.

Chapters 7 and 8 present a contrast between fantasies about race in antiquity and in the future. H. Rider Haggard's racism and his fetishistic archaeology led him to insist that Great Zimbabwe and other ruins in southeastern Africa could only have been constructed by a civilized, white, or at least Semitic race. He saw the ancient Egyptians as a great civilizing race; he also saw the Zulus as a great savage race, and imagined that they would always remain savage. Other Africans were likely to be degraded cannibals, similar to the Amahaggers in *She*. Though well aware of the theory of evolution, Haggard treats both savage and civilized races as if they were permanent fixtures, eternal certitudes that helped him believe in the permanency of British civilization and its empire.

Chapter 8 on "the coming race" surveys the rise of science fiction and the Victorians' response both to what evolution meant for the future and to new machines, especially new communications devices such as the telegraph and the typewriter. Edward Bulwer-Lytton's science fiction classic

The Coming Race appeared in 1872. Victorians, including George Eliot, speculated about machines as a super-race that would one day replace humans. In the machinic throes of vampirism, Bram Stoker's Dracula represents a past in which imperialism and cannibalism were inseparable—a past that he threatens to turn into Britain's future by creating an ever-expanding race of vampires. Universal bloodthirstiness or vampiric cannibalism is the ultimate nightmare version of racial degeneration and also of going native.

In the epilogue I examine the many "afterlives" of "The White Man's Burden." There have been literally hundreds of reactions to Kipling's notorious white supremacist poem, which he sent to Theodore Roosevelt as an encouragement for the Americans to colonize the Philippines after the Spanish-American War. Many satires and parodies appeared in the African American press, which was highly critical of the U.S. takeover of the Philippines. Unfortunately, the white supremacism it expresses survives among supporters of America's neoimperialism in Iraq, as well as more generally in anti-Islamism and anti-immigrant discourse both in the United States and in Britain.

Part I

Two Island Stories

1

MISSIONARIES AND CANNIBALS IN NINETEENTH-CENTURY FIJI

"Fiji, Cannibal Fiji! Pity, O pity, Cannibal Fiji!"
REVEREND JAMES WATKIN, "Pity Poor Fiji"

Although in the 1800s both Tasmania and Fiji became British colonies, their historical trajectories were in several ways mirror opposites. In 1801 the British established a penal colony in Van Diemen's Land (as Tasmania was first named). Free settlers began to arrive two decades later, and by the 1830s nearly all of Tasmania's Aborigines had been exterminated by violence and disease. Much of the violence took place during the "Black War" of the late 1820s, when the Aborigines put up a fierce resistance to the invasion of their island. Missionary, humanitarian, and anthropological efforts to save at least the remnants of the "dying race" failed. The last full-blooded Tasmanian Aborigine died in 1876. In contrast, Wesleyan missionaries first came to Fiji in the 1830s, where they discovered ongoing warfare and such "diabolical" customs as infanticide and cannibalism, which they diligently sought to eliminate. Although a handful of white traders and beachcombers arrived, Fiji did not become a territory of white settlement. The missionaries' proselytizing succeeded, and by the 1850s Thakombau, the most prominent Fijian chief and notorious cannibal, began pleading with Britain to make the archipelago a crown colony, which it finally did in 1874.

The Missionaries and the Great Cannibal Debate

A familiar cartoon shows a white explorer staring into a cannibal cooking pot and asking, "Dr. Livingstone, I presume?" No, the great missionary-explorer was not killed and eaten by "cannibals." Throughout his travels, Livingstone found most Africans peaceful and welcoming, and he was suspicious of claims that any of them engaged in cannibalism. But the motif of the missionary as cannibal fare has been a staple of Western popular culture for centuries. Is this motif just the result of white racism, or does it have a historical basis? The answer appears to be both. The main locus of missionary-cannibal stories, however, is not Africa but the South Pacific. Their main source, moreover, is the missionaries themselves.

Given the debate about whether customary cannibalism has ever been practiced anywhere, the missionaries' testimony is at least intriguing. In *Cannibal Talk,* Gananath Obeyesekere seeks to end the debate in favor of the skeptics, but he scants missionary accounts. And then there are the accounts by those identified as "cannibals" in Western texts. Can the "cannibal" subaltern speak? Yes—to a degree. "For the Cannibals did really exist," writes Frank Lestringant, "and have never ceased to speak to us" (7). They do so, however, through the mediation of Western languages and texts, which is precisely the issue posed by Gayatri Spivak in "Can the Subaltern Speak?"[1] Thus the ceremony of apology conducted in the fall of 2003 by the village of Navasutila in Fiji made international news. The Fijians were apologizing for their ancestors' having killed and eaten the Reverend Thomas Baker in 1867; they invited Baker's descendants, and several from Australia attended, as did Prime Minister Laisenia Qarase of Fiji (Kikau 1). The *Times* of London reported that the "cannibals" had also tried to eat Baker's boots, but found them too tough even after boiling them for a month (Barkham 3). The "cannibals," however, seem to have resented the notion that they were so foolish as to try to eat a pair of boots.[2] Nevertheless, one of the boots is on display in the National Museum in Suva, along with the bowl in which Baker's remains were supposedly served.[3]

Anthropologist Steven Hooper cites the Navasutila ceremony as an example of Fijians "talking" about their cannibal past. "With respect to so-called 'cannibal talk,'" Hooper notes, "the 'talk' of Fijians seems to have been ignored or discredited in some circles....[But] Fijians have long talked privately and publicly of cannibalism as a cultural practice" (20).[4] Modern Fijians, however, know about cannibalism only as history. Fijians talking about cannibalism from precolonial Fiji speak most clearly through the mediation of missionary texts. Besides Baker, between the 1830s and 1870s there were many other missionaries in Fiji, and many of them testified, both as eyewitnesses and through ventriloquizing their native informants, about customary cannibalism. Sometimes, moreover, they produced texts that invite evaluation by the standards of modern anthropology.

Beginning with William Arens's study *The Man-Eating Myth* in 1979, the debate over customary cannibalism has compounded the crisis in anthropology caused by poststructuralism, postcolonialism, and the disappearance of "primitive" cultures (Brady, "Myth-Eating"; Hulme; Osborne; Lindenbaum). Arens, Obeyesekere, and their supporters cast doubt on all accounts of customary cannibalism. They contend that while cannibalism may once have been practiced in a few parts of the world, there is no reliable evidence about it. Are their opponents perhaps prey to a mass delusion that has produced the specter of the cannibalistic "Other" throughout history? In contrast, Hooper, Lestringant, Marshall Sahlins, and their allies contend that there is plenty of evidence to show that, though not necessarily universal, customary cannibalism used to be widespread (Brown and Tuzin; Goldman; Leach). They see the skeptics as too eager to defend non-Western peoples from being stigmatized as cannibals or ex-cannibals; the skeptics are the deluded ones.[5]

The skeptics rightly note that the real practitioners of the various types of cannibalism have never had as much impact on (Western) history as their stereotypic simulacra. Both sides agree that imaginary cannibals have been all too influential as a negative stereotype of non-Western Others and as an excuse for the extermination of those Others (Obeyesekere 2). In her study of Australian captivity stories, Kay Schaffer notes that during the first two or three decades of colonization, "it is difficult to find even one reference to [Aboriginal] cannibalism in the local Australian press." The Tasmanian Aborigines were seldom tarred with the cannibal brush. But as white settlement expanded and met with increasing Aboriginal resistance, starting in "the late 1820s...the *Sydney Gazette* began to publish letters from settlers attesting to scenes of...cannibalism." Such stories "helped to justify colonial practices of extermination" (118; see also Pickering, "Consuming"). From the Renaissance through the 1930s, the same ideological utility was found for cannibalism in other supposedly benighted parts of the world. It not only supported "exterminating all the brutes," to quote Mr. Kurtz's genocidal phrase in *Heart of Darkness,* but also supported the missionaries, making their activities seem urgent and heroic.

Mortuary rituals provide some of the best evidence for customary cannibalism (Conklin 2001). In reverence, some peoples used to eat part or all of their deceased kinfolk. The motivations for endo-cannibalism no doubt vary from culture to culture but seem often to involve preventing the revered ancestor's corpse from rotting or from being eaten by animals. For the subtitle of her 2001 study of the Wari of Brazil, Beth Conklin uses the phrase "compassionate cannibalism"—a far cry from the bloodthirsty sort associated with mass slaughter and missionary stew (cf. Lewis 73). Some evidence for violent exo-cannibalism comes from New Guinea as recently as the 1970s (Gardner 29–36; Knauft; Shaw 180–81). Archaeologists have also provided new evidence, some of the latest involving DNA analysis, so the general case no longer stands or falls on eyewitness observation (White; de Gusta; Kirch 160–61). Although Obeyesekere does not mention it, primatology, too, may be relevant; cannibalism occurs fairly often among chimpanzees (Brady, "Cannibalism" 165; Hiraiwa-Hasegawa). All of this recent evidence, combined with that provided by missionaries, explorers, and the cannibals or ex-cannibals, makes a strong case for customary cannibalism in at least some societies. As in Obeyesekere's *Cannibal Talk,* the debate has devolved into issues of frequency and interpretation.

The skeptics point out that anyone who goes looking today for customary cannibals will not find them. This, however, is largely the result of both the extirpation of many indigenous peoples through the impact of imperialism and the conversion of the survivors to modern, Western ways and often to Christianity. No one disputes the fact that there have been numerous cases of survival cannibalism throughout history, and also of criminally insane cannibalism.[6] And after the 1970s customary cannibalism may no longer have been practiced anywhere in the world. That makes it a matter of historical record, or perhaps of nonhistorical nonrecord, or even of prehistory. In much Western discourse customary cannibalism has always been something that occurred in the primitive past, perhaps even before history began. Thus in *Totem and Taboo,* Freud's story of the origin of culture, the brothers of the primal horde murdered the ur-father to end his sexual monopoly over the women. "Cannibal savages as they were," Freud writes, "it goes without saying that they devoured their victim." But oedipal guilt prompted the brothers and their descendants to reenact the cannibal event as ritual repetition. "The totem meal, which is perhaps mankind's earliest festival, would thus be a repetition and a commemoration of this...criminal deed, which was the beginning of so many things—of social organization, of moral restrictions and of religion" (Freud 142). So the cannibal act that Freud posits as the origin of culture is precisely precultural and therefore prehistorical.[7]

But if cannibalism is prehistorical, how can it be historically apprehended, except through sheer speculation like Freud's? Without even asking whether other primates devour their own kind (they do), Freud simply assumes that the members of the primal horde were "cannibal savages." Freud was not alone, however: most nineteenth-century observers, including natural scientists and early anthropologists, assumed that many peoples throughout the world practiced anthropophagy. Cannibalism marked the low end of the evolutionary totem pole from savage to civilized. Darwin mistakenly believed that the Tierra del Fuegians were cannibals (Darwin, *Voyage* 214). And in *Man's Place in Nature* (1863), Thomas Henry Huxley included an illustration from a sixteenth-century Portuguese text that purports to show a cannibal butcher shop in West Africa. The otherwise scrupulously scientific Huxley admits that this image has no relevance whatsoever to his argument (Obeyesekere 223–25).

Before the major European explorations of central Africa starting in the 1850s, the locus classicus of cannibalism in the Western imaginary was the South Pacific, which from Cook's voyages forward surpassed the Caribbean. After all, the ferocious Caribs, from whose name the word "cannibal" derives, were exterminated by the Spanish long before the 1700s. In their *Voyage to the Pacific Ocean* (1784), Captain James Cook and James King write:

When Great Britain was first visited by the Phoenicians, the inhabitants were painted savages, much less civilized than those of Tongataboo, or Otaheite; and it is not impossible, but that our late voyages may, in process of

time, spread the blessings of civilization amongst the numerous islanders of
the South Pacific Ocean, and be the means of abolishing their abominable
repasts, and almost equally abominable sacrifices. (quoted in Wilson, *Island
Race* xv)

From the 1790s through the 1850s, in the wake of Cook's voyages, much of
the eyewitness evidence about South Pacific cannibalism comes from missionaries, so if the skeptics are correct, then missionaries were among the
main fabricators of the nonexistent cannibals.

There are also, however, numerous non-missionary accounts, such as
those concerning Fiji by Samuel Patterson, Peter Dillon, William Lockerby, William Endicott, Captain Charles Wilkes of the U.S. Exploring
Expedition, John Twyning, Mary Wallis, and John Jackson ("Cannibal
Jack," a.k.a. William Diaper or Diapea).[8] Obeyesekere "deconstructs" the
accounts by Dillon, Endicott, and Jackson, showing—to his satisfaction,
at least—why they cannot be trusted. But Marshall Sahlins contends that,
taken together with missionary accounts, they possess an ethnographic
consistency not easily dismissed. In "Artificially Maintained Controversies," Sahlins stresses the sheer number of accounts that describe the same
quite specific behaviors by Fijians after raids or battles. And then there
are the accounts by Pacific Islanders themselves, like the Rarotongan convert and "native teacher" or missionary Ta'unga, who claims to have witnessed plenty of cannibalism on the islands he visited, and who provides
detailed information about preparing, cooking, and eating human cadav-
ers.[9] "You will probably want to ask, 'How do [I] know'?" writes Ta'unga;
"I am telling you that with my own eyes I have witnessed these things"
(Ta'unga 91). Arens tries to discredit Ta'unga's account, but the most he
can show is that Ta'unga may have exaggerated (Arens 31–32). Whether
fully credible or not, moreover, Ta'unga is an extraordinary witness: he
is simultaneously native informant and missionary ethnographer, and the
same is true of both Joel Bulu and Maretu. "I have actually experienced
cannibalism," writes Maretu; "some of our own family gave us human
flesh to eat from [my father's] oven, and instructed us never to forget"
(Maretu 41; see also Gill 234–35; Tippett).

Ta'unga, Bulu, and Maretu may have exaggerated the violence of the
"heathens" to please the white missionaries who had converted and trained
them. But exaggeration is not wholesale lying, the charge Obeyesekere

brings against Endicott, Jackson, and Dillon. The skeptics want to treat all accounts of cannibalism as entirely true or entirely false, with no shadings between these extremes. But whether exaggerating or not, on what grounds can missionaries, either collectively or as individuals, be dismissed when they claim to be sojourning among cannibals? There is no evidence that they suffered from some sort of collective delusion about cannibalism. On the contrary, as Sahlins emphasizes, at least in the Fijian archipelago their individual accounts form a consistent, cumulative record over time and distance. Missionaries to the South Pacific were also often fearless defenders of the indigenous peoples they encountered, even those they held to be cannibals, against non-missionary colonizers. And some of them wrote detailed, surprisingly sympathetic accounts of the cultures of those they sought to convert.[10]

In the 1790s directors of the London Missionary Society (LMS) were influenced by Cook's *Journals* and other accounts of Polynesian societies as more welcoming than dangerous to choose the South Seas for their first proselytizing endeavors. In the Reverend Thomas Haweis's estimation, the main danger would be sexual temptation rather than violence. His Edenic description of Tahiti, stressing the perilous "fascination of beauty, and the seduction of appetite," concerns missionary rather than cannibal appetite (quoted in Samson, "Ethnology" 102).[11] The first "godly mechanics"—so called because, though some were ordained clergy, many were working-class artisans chosen for their practical skills—set sail to the islands of promising savagery in 1796 (Gunson). Their journals and records, written in the first instance for the governing bodies of the societies that supported their work, were often edited and reprinted for as wide a readership as possible, partly in the hope of gaining even more converts at home. Throughout the nineteenth century, the missionary press in Britain, the United States, and elsewhere was one of the primary sources of ethnographic information—and misinformation—for a general public just as eager for knowledge and vicarious adventure as for religious instruction (Johnston, *Missionary Writing*).

In the missionaries' narratives, from the moment of their arrival, in direct contrast to the romantic island paradise strain coming from Louis-Antoine de Bougainville, Cook, and others, the "horrid customs" of the Polynesians compete for the record of devilish degradation among all "savages." Some Polynesian behaviors were stark opposites of those of the missionaries. Several missionaries responded badly to sexual temptation and "went native"—that is, surrendered their souls to the devil—while some fled from scenes either too tempting or too horrific to endure.[12] For those who remained on task, moreover, the results were often disappointing. Yet their proselytizing in Tahiti, Hawaii, Samoa, and even "ferocious" Fiji was more successful than in Australia and many other parts of the world. When in 1812 "king" Pomare II of Tahiti *lotu'*d, or converted to Christianity, the missionaries believed they had won a providential victory and that many more victories would follow (Lovett 1:194–237). This was so even though Pomare continued to sin: he was a drunkard and he persisted in favoring a "detestable pander" who catered to his homosexual predilections (Lovett 1:227; Johnston, *Missionary Writing* 143–44).

The triumphalist strain in LMS discourse reached a climax with publication of the Reverend John Williams's 1837 *Narrative of Missionary Enterprises in the South Sea Islands.* Two years later climax became apotheosis, at least among the evangelical reading public in Britain, when Williams and another missionary, James Harris, were slain and allegedly eaten by the natives of Erromanga. Williams became an evangelical martyr-saint, eulogized in countless texts and sermons in Britain, much as David Livingstone would later be mourned and celebrated well beyond the circuit of missionary publishing and propaganda. Thus, in his 1859 best-seller *Self-Help,* under the rubric of "energy and courage," Samuel Smiles declared, "It was in the course of [Williams's] indefatigable labors that he was massacred by savages on the shore of Erromanga—none worthier than he to wear the martyr's crown" (272). Williams and the other South Seas missionaries were also eulogized in Victorian fiction, most notably in Robert Ballantyne's 1857 best-seller *The Coral Island.* In the final third of Ballantyne's novel, Ralph Rover and the other boy heroes learn much about the diabolical customs of cannibals and about the missionaries' miraculous success in converting them to Christianity and civilization. Ralph's sentiment is Ballantyne's: "God bless and prosper the missionaries till they get a footing in every island of the sea!" (231).[13]

Unlike those in Fiji and the Marquesas, missionaries stationed in Tahiti, Hawaii, and Samoa did not claim that they witnessed cannibalism. They believed that cannibalism was once practiced throughout the South Pacific but that it had ceased to be customary before their arrival, although other "horrid" customs such as infanticide and widow strangling persisted (see Williams, *Narrative* 456; Turner 240). This fact should dispel any notion that the missionaries suffered from a collective delusion, much less that they conspired to identify all "heathens" in all the world's "dark" abodes as man eaters. Nevertheless, even the most detailed, sympathetic missionary accounts of Polynesian cultures overemphasize the "horrid" and "unspeakable" in contrast to the peaceful, productive, and artistic. "Do not think that all the horrid evils of Fiji have been told you," writes the Reverend Joseph Waterhouse while depicting many of those "horrid evils" (119). One form of exaggeration that occurs in many missionary texts involves the trope of unspeakability.[14] Declaring a specific custom, behavior, or belief "unspeakable" typically emphasizes rather than conceals its identity, while also underlining the horror with which the Western reader is supposed to respond to it.

Despite "unspeakable" moments, Waterhouse's 1865 book *The King and People of Fiji* is remarkable for several reasons, not least because he was "the first Englishman... permitted to reside in [Bau,] the city of Thakombau, the titular King of Fiji" (Preface). Waterhouse became a fluent speaker of Fijian and lived in Fiji for fourteen years before publishing his account—a far longer time than that spent by most modern anthropologists doing fieldwork. And the Reverend Thomas Williams's 1859 *Fiji and the Fijians* is equally remarkable. George Stocking, Christopher Herbert, and Christine Weir all credit Williams with being one of the best missionary ethnographers. According to Herbert, of all the "early Polynesianists," Williams, with thirteen years' experience in Fiji, "explored most daringly the issue of the possible transformation of the 'civilized' Christian through contact with barbarous heathens" (Herbert 175; Stocking 87–92; Weir 163–67). The next section of this chapter examines *The King and People of Fiji* and *Fiji and the Fijians* as key missionary texts that deal with customary cannibalism and with "King" Thakombau.

The Wesleyans and Thakombau

The reputation of the Fijian archipelago as "cannibal islands" preceded the first missionaries to land there. In 1809 a group of LMS missionaries were briefly stranded on a Fijian island. Their journal, written by the Reverend

John Davies, contains no eyewitness testimony about cannibalism. It does, however, state:

> The Fejeans are probably the most notable cannibals existing. All their is-
> lands seem to be divided between petty Chiefs who are constantly at war
> with one another, and whenever a man can kill his enemy he will eat him;
> and sometimes hundreds are cut up and baked in ovens at the same time, to
> make a grand feast. They bake the human flesh in the same manner the Ta-
> heiteans bake their pork. (Cargill 154)

Since he did not observe any cannibalism, what evidence did Davies have for these claims? Perhaps he based them on what Captain Cook had writ-ten about Fiji: it "is said to be" populated by "Canibals, brave, Savage and Cruel. That they are Canibals, they themselves do not deny" (Cook, *Jour-nals* 3:163). But the Tahitians or Tongans whom Davies had encountered may have told him the same about Fiji (Scarr 10). In any case, Fiji had its cannibal notoriety—or stereotype—well before the arrival of the Wes-leyan missionaries starting in the 1830s. Perhaps this notoriety drew the Wesleyans into delusional discoveries of what they expected to find. But it is much more likely that the reputation, though perhaps exaggerated, was fairly accurate and not simply a stereotype. It is at least evident that the cannibal reputation of Fiji was shared by non-missionary Europeans and by many non-Fijian Polynesians prior to the advent of the Wesleyans.

After serving in Tonga, the Reverends David Cargill and William Cross were sent by the Wesleyan Missionary Society (WMS) to Fiji in 1835. They were fluent in Tongan and already learning Fijian, a language that Car-gill set about codifying partly for translating the Bible. Cross was often ill and Cargill was temperamental, so they were not as successful with "the natives" as later missionaries would be. Besides, Cargill's first wife and two of their children died, so he returned to London, where he remarried before setting out again for Tonga rather than Fiji. In 1843 Cargill com-mitted suicide, the victim of depression compounded by tropical disease. His dementia was perhaps partly caused by the "scenes of cannibalism and widow-strangling" he had witnessed (Cargill 4). Cargill's journal entry for August 28, 1839, describes trying to prevent an episode of cannibalism, with no success: "Early on Sunday morning the cooked human flesh was carried past the Mission house in a canoe." Cargill concludes this entry by echoing *Psalms:* "Truly the dark places of the earth are full of the habitations of cruelty" (148–49). Two months later, in a letter to the WMS, Cargill declares that "this morning we have witnessed a shocking spectacle." He continues:

> 20 dead bodies of men, women, & children were brought to Rewa as a present to Tui Dreketi from Tanoa.[15] They were distributed among the people to be cooked and eaten. . . . The children amused themselves by . . . mutilating the body of a little girl. . . . Human entrails were floating down the river in front of the mission premises, mutilated limbs, heads and trunks of the bodies of human beings have been floating about, & scenes of disgust and horror have been presented to our view in every direction. (158)

Cargill's account of this episode is seconded by the Reverend Thomas Jaggar, whose letter of November 1, 1839, to the WMS describes the same "shocking spectacle." He reports: "And oh! What scenes we have witnessed the recollection of them almost makes me shudder" (Cargill 158).

Jaggar had arrived in Fiji with two other WMS missionaries in 1838, John Hunt and James Calvert, and they in turn were followed by Richard Lyth, Thomas Williams, Joseph Waterhouse, and several others. The journals and letters of all these men provide eyewitness testimony to cannibalism, as well as to many other aspects of Fijian life. Most of them lived for years among the Fijians, who welcomed them into their communities from motives of hospitality, curiosity, and the desire for Western goods. Like white traders and beachcombers, the missionaries were useful, or potentially so, to Fijian chiefs in a variety of ways (Calvert 222; Scarr 11–15). Whether a chief converted or not, having a missionary in his community became a status symbol. And missionaries were exempt from being killed and eaten because of a "special *tabu*" accorded to priests and teachers of religion (Garrett 106). Nevertheless, "every day, and all day long, the Missionaries and their wives were compelled to hold intercourse with the natives" (Calvert 221–22).

The presence of large numbers of Tongans in Fiji was aided the missionaries' proselytizing. "King George" of Tonga had *lotu'*d, or converted, in 1834, and many of his people followed his lead (Scarr 21–27). The Tongans constituted a political and military power whose allegiance Fijian chiefs vied for, and Tongans such as Joel Bulu were readily trained to serve as "native teachers." The white missionaries meanwhile strove to eliminate those customs such as widow strangling that they considered diabolical, while supporting benign, productive ones. Even when interfering, they seem to have remained welcome, although once they began making converts, both they and the converts experienced persecution and, at times, considerable danger. But, writes Calvert, "Christianity has always received ultimate gain from the persecution aimed at its overthrow" (225).

Most of the missionaries gained the respect both of Fijian chiefs and of common folk; this was so of Thomas Williams and Joseph Waterhouse. Of the two, Waterhouse is more literary, Williams the better ethnographer. Thus Waterhouse incorporates Fijian poems or *meke* into his text. Furthermore, apart from the last two chapters, *The King and People of Fiji* is a biography of "King" Thakombau. Its stress is, therefore, on the life and deeds of that famous cannibal, while Williams's text deals more fully with the customs, beliefs, and practices of ordinary Fijians. That said, both books share the Manichaean worldview of all missionaries as well as the general weaknesses of most nineteenth-century ethnography. Thus, for example, Waterhouse and Williams lack a modern anthropological sense of Fijian culture as a whole way of life; instead of culture, they emphasize Fijian "character," a term with racial overtones (Weir 164).[16] Yet they rarely denigrate the Fijians in terms that we would today identify as racist. Perhaps that was because of the theory that many South Sea Islanders were an ancient branch of the Aryan race.[17]

Regarding several aspects of Fijian culture, Williams seems to have been more flexible or even relativistic than does Waterhouse. Thus, in blatant contradiction of his interest in Fijian poetry and his own use of the Fijian language for preaching, Waterhouse declares that that tongue contains no words "to express a spiritual conception" (345). In contrast, Williams notes that it is a "copious" language well suited for expressing all aspects of experience including the religious variety (*Fiji* 200–209). Waterhouse quotes Fijian poems and stories, but Williams ends his book with this paragraph:

> With a language such as has now been described, and with the blessing of God…among a people so strong-minded, so enterprising, and so versatile…there is no reason why Fijian literature should not by and by take its rank with the noblest cultures, to which the Gospel is at present shaping the genius and heart of so many heathen populations of our globe. (209)

Despite being a better ethnographer than Waterhouse, Williams fore-grounds the "brutalized and abominable" aspects of Fijian culture, as do all missionary texts. He focuses almost as much on the "bloodthirsty" deeds of chiefs or "kings" as on the everyday routines of ordinary Fijians. Thus he includes this episode, which he did not witness, but which appears in some other missionary texts (it took place before 1835):

> After having kissed his relative, [King] Tanoa cut off his arm at the elbow, and drank the blood as it flowed warm from the severed veins. The arm, still quivering with life, he threw upon a fire, and, when sufficiently cooked, ate it in presence of its proper owner, who was then dismembered, limb by limb, while the savage murderer looked with pitiless brutality on the dying agonies of his victim. (20; cf. Ta'unga 93–94)

Williams adds, "Murder is not an occasional thing in Fiji; but habitual, systematic, and classed among ordinary transactions" (134).

Reading the missionaries' accounts, one wonders how any Fijians sur-vived the murderous onslaught of their "horrid customs." With the intro-duction of firearms and the warfare that led to the emergence of Tanoa's son Thakombau as the most powerful "king" in Fiji, the population de-clined sharply, though some portion of that decline was caused by disease, as elsewhere in the South Pacific. In any event, although Williams dwells on "deeds of darkness"—warfare, torture, cannibalism, infanticide, and widow strangling—much of that emphasis occurs in his chapters on gov-ernment, war, and religion. Moreover, he rejects the "caricature" of the Fi-jians as "ferocious, and eager for bloodshed and battle" (33). Several factors such as "the pride and jealousy of the Chiefs" produce the wars that the average Fijian would just as soon avoid (33). And he is also critical of what he sees as exaggeration on the part of his informants: "Old natives speak of as many as a thousand being killed in some of the battles when they were young men; but I doubt whether the slain ever amounted to more than half that number" (40).

Williams's other five chapters provide a detailed, highly appreciative account of Fijian customs, family life, art, agriculture, house construction and canoe making, religious beliefs, and "language and literature." At the start of chapter 4, on agriculture and "industrial produce," Williams writes: "It is pleasing to turn from the horrible scenes of barbarous war, to the gentler and more profitable occupations of peace" (46). In general, he admires Fijians for their skillful sailing, carpentry, cooking, success in cultivating a variety of crops, and for their etiquette: "Among themselves the rules of politeness are minute, and receive scrupulous attention" (119). Furthermore, Williams's native informants were numerous, ranging from chiefs to commoners, carpenters to priests, fishermen to musicians.

The more literary, narrative quality of *The King and People of Fiji* is evident in Waterhouse's tendency to fictionalize episodes by inventing conversations that he could not have heard, and by expressing the thoughts he imagines Thakombau and other Fijians may have had. Thus the opening chapter, titled "First Blood," offers a fictionalized account of Thakombau's coming of age, well before the arrival of the missionaries, toward the end of which the "boy-chief" clubs his first victim: "This is noted here as the first deed of blood done by him who afterwards became the redoubtable Thakombau.... The boy-chief puts aside his heavy weapon to gaze on his first sacrifice to the customs of his people. Thence he departs to wash his hands, and partake of food; feeling himself every inch a man" (Waterhouse 7). It would be easy to accuse Waterhouse of inventing such an episode. But he spent long hours over several years in Thakombau's household, so it seems likely that he is giving a rendition of what he was told, perhaps by Thakombau himself.

Thakombau emerges from the missionaries' accounts as the most famous of all South Pacific cannibals, partly because he had a lot to say about cannibalism. If we accept what they say he told them, then certainly he and other chiefs viewed killing and eating their enemies their royal prerogative. On this score, Waterhouse quotes the journal of another missionary, the Reverend Walter Lawry, who visited Fiji in 1847:

> I received a visit from Thakombau.... He is an absolute ruler: whom he will he kills, and whom he will he keeps alive. Upon the whole, he is rather favourable to our mission here, but does not *lotu*. He professes great dislike to the introduction of Popery. War is his delight, and feasting on the bodies of the slain. He is sitting by my side while I write, and is urging me to persuade Governor Grey [of New South Wales] to visit him in a war-steamer, in order that they may be allied friends. He reposes confidence in England, but not in France. (quoted in Waterhouse 152)

Lawry adds that Thakombau told him "he and his chiefs...shall one day *lotu*" (152), or convert to Christianity, but it seems clear that the great chief wanted to squeeze every advantage he could out of the missionaries before taking that step (Scarr 21).

For nearly twenty years Thakombau either rejected the missionaries or, when it appeared to his benefit, drew them to Bau and tantalized them with the prospect of his eventual conversion. He obviously understood that conversion was on the horizon; many of the warlike, independent Tongans in Fiji were Christians, as were the small but growing number of white immigrants—all potentially valuable allies. And then Varani and several other Fijian chiefs *lotu'*d, perhaps because they saw the advantage of having the Christians on their side. Ships' captains and white traders often also told him to give up his heathen, warring, cannibal ways for Christianity (Scarr 31; Morrell 124).[18] That Thakombau was cagey about politics, including his own conversion, is evident from this conversation between himself and the Reverend John Hunt, which Waterhouse quotes from Hunt:

> *The Chief*: If I am the first to become a Christian among my people [of Bau], I shall be first in heaven, shall I not?
>
> *The Missionary*: If you love God the most, and serve Him the best, you may have a higher place in heaven.
>
> *The Chief*: But [Chief] Namosimalua has become a Christian. Have you given him glass windows for his new house, and English carpets for his floors, and have you sent to England for a vessel for him? He gets no riches because he has renounced heathenism.
>
> *The Missionary*: We do not come here to give riches to those who become Christians, but to tell you about God and Jesus Christ, that you may love Him, and your souls be saved.
>
> *The Chief*: Then I will not become a Christian. What will become of the bodies of those who have been eaten, and of those who have been buried? Will they rise again from the dead?
>
> *The Missionary*: Your body, the bodies of all those whom you have eaten, and the bodies of all who are in the graves, will rise again at the day of judgment; and if you and they have not repented, you will all be condemned and cast into hell-fire.
>
> *The Chief*: Ah, well! It is a fine thing to have a fire in cold weather. (quoted in Waterhouse 103)

Thakombau's sense of irony is evident here and elsewhere in his dealings with the missionaries and other Europeans from whom he believed he had something to gain. Sahlins writes that "after more than fifteen years of missionary hectoring," Thakombau "finally declared for Jehovah" on April 30, 1854. His doing so "abruptly redefined the terms of battle" for dominance in Fiji. "Aided now by missionary intrigue and the decisive military intervention of the Christian King of Tonga, Thakombau was able to rout his enemies in the battle of Kamba in April 1855. He was indeed saved" (Sahlins, *Islands* 37–40).

Well before then, Waterhouse felt he was becoming the conscience of the king. He claims, at least, to have prevented Thakombau from killing and eating a number of captives, and from strangling more widows of Tanoa and of other members of the royal family than custom would otherwise have dictated. Early in 1854, in a much-quoted letter, King George of Tonga advised Thakombau to lotu; enclosed with the letter was an article from a Sydney newspaper citing American "consul" John Williams's appeal to "the different [white] nations" of the world "to destroy Bau. The ease with which this could be done, 'while one is smoking a cigar,' was one of [Williams's] arguments" (Waterhouse 244). A general nuisance, Williams demanded that Thakombau pay $43,000 for various losses that he and other Americans had supposedly suffered in Fiji (Scarr 27–34; Morrell 129–30). Meanwhile, the white residents of Ovalau "had got the trade of Fiji into their hands" and were stopping ships from calling at Bau; some of them were plotting to overthrow Thakombau and install one of the other chiefs as Tui Viti or "king" of all Fiji (Calvert 471). The missionaries warned Thakombau, who had come to view the white traders as "a bad lot...mere stalkers of the beach...cormorants [who] will open their maws and swallow us" (quoted in Cumming 2). Whatever the intentions of the white traders, both missionaries and imperial officials wanted the warfare between Fijian chiefs to cease, and for power in Fiji to be consolidated in some central place and figure. Bau was such a place, and Thakombau was as accessible as, or more so than any of his rivals. And so with such threats, hectoring, and inducements, the most powerful chief in Fiji became a Christian.

In his attempts to consolidate his rule and to squirm out of paying Williams's "American debt," Thakombau in 1858 requested that all of Fiji become a British colony. This offer of cession was refused several times during the next sixteen years, until Britain reluctantly accepted it in 1874 (Morrell; Scarr 75). Thus the "King of the Cannibal Isles," having fallen on hard times, both *lotu*'d and turned his kingdom into a peaceful backwater of the mighty British Empire. In the days of his prime, however, when Thakombau was warring with neighboring chiefs to defend or increase his dominion, "the Bau ovens were never cold." Quoting this bit of "cannibal talk," Waterhouse adds, "as the natives say" (112).

Thomas Williams and Joseph Waterhouse helped to convert Fiji to Christianity, but "their own indoctrination had to precede that of their intended converts" (Herbert 185). Rather than the cannibals eating the missionaries, the missionaries introjected the cannibals, and vice versa. Both *Fiji and the Fijians* and *The King and People of Fiji* are thoroughly "polyvocal" in the "restrained and orchestrated," "hierarchical" manner of "traditional ethnographies" (Clifford, Introduction 15). As James Clifford puts it, even though there is a "pervasive authorial function" in such texts, "many voices clamor for expression" (15). One result is that Williams and Waterhouse can be "deconstructed" only by discrediting the "many voices," including Fijian voices talking about cannibalism, which speak to us through their mediation. Both the voices of the Fijians and the testimony of the Westerners who listened most carefully to those voices need to be heard, albeit with due caution about possible exaggeration, distortion, and prejudice.

Besides polyvocality, another aspect of *Fiji and the Fijians* and *The King and People of Fiji* that approximates many modern anthropological works is their use of the "ethnographic present." This is hardly a virtue, however. "The ethnographic present is the practice of giving accounts of other cultures and societies in the present tense," writes Johannes Fabian (80), with the result that they seem changeless, without history. Although both Williams and Waterhouse were writing after the conversion of Thakombau and much of Fiji to Christianity, they treat the "character" of the Fijian people as if locked in the primitive past, ironically because they employ the ethnographic present. The contradiction is more glaring in Waterhouse. After ending his 1865 biography of Thakombau with the triumph of Christianity over heathenism, he adds two general chapters titled "About the People" and "Mythology and Superstitions." These ethnographic chapters include such statements as "The Fijian religion requires cannibalism" and "Many eat [human] flesh through pride. Cannibalism is considered manly" (Waterhouse 313), just as if nothing had changed since 1835. Williams also treats the Fijians as unchanging, although he concludes with his assertion of the promising future of Fijian literature and culture.

While the missionaries' use of the ethnographic present does not undermine the polyvocal evidence in their texts about cannibalism and other aspects of past or passing Fijian culture, perhaps it implies some lingering doubt that their proselytizing had worked. Were they afraid that newly Christian Fiji would backslide? Just as likely, the ethnographic present in these texts may express an unconscious nostalgia for the exciting times that Williams and Waterhouse had experienced as adventurous young men, before they and their fellow missionaries, with the help of Western guns, gunboats, and goods, succeeded in taming the cannibals. After all, the final words from Waterhouse are Fijian *meke* or poems, including one that celebrates the victory of Thakombau over the rebels against his father, Tanoa, in 1837. "In some degree," Waterhouse says, "I was one of themselves" (241–42). If he and the other missionaries had "in some degree" gone native, that was the price they paid for transforming Thakombau and other Fijians "in some degree" into peaceable Methodists.

The repeated attempts by the converted "King" Thakombau to get Britain to turn the Fijian archipelago into a colony can be understood in various ways, but he clearly desired contact with the more powerful parts of the world and, for Fiji itself, modernization or development (for better or worse). Thakombau was also aiming for paramountcy in Fiji, under what must have seemed to him the very distant, abstract dominion of Queen Victoria. And it also seems likely that, by 1874 and in old age, Thakombau wanted what most Fijians wanted: peace. People caught in a cycle of violence (with or without cannibalism) typically long for its cessation. In her 1889 memoir *At Home in Fiji,* Constance Gordon Cumming recalls: "The old king...was never so happy as when Lady Robinson's...grand-daughter, a pretty little child with golden hair, crept on to his knee, whispering, 'You won't eat *me,* will you?' Or else he would lie down and rest on his mat, keeping his big Bible beside him" (18).

According to Claude Lévi-Strauss in *Tristes Tropiques,* "[the] missionaries who, along with the Protection Service, succeeded in bringing the strife between [the Bororo] Indians and colonists to an end, had both carried out excellent anthropological research...and at the same time pursued the systematic obliteration of native culture" (216). Similarly, the Wesleyan missionaries who helped end warfare among the Fijians often produced detailed, sympathetic accounts of Fijian culture even while aiming to eradicate various aspects of that culture, including cannibalism, infanticide, widow strangling, and what they saw as idolatry or devil worship. Like the missionaries to the Bororo in Brazil, the Wesleyans in Fiji are important historical witnesses as well as careful ethnographic observers. Although their accounts are marred by forms of exaggeration, including Manichaeanism, taken together with non-missionary accounts they form a consistent, detailed record over the better part of a century that provides strong evidence for, among other items, the practice of customary cannibalism as an aspect of Fijian warfare and chiefly bravado. While there may be reasons to doubt or dismiss this or that individual account of cannibalism or of other "horrid" practices such as infanticide, the cumulative record is impressive. It is irrefutable from the standpoint of empiricist historiography; there is no countervailing body of evidence, written or otherwise.

The specific reasons for the mass conversion and ultimate colonization of the Fijians need further investigation, but the missionaries offered more than what they considered to be the only true religion. They also offered the chance for Fijians to end their self-destructive warfare and to engage with the rest of the world—that is, to become "modern" or "civilized." I put these words in quotation marks because in much anthropological discourse they have pejorative connotations—as do also their antitheses, including "uncivilized," "primitive," and "cannibal." Anyone who travels to Fiji today will find the indigenous islanders welcoming, curious, and Christian. The other half of the population is Indian—the descendants, both Hindu and Muslim, of the laborers imported from the 1870s on to work on sugar cane plantations. Nobody eats anyone else in Fiji today; but native Fijians and those of Indian descent are in constant strife over political control of the archipelago. Nevertheless, *bula* means "hello," "thank you," "it's good," "I'm your friend," and "welcome"; it does not seem to have an opposite. And one of the Reverend Thomas Baker's boots rests in peace in the Fiji Museum in Suva.

2

King Billy's Bones

The Last Tasmanians

> To his quixotic, government-sponsored venture with the savages—in the
> service of which he had travelled the length & breadth of the dark, wild
> woods...Robinson had given the grand title of the Conciliation.
>
> RICHARD FLANAGAN, *Gould's Book of Fish*

The Fijians gradually gave up warfare and cannibalism while becoming Wesleyan Methodists and voluntarily joining the ranks of the colonized. In contrast, the indigenous inhabitants of Tasmania were overrun and exterminated by British convicts and settlers. The Tasmanian story is closer to the experiences of indigenous peoples elsewhere in the empire. As the number of Tasmanian Aborigines rapidly dwindled, missionaries and humanitarians tried to save them from complete annihilation. Starting in the 1830s, their depopulation was widely publicized as evidence that some or perhaps all "primitive races" were doomed to extinction when they came into contact with "white civilization" (Brantlinger, *Dark Vanishings* 124–30). This is how Darwin interpreted it in his consideration of race in *The Descent of Man* (1871). Unlike the Fijians, moreover, the indigenous Tasmanians were at first peaceable and only rarely accused of cannibalism. Before the late 1820s, writes Henry Reynolds, "the common view among the colonists was that the Tasmanians were a mild and peaceful people" (*Fate* 29).

The demise of the Tasmanian Aborigines is still infamous as an instance of genocide under British watch. In Australian history it is also remembered because of the deeds and words of George Augustus Robinson, who in the early 1830s launched his "Friendly Mission" to round up and save—in both the bodily and religious senses—the remaining Aborigines. In their introduction to *Reading Robinson,* Anna Johnston and Mitchell Rolls write, "Ideas about Robinson and his mission...have continuously circulated in popular culture and art from the 1830s onwards" (16). At least four twentieth-century novels revisit his story. In the nineteenth century, "Robinson and the Tasmanian Aborigines were envisioned by popular newspapers, pamphleteers and writers in the Victorian economy's commodification of empire," including what Anne McClintock calls "commodity racism" (Johnston and Rolls 17; McClintock 209).

The 2002 attempt by Keith Windschuttle to whitewash the destruction of the final Tasmanians involves denigrating Robinson's character and achievements. In Robinson's own opinion, he was the savior of the remnants of a perishing race. In Windschuttle's opinion, Robinson was a fraud. To make his case that Robinson is not to be trusted, Windschuttle cites Vivienne Rae-Ellis's debunking biography, in which she declares that for a variety of selfish motives, the Great Conciliator "became 'a liar and a cheat, a man of little honour,' whose reports about the conditions of the Aborigines under his control turned out to be largely fraudulent" (Windschuttle 35).[1] Robinson established a reservation on Flinders Island for the remnant of the dying race, and his accounts about the progress his unhappy charges were making en route to Christianity and civilization are indeed hyperbolic. Robinson was a self-promoter who clearly exaggerated the perils and successes of his errands into the wilderness (Pybus). But it is not the case that he deliberately fabricated any of the information he so patiently, obsessively compiled in his *Journals.* There is nothing in them concerning the behaviors and beliefs of the first Tasmanians that contradicts others' firsthand observations. Indeed, as Henry Reynolds points out, Robinson was something of a rarity in being interested in the Tasmanians "at a time when many of his contemporaries thought them contemptible and unworthy of any attention at all" ("George Augustus Robinson" 162).

Robinson provides much evidence that, contra Windschuttle, the social organization and customs of the first Tasmanians were not "dysfunctional" (Windschuttle 386). According to Robinson, the violence they aimed at white settlers, including their raids during the so-called Black War (1826–1830), was retaliatory. "Can we wonder then at the hatred they bear to the white inhabitants?" writes Robinson in an entry for August 20, 1830 (237). "This enmity is not the effect of a moment. Like a fire burning underground, it has burst forth. This flame of Aboriginal resentment can and ought only to be extinguished by British benevolence. We should fly to their relief" (237). The view, expressed by Windschuttle and inscribed in the early legal doctrine of *terra nullius,* that both the Tasmanian and the mainland Aborigines had no conception of property or of owning the lands they inhabited is the opposite of what Robinson repeatedly declares: "Patriotism is a distinguishing trait in the Aboriginal character" (762). In a report dated January 25, 1832, Robinson writes: "The chiefs assigned as a reason for their outrages upon the white inhabitants that they and their forefathers had been cruelly abused, that their country had been taken from them, their wives and daughters had been violated and taken away, and that they had experienced a multitude of wrongs" (602–3). Robinson also frequently expresses admiration for the moral virtues of his "sable friends," including, when they were treated with benevolence, their "great tractability. . . . My ears is not assailed by impious execrations, as would be the case with the same number of white men" (553). Elsewhere he expresses concern about the "indelicate"—probably sexually explicit—language of some of their songs, though about one of these he also records that "the tune is very pleasing" (432). And about their family relations, Robinson says: "The natives are very fond of their children, and the husbands of their wives. I know of no case of polygamy among them; nor any petulant or dishonest acts" (679).

Robinson's attempt to preserve the Tasmanian race from complete physical extinction was a failure. No modern commentators on his mission to transform the remnants of that race to civilization and Christianity believe that, in either spiritual or cultural terms, he was more successful. The lugubrious story of the final Tasmanians, supposedly totally obliterated from the face of the earth by 1876, became central to later attempts to explain what seemed to be the inevitable extinction of many other indigenous races. In *The Descent of Man,* Darwin focused on the Tasmanian case in his attempt to analyze why some primitive races were vanishing before the onslaught of civilization (or European colonization). He acknowledges the violence and diseases that decimated the Aborigines, but he is most interested in the infertility that affected the handful Robinson managed to round up. Even though Robinson corralled a little over two hundred, "the race" failed to reproduce itself. From Robinson's time forward, though guilt will forever haunt the story of the doomed Tasmanians, missionary and humanitarian interest gave way to the aim of scientific understanding of racial differences and destinies. Nevertheless, according to Alan Lester, in the 1830s and 1840s Robinson's reports, both from Tasmania and from Port Philip, where from 1836 he served as Protector of Aborigines, "were read by many as powerful support for a trans-imperial, humanitarian campaign against settlers' brutal dispossession of indigenous peoples." He was an important advocate "for an alternative, evangelical-inspired model of British colonialism" (Lester 28).

Given the ongoing controversy about whether what happened in Tasmania as well as on the Australian mainland was genocide, Robinson's testimony is crucial (Brantlinger, " 'Black Armband' "; Manne; Reynolds, *Indelible Stain*; Johnston and Rolls). It is also the case that, whatever the flaws and limitations of his character and of his account of Aboriginal beliefs and behaviors, his story is remarkable in many respects, including what it says about early colonial life and about the early forms of colonial knowledge. Robinson was not an ordained clergymen, but that was true of many missionaries. It is evident that he saw himself as a missionary. According to Reynolds, "much of Robinson's self-importance came from his conviction that he was doing God's work and following in the footsteps of the missionaries whose exploits in Africa and the Pacific were well known to him" ("George Augustus Robinson" 167). In *The Last of the Tasmanians* (1870), James Bonwick writes, "All honour to [Robinson's] intrepidity' and to the 'wonderful fidelity' of 'his Black guides' " (237). Bonwick is one of the most important commentators about the fate of the Tasmanian Aborigines and about Robinson's Friendly Mission; here I compare aspects of his books to Robinson's *Journals* in terms of the emergence of anthropology as one type of colonial knowledge.

Robinson and Missionary Ethnography

Bonwick rightly recognizes Robinson as a hero, although he also criticizes him in two ways. First, Bonwick points to "weaknesses of character" common to "many great and good men." The main weakness is Robinson's "perfect satisfaction with himself. This made him at times rather pompous and overbearing" (Bonwick, *The Last* 221). The *Journals* offer many examples of this failing. On July 24, 1833, Robinson boasts, "Providence had certainly crowned my labours with abundant success and I remarked that with me the motto *veni, vidi, vici* was applicable" (805). Later, on October 21, 1833, after returning to Hobart with a group of Aborigines, he declares: "The natives was highly pleased. The newspapers extol my exertions" (836). And he claimed that his rescue mission was "the most dangerous and arduous service that ever was entered upon" (878).[2]

Bonwick's second criticism relates more directly to the issue of how to judge especially the anthropological utility of Robinson's *Journals.* Although Bonwick probably never saw the field notebooks that make up the *Journals,* he was able to read many of Robinson's letters and reports. Bonwick describes plunging into Robinson's "ready-letter writing" (*The Last* 303), but he complains:

> I have been struck with the barrenness of information about the habits of the Tasmanians, when perusing the letters of Mr. Robinson, at the Record Office of the Colonial Secretary. No one could have told us so much, and yet we hear so little from him. A few stray statements have appeared, bearing his authority; but all must regret that a man of such observation and opportunity, and who lived in ease upon the pension of the Colonial Government so many years, made known scarcely anything of these curious and interesting tribes. (232)

It seems likely, however, that Bonwick would have been less frustrated if he had seen Robinson's *Journals.* As Norman Plomley writes, these give

> important information not only on the geography of Tasmania, many parts of which he was the first to see and the first to describe; but also on the Tasmanian Aborigines, about whom he has left the only account of many of the tribes; as well as upon certain aspects of history and in particular the origins of a native policy in the Australian colonies and the vital part which Lieutenant-Governor Arthur played in its development. (Plomley, introduction to *Friendly Mission* 3)

Plomley goes on to add, "Our knowledge of social organisation among the Tasmanians is slight," and "most of what we know has its basis in Robinson's statements." Plomley also notes that Robinson provides information about the flora and fauna of Tasmania "in their natural state," that "his comments on the Van Diemen's Land Company are of interest," and that his account of "the sealers is the most complete available" (3).

Yet as Plomley acknowledges, Robinson was hardly a systematic anthropologist, geologist, or naturalist. Johnston and Rolls agree that Robinson "was untrained in the specialist fields of recording and interpreting observations of Aboriginal life," though they immediately add, "But so were all early observers of Aborigines" (15). Robinson's *Journals,* letters, and reports nevertheless contain much information about the customs and beliefs of the Tasmanians that all subsequent observers have relied on. He certainly understood, contra Windschuttle, that they had been goaded into fighting a guerrilla war against the white invaders of their island. He also understood that although they may have had various failings, they were not cannibals. In *Daily Life and Origin of the Tasmanians,* Bonwick cites both Robinson and Alexander M'Kay, "who spent so much time among the race," as denying "the impeachment" that the Tasmanians were man eaters (22). Bonwick thinks that they may have "indulged in this practice, once adopted," he adds, "by our own ancestors in Britain," but he has encountered no good evidence that they did so (23). In *Last of the Tasmanians,* he recounts the story of a white girl whose mother warns her not to go into the bush "because she might be killed and eaten by the cannibals." She goes anyway, encounters some Aborigines, and finds herself "kindly treated by the sable throng" (8–9). Writing in the early 1870s, J. E. Calder also says that although the Tasmanians "were great flesh-eaters," they were "not cannibals, and never were." Game was so plentiful, he asserts, "that they had no occasion to resort to the revolting custom," and they "expressed great horror" when they were asked about it (35–36). And in *The Present State of Australia* (1851), Henry Melville writes that although the Tasmanians were "lowest" on the scale of human races, "those who suffered most from their warfare, and were, consequently, likely to attribute to them their worst propensities, never charged them with cannibalism" (346; see also Roth, *Aborigines* 97).

Anthropology as the systematic gathering of objective information about indigenous peoples began to develop only from about the mid-nineteenth century forward. To Bonwick, who attempts to write, at least retrospectively, as a scientific observer of the Tasmanian Aborigines, Robinson's *Journals* would probably not have seemed as devoid of information about the Aborigines as his correspondence and reports, but he still might not have trusted them. The *Journals* are first and foremost an account of Robinson's famous conciliatory manhunt. Robinson understood his mission to be of historical importance, and he presents himself as the last hope and rescuer of the nearly vanished Tasmanian "race." Scattered throughout the *Journals* are numerous passages in which he describes the behaviors, beliefs, and what Plomley calls the "social organisation" of the Tasmanians. But Robinson seems not to have viewed such information as crucial to the task of rescuing the "race" from extinction. This is probably because, though concerned about their physical preservation, Robinson believed their spiritual salvation to be much more important: his chief aim was to Christianize and tame or civilize them before they all perished. Their "native" culture was of only passing interest because, even if they were gentle savages who did not practice cannibalism, it was something that he wished to help them eradicate. Robinson wrote to Sir George Arthur, governor of Tasmania, on April 15, 1829, that "the amelioration of the Aborigines of Van Diemen's Land" meant "1. Civilisation; 2. Instruction in the principles of Christianity" (*Journals* 57).

In his study of Robinson's imbrication in the "imperial networks" of humanitarian and missionary discourse in the 1830s, Alan Lester writes that Robinson was familiar with "the reports of the London Missionary Society's Pacific and southern African missions," and he claimed "that he wanted to replicate the process by which 'the degraded Hottentot has been raised in the scale of beings and the inhabitants of the Society Islands are made an industrious and intelligent race'" (30). Cassandra Pybus also observes that, besides monetary and social advancement, Robinson "seemed genuinely motivated by a missionary impulse that had already involved him prominently in the Wesleyan Missionary Society, bible societies and a mission to seamen" (102). Something of Robinson's missionary zeal is evident in how he interprets Aboriginal stories about the Creation and about supernatural beings. He cites at length Woorrady's response to his question of "how and where the first black man came from," apparently without any attempt to refute him (405). But shortly before this, he records telling the Aborigines that "one God made black man and white man. When I spoke of heaven and how the good spirits live without food, Tom said how could they live without eating; and I explained" (403). Just how he explained the anorexia of the angels he does not say. But he also tells them there is only one devil instead of many. And he later preaches to them about the "one God [who] made us all" and says that their belief in and stories about various "devils" are "nonsense" (557). Repeatedly Robinson uses the words "devil" or "devils" to translate what the Aborigines probably regarded as spirits or unseen powers that could do either good or evil, as the spirits saw fit. Robinson's misinterpretation of non-Christian or "heathen" idols and spirits as "devils," or as manifestations of *the* devil, was an evangelical commonplace and a drawback in most versions of missionary ethnography.

In an outline of the book he planned to write, Robinson listed the primary reasons for his taking charge of "the Aboriginal establishment at Brune [*sic*] Island in 1829." First on the list is "a missionary desire to benefit this portion of the human race (the aborigines)." Second is "to benefit this land of my adoption." Last on the list is "to become acquainted with the history manners and language of this interesting portion of the human race particularly as very little or nothing was known of them more especially as I had entertained an impression that this race would ultimately and at no distant period become extinct" (971 n. 7). These priorities were probably those of most missionaries and humanitarians in Australia in the early 1800s. But as missionary endeavors to civilize and Christianize indigenous peoples throughout the British Empire proved more difficult than was anticipated, the priorities were reversed (Stocking 244). Modern anthropology emerged partly as what James Clifford calls "'salvage' ethnography" ("Allegory" 112), less concerned with saving primitive peoples from extinction, and not at all concerned with converting or civilizing them, but intent on preserving a record of their cultures and societies.

In expressing the view that the Tasmanian Aborigines were a "race [that] would ultimately and at no distant period become extinct," Robinson may seem to be contradicting himself; after all, he was supposed to be their physical protector as well as spiritual redeemer, whose job was to save the "race" from both extinction and damnation. But the belief in the inevitable extinction of the Tasmanians and other primitive races, although it underwent pseudoscientific reification later in the century, was widespread in Australia, in North America, and elsewhere by the early 1800s.[3] Robinson, however, would surely have rejected Bonwick's conclusion that his "sable friends" continued to die out on Flinders Island because of Robinson's own "over-sanguine" and narrow-minded attempt to civilize them. Bonwick quotes the *Melbourne Argus* to the effect that, on Flinders Island, civilization was equated with "a system of restraint and plodding methodised daily pursuits...[that] has terminated in those savages pining away, and dying *en masse*. They were, in the most literal sense, "civilized off the face of the earth" (*The Last* 351). While this criticism is perhaps too harsh, Robinson clearly shared with most nineteenth-century missionaries the belief that savage customs could and should be eradicated in favor of Christianity and the settled—as opposed to nomadic—habits of the white colonists.

Bonwick and Modern Anthropology

Robinson's *Journals* are not the sort of anthropological record that Bonwick compiled in *Daily Life and Origin of the Tasmanians* (1870). In that book, the anthropological twin or sequel to *The Last of the Tasmanians,* Bonwick draws on dozens of authorities, including Robinson, many of them with firsthand knowledge of the Aborigines. Anthropology is just one type of colonial knowledge, however, one whose origins lie in the decades between Robinson's Friendly Mission and Bonwick's books, roughly 1840 to 1870 (Stocking). While one of its starting points was the increasingly systematic information gathering about indigenous peoples conducted by the Colonial Office and also by the Aborigines Protection Society and its offshoots in places such as Sydney and Hobart, another was the writings of missionaries. As noted earlier, George Stocking, Christopher Herbert, and others have made the case for missionary ethnography, at least in some instances. Texts such as David Livingstone's *Missionary Travels and Researches in South Africa* (1857) and the Reverend Thomas Williams's *Fiji and the Fijians* (1859) are examples, and in *Last of the Tasmanians,* Bonwick himself cites the Reverend Joseph Waterhouse as an authority on "the rude and cannibal Fiji islanders" (112).[4]

The forms of colonial knowledge include the broad category of humanitarian, missionary, and abolitionist discourse dominant in the first third of the nineteenth century, but also the versions of "ethnology," "anthropology," and "scientific racism" that grew in number and influence from the 1840s forward.[5] Darwin and social Darwinism are one major aspect of this later development, as is the emergence of cultural anthropology in its evolutionary or Darwinian phase, marked in Britain by publication of

Edward Burnett Tylor's *Primitive Culture* (1871). In *Victorian Anthropology,* George Stocking examines the mid-century split between "anthropology" and "ethnology," with the former stressing monogenesis, or the unity of *Homo sapiens* as a single species, and the latter insisting on polygenesis or the multiple origins of "the races of man," viewed as separate species. In *Origin of Species* and *Descent of Man,* Darwin supported monogenesis: the similarities between the races were far greater than the differences, pointing to the probability, at least, of a single origin. As Stocking notes, prior to mid-century and the "ethnological" stress on the physical differences among the races, supposedly demonstrable through craniology, Peter Camper's facial angle, and other pseudoscientific measurements, most discourse on race adhered to the biblical version of Creation, and hence to monogenesis. This was the position of James Cowles Prichard, the most important British authority on human races and cultures before Darwin and Tylor. Belief in monogenesis points to the paradoxical commonality between early missionary and abolitionist views about race and later anthropological views, from Darwin, Huxley, Tylor, and other evolutionists into the twentieth-century era of cultural relativism, stressing monogenesis, or the unity of *Homo sapiens* as a single species. Both missionaries and evolutionists believed in the unity of the human species, even as they often also stressed what they saw as the huge differences between races that they could explain as resulting either from cultural and historical factors or from racial inferiority and its opposite, the supposed superiority of the white race and its civilization.

Robinson adheres to the early, monogenist, and humanitarian view about the equality of the races and the unity of the human species. He declares repeatedly that the Tasmanian Aborigines are his brothers and sisters. In contrast, Bonwick is torn between what might be called missionary (or humanitarian) monogenism and the later, ethnological view—whether monogenist or polygenist—that emphasized both the physical and the cultural differences among the races. In terms of the forms of colonial knowledge, Robinson's *Journals* bear comparison to other explorers' narratives, especially in the Australian context. But just as important, they are characteristic of humanitarian, missionary, and abolitionist discourse from the 1790s into the 1840s. They are so in part because Robinson expresses little interest in the physical differences between the Aborigines and the European settlers, either in Tasmania or on the mainland. He is far more concerned about the issue of slavery than about any physical or for that matter mental inequalities between himself and his Aboriginal guides and charges.

Especially in his dealings with the sealers, Robinson understood his "mission" as directly related to the broader antislavery cause. (The British Parliament outlawed the slave trade in 1807 and abolished slavery in all British territory in 1833.) On October 10, 1829, regarding the sealers' kidnapping and abuse of Aboriginal women and children, he writes: "The Aboriginal female Mary informed me that the sealers at the straits carry on a complete system of slavery; that they barter in exchange for women flour and potatoes; that they took her away by force.... Surely this is the African slave trade in miniature, and the voice of reason as well as humanity calls for its abolition" (91). And on November 17, 1830, Robinson declares, "To abolish the slave trade the government at home has expended millions; and that it should exist in her colony is certainly improper and disgraceful" (313).

As Alan Lester points out, Robinson was familiar with abolitionist discourse before he emigrated to Tasmania (31). In *Civilising Subjects,* Catherine Hall demonstrates that the crusade against slavery influenced many aspects of British as well as colonial culture. Governor Arthur and Colonial Secretary Lord Glenelg understood the Friendly Mission partly in abolitionist terms; indeed, the 1830s were a period of intense evangelical humanitarianism emanating from the Colonial Office in London. Robinson's expressions of humanitarian sympathy for the Aborigines are often awkward and unsophisticated, but they are unmistakably sincere: "My feelings was overcome. I could not suppress them: the involuntary lachryme [*sic*] burst forth and I sorrowed for them. Poor unbefriended and hapless people! I imagined myself an Aborigine. I looked upon them as brethren not, as they have been maligned, savages. No, they are my brethren by creation. God has made of one blood all nations of people" (310). In contrast, though Bonwick also expresses humanitarian sympathy for the fate of Aborigines in Tasmania and elsewhere, he cites authorities on all sides of the ethnological versus anthropological divide on many issues, including whether the first Tasmanians were an entirely separate species and whether they, perhaps like all other "primitive races," were doomed to extinction. In *The Last of the Tasmanians,* Bonwick quotes various experts who held that, in the words of Theodor Waitz, "the extinction of the lower [species and/or races] is predestined by Nature; and it would thus appear that we must not merely acknowledge the right of the white American to destroy the Red man, but perhaps praise him that he has constituted himself the instrument of Providence in carrying out...this law of destruction" (375)—a "law" reinforced, from the 1840s on, by evolutionary speculation and theory. By citing all sides on these and other issues, Bonwick vacillates between a humanitarianism like Robinson's and a reified, hard-boiled—that is to say, scientific—point of view.

Thus, concerning cannibalism, Bonwick cites the claims of various authorities that both the Tasmanians and the mainland Aborigines practiced it. But he also notes that "Mr. G. A. Robinson and Mr. [Alexander] M'Kay...deny the impeachment" (*Daily Life* 22). Today there is no reliable evidence that either the Tasmanians or any of the mainland Aboriginal societies practiced cannibalism. More important, Bonwick is grateful to be able to include the craniological chart given him by "Dr. Paul Topinard, of Paris," and he quotes Topinard at length in French about it (*Daily Life* 113–18). Topinard's conclusion is that the skulls of the Tasmanians reveal "une organisation supérieure" to that of the mainland Australians and also that they have nothing in their "crania" ("qu'ils n'ont rien dans leur crâne") that suggests an affinity with African negroes (118).

Why would Bonwick include Topinard's minute, pedantic skull measurements if neither he nor Topinard believed in their scientific validity? Yet Bonwick later cites Topinard among the experts who debunked craniology as pseudoscience. Bonwick declares that "it is scarcely safe to pronounce upon any skull as a type of a nation." He continues:

> Mr. Crawfurd thought the attempt [craniology] an absurd one. Dr. Meigs, after a review of 1,125 crania, declared he could find none typical. Professor M. J. Weber acknowledges that "there is no proper mark of a definite race-form of the cranium so firmly attached to it that it may not be found in some other race." Dr. Paul Topinard seemed to favour that view, when exhibiting to me some Tasmanian skulls in Paris....The great authority of Professor Huxley may be instanced, when he testifies that "cranial measurements alone afford no safe indication of race." (*Daily Life* 126)

And so forth.

Yet the spell of craniology, phrenology, physiognomy, and other attempts to quantify racial inequalities by physical measurement hovers over Bonwick's text, as it does over the ethnological and anthropological debates of the mid- and late Victorian eras. These attempts expressed a materialist determinism, strongly associated with scientific explanation, that underscored the inevitability of the extinction or extermination of the "lower races" by the "higher" ones in "the struggle for existence." As an amateur physical anthropologist (or race scientist), Bonwick himself engaged in craniology both with Topinard in Paris and at the museum of the College of Surgeons in London. It was in the latter location, he writes, that he "found the best collection of Tasmanian skulls," explaining: "It was to enrich this noble collection that Dr. Crowther is said to have performed the office of decapitator upon the body of the last man of the race in Hobart Town. My measurements were necessarily, from my unprofessional character, of a defective order. I confined myself to those of a simple kind" (131). Why did Bonwick bother to take any measurements if he knew in advance they were going to be "of a defective order"? He seems more convinced of the validity of his phrenological observations of the Tasmanian skulls that he goes on to enumerate (131). Whatever the case, it was clearly just as important to him to try to be scientific as to express humanitarian outrage, guilt, or mourning over the vanishing of the first Tasmanians.

Bonwick situates his own admittedly flawed attempts at scientific measurement in the context of the story of what Dr. W. L. Crowther did with the corpse of the last Tasmanian Aboriginal man, William Lanney, in 1869. The lugubrious tale of the final days and burial of "King Billy" Bonwick tells at length in *The Last of the Tasmanians* and with an evident humanitarian outrage directly opposed to the scientific pretensions of Crowther and the other colonial Frankensteins who coveted Lanney's bones, as they would later covet those of the last Tasmanian woman, Trugernanna. After describing Lanney's upbringing, his friendly personality, his alcoholism, and his death, Bonwick turns to the reports published in the *Hobart Town Mercury* concerning Lanney's burial and the multiple grave robbings and grotesque "mutilation of his body" (396) that ensued.

Although the colonial secretary, Sir Richard Dry, "sent positive instructions... that the body of 'King Billy' should be protected from mutilation" (quoted 396), whatever protection was provided failed. The *Mercury* report continues: "It is a somewhat singular circumstance that, although it has ever been known for years that the race was becoming extinct, no steps had ever been taken in the interest of science to secure a perfect skeleton of a male Tasmanian Aboriginal." So with King Billy's death, the scientific establishment was on the alert: "The Royal Society, anxious to obtain the skeleton[,]...wrote specially to the Government upon the subject....The Government at once admitted their right to it, in preference to any other institution....Government, however, declined to sanction any interference with the body, giving positive orders that it should be decently buried" (quoted 397). Enter, therefore, Dr. Crowther into the "dead-house at the hospital" in the dead of night. Crowther skinned Lanney's skull and, before he carried it away, inserted the skull of another corpse into "the scalp of the unfortunate native, the face being drawn over so as to have the appearance of completeness" (quoted 398). When this double decapitation was revealed, the Council of the Royal Society then "resolved to take off the hands and feet and to lodge them in the Museum, an operation which was carefully done" in order to make the rest of Lanney's remains relatively valueless. According to the *Mercury* (Bonwick is less clear about it), Lanney's "body was of the greatest scientific value," and particularly in its entire, unmutilated condition. Its value seems to have fallen drastically after its decapitation and the removal of its hands and feet. Bonwick concludes, "It is sufficient to add that Dr. Crowther was suspended as honorary surgeon of the hospital, that the skeleton was in possession of the Royal Society of Tasmania, and that, according to the *Launceston Register,* 'it is expected that one of the first orders on the assembling of Parliament will be a "return of King Billy's head!"'" (399). This reunion of King Billy's bones never took place. In *The Aboriginal Tasmanians,* Lyndall Ryan writes that another doctor "had a tobacco pouch made out of a portion of the skin, and other worthy scientists had possession of the ears, the nose, and a piece of Lanney's arm. The hands and feet were later found in the Royal Society's rooms in Argyle Street, but the head never reappeared" (217)—although it seems to have found its final resting place with the College of Surgeons in London.

Another episode of scientific enthusiasm and grave robbing occurred after the death of Trugernanna. Her bones disappeared altogether until the 1890s, when they were discovered packed in an apple crate in the Tasmanian Museum in Hobart. They were then unpacked, and the skeleton was exhibited in the museum until protests by Aboriginal activists prompted its curators to remove it and allow its cremation in 1976, marking the centennial of Trugernanna's death. In *What the Bones Say,* John Cove declares, "A review of the literature prior to 1950 shows no evidence that Truganini's [*sic*] skeleton had been used in any published research" (147). The same is undoubtedly true of King Billy's bones; even if craniologists in London had measured his skull, no scientifically meaningful evidence could have been drawn from such an act of obsessive materialism.

Despite his lack of sophistication, his self-puffing, and his Christian zeal, Robinson has much more to tell us about the Aboriginal Tasmanians than do later, supposedly scientific attempts to weigh and measure their remains. Even when sympathetic anthropological commentators such as Bonwick, Tylor, and H. Ling Roth emphasize cultural and societal factors rather than those preferred by Victorian race scientists or ethnologists who thought they were finding evidence of racial inferiority and inevitable extinction in such physical factors as skull capacity, after Bonwick scientists ceased to have any meaningful firsthand experience among the Tasmanian Aborigines. Tylor and Roth are dependent on Bonwick, who is in turn dependent on Robinson, M'Kay, and other firsthand observers of the Aborigines—despite his many flaws, none of these observers more important than the Great Conciliator.[6]

As Henry Reynolds argues in his superb account of what happened to the Tasmanian Aborigines, *The Fate of a Free People,* if there is anything misleading in Robinson's *Journals,* it stems from his magnification of his role at the expense of that of the Aborigines who aided him:

> By any measure Robinson's six expeditions were significant journeys of exploration. But like comparable ventures on mainland Australia they were highly dependent on Aboriginal bushcraft and diplomacy. Robinson was the most inexperienced of explorers. He was neither bushman, squatter, surveyor nor soldier. He had no bush experience at all. He was guided, fed, sheltered and, in all likelihood, managed by his Aboriginal companions. It was they, and not God, who "led him in paths which he knew not." (136)

Reynolds notes Robinson's occasional acknowledgments that, as he wrote, "I cannot affect anything without these people" (quoted 137). "My greatest confidence was in the natives," Robinson confided. "They were well acquainted with the resources of the country and would not allow me to want" (149). Nevertheless, as Robert Hughes puts it, the remnant of the Aborigines "followed their evangelical Pied Piper" to Flinders Island (Hughes 423), which another historian, Lloyd Robson, has called "the world's first concentration camp" (Robson 220). That was not, of course, how Robinson saw it. He meant Wybalenna to be a peaceable, Christian settlement, governed in the best interests of the Aborigines by benevolent white men like himself. But the rest, as they say, is history. Today the mixed-race descendants of white sealers and Tasmanian Aboriginal women, after long struggle against enforced oblivion, have gained the rights (such as they are, belated and insufficient) accorded to mainland Australian Aborigines.

The struggle for those rights has had to combat the myth of the complete extinction of the Tasmanian race. When, toward the end of the 1800s, an anthropologist proposed that Mrs. Fanny Wright was a Tasmanian Aborigine, other experts, including H. Ling Roth, insisted that she was of mixed-race parentage. (Roth based his opinion on photographs that were sent to him in London.) There were supposedly no more indigenous Tasmanians after 1876. But as I. P. S. Anderson, himself a Tasmanian Aborigine, observes, "the notion of racial extinction is nonsense if you accept that race is a scientifically implausible construct" (73).

Part II

RACIAL ALTERNATIVES

3

Going Native in Nineteenth-Century History and Literature

> When one tries to rise above Nature one is liable to fall below it. The highest
> type of man may revert to the animal if he leaves the straight road of destiny.
>
> SHERLOCK HOLMES in "The Adventure of the Creeping Man"

According to its advocates, the grand purpose of the British Empire was
to bring civilization and Christianity to "the natives" of the non-Western
world. But the advocates often also claimed that "the natives" could not be
fully civilized. Perhaps their souls could be saved—though even this was
debatable—but "the natives" could only "mimic" or "ape" their white betters. The same notion circulated in the United States: slaves and ex-slaves
could be partly but never fully educated; they could only copy, typically
with comic effect, members of the white race.[1] In contrast, Native Americans were often viewed as a doomed race; when they tried to mimic whites,
they sealed their fate. Indians mimicking whites supposedly "imbibe all our
vices, without emulating our virtues" (quoted in Dippie 25). But just how
is "mimicry" by "natives" different from what happens when supposedly
civilized white people mimic "the natives"? This is what "going native"
means, and there are many examples of it in both history and literature.

One difference between "mimicry" by "natives" and "going native" is
that while the natives supposedly can't achieve full civilization, a white

person can shed civilization and achieve full savagery. At the start of Charles Dickens's *Great Expectations,* Pip is seized by escaped convict Abel Magwitch, who shakes him upside down and demands he bring him a file and some "wittles." Otherwise, Magwitch threatens, "your heart and your liver shall be tore out, roasted and ate" (3). Magwitch adds that if he himself doesn't roast and eat Pip's heart and liver, then he is with a "young man" who is even more ferocious and will be sure to get at them. This threat of cannibalism by white men proved real in the case of transported Irishman Alexander Pearce, who in the early 1800s escaped with seven other convicts from Macquarie Harbor in Tasmania. They survived by killing and eating one another. Pearce was the ultimate survivor who, when he was finally recaptured, was carrying an axe and a bundle of human flesh.[2]

Turning cannibal does not necessarily mean going native, however, because most natives weren't cannibals. Besides, there seems always to have been a few highly civilized cannibals, like Hannibal Lecter. But Dickens and other Victorian writers treat cannibalism as the nadir of savagery, the complete antithesis of civilization. Pearce and Magwitch are, moreover, examples of home-bred savagery, and there were many more where they came from, as the title of Phillips Watts's 1855 book *The Wild Tribes of London* suggests. Also, many versions of going native were not so horrific as Pearce's cannibalism. Indeed, some versions were benign. As noted in chapter 1, missionaries to Polynesia or Africa expected to live for years among "the natives," learn their languages, eat their food, and adopt many of their customs, even as they strove to convert their native hosts to Christianity. In W. S. Gilbert's "The Bishop of Rum-ti-Foo," the natives

> played the eloquent tum-tum
> And lived on scalps served up in rum—
> The only sauce they knew.
> When first good BISHOP PETER came
> (For PETER was that Bishop's name),
> To humor them, he did the same
> As they of Rum-ti-Foo.   (15)

When in Rum-ti-Foo, do as the Rum-ti-Fooans do.

There was of course a spectrum ranging from positive to negative versions of going native. Many instances involved captivity and coercion, but others were voluntary, with all sorts of variations in between. And while going native could result in a permanent change of behavior and culture, it could occur as well on a temporary basis. Motivations for going native also varied, as suggested by the contrast between missionaries and escaped convicts. This diversity of patterns, motivations, and duration makes it difficult to construct a taxonomy of types of going native. Racism may often have impeded adopting the ways of other cultures, but throughout the British Empire versions of racial mixing, including ideas about the inevitability of hybridity, were just as evident as types and theories of racial apartheid (Young). Theories about race of all sorts, however, often stressed the threat of racial degeneration (Pick). For those who adhered to the biblical story of Creation, all present-day races resulted from degeneration after the Fall or after the Flood. The threat of racial degeneration among whites at home or in the colonies raised the specter of "the imperial race" itself falling prey to a collective form of going native.

Literature versus History

As noted in chapter 1, for the Victorians, the most notorious cannibalistic natives were probably the Fijians. But, like Joseph Waterhouse and Thomas Williams, many of the early missionaries to Fiji lived there for decades. While they were neither eaten nor converted to cannibalism—and while they strove mightily to put an end to so-called man eating, they adopted many Fijian customs. Furthermore, missionaries often took sides with the natives against the incursions of non-missionary colonizers. In Robert Louis Stevenson's story "The Beach of Falesá" (1893), Wiltshire complains that missionaries "look down upon" traders like him; "and besides, they're partly Kanakaised, and suck up with natives instead of with other white men like themselves" (34). Being "Kanakaised" means going native. Nevertheless, Wiltshire marries a Kanaka woman, with whom he has several "half-caste" children.

Although most missionaries stayed true to their cause, some went native in unacceptable, supposedly heathen ways. Thus Charles Stokes abandoned the Church Missionary Society, took an African mistress, and lived by slave trading and gunrunning. He was executed in the Congo for selling guns to Arab slave traders. Stokes may have been one of the models for the best-known example of "going native" in Victorian literature, Mr. Kurtz in

Joseph Conrad's *Heart of Darkness* (Watt 141–46). Kurtz goes to the Congo as a brilliant, highly moral emissary of European civilization. By the time Marlow reaches him at the Inner Station, Kurtz has succumbed to greed and egomania; he has acquired an African mistress and a horde of black followers who worship him in rites that Marlow calls "unspeakable" and "diabolical." Kurtz's dying words, "The horror! The horror!" may refer to death or to African savagery, but they undoubtedly also refer to his own backsliding from civilization—in other words, to his going native.

Conrad knew what he was writing about. In 1890 he made the journey up the Congo River that Marlow undertakes, and he was one of the early witnesses to the death and devastation occurring in the private colony that King Leopold of Belgium had established there. During the killing times in Leopold's Congo, perhaps half of its population perished—a genocidal toll equivalent to the Holocaust (Hochschild 233). In any event, Conrad understood that men like Kurtz were not uncommon in Africa. Sir Harry Johnston, administrator of British Central Africa in the late 1800s, re- marked, "I have been increasingly struck with the rapidity with which such members of the white race as are not of the best class, can throw over the restraints of civilization and develop into savages of unbridled lust and abominable cruelty" (68).

A positive version of going native is offered by a literary contemporary of Kurtz, Rudyard Kipling's Kim. An Irish orphan who is more Indian than the Indians, Kim serves as a spy for the British secret service and as the *chela* or disciple of the lama with whom he travels through northwestern India. Thoroughly enjoying his adventures, Kim succeeds both in foiling the Russian and French agents and in helping the lama achieve salvation. Kim has been growing up as an Indian, so going native is not a matter of choice for him. But his enjoyment—and Kipling's enjoyment—of India is so great that it seems very unlikely he would have chosen to be a good, civilized, stay-at-home British or Irish boy. The only aspect of Kim's career that isn't enjoyable occurs when he is sent to school for an English make- over. Kipling is an imperialist and a white supremacist, yet he shares in the delight and freedom that going native affords his boy hero. Moreover, Kim's ability to behave like the natives helps to preserve British rule from foreign meddling. So in his case going native benefits the British Empire rather than undermining it.

If Kurtz and Kim represent the negative and positive extremes of going native in literature, there are all sorts of variations and degrees between them. But just how many actual cases of going native were there in the history of the British Empire or for that matter of the United States, France, or other imperial powers? Although it is impossible to count actual cases, there were undoubtedly far more instances of going native in reality than in literature. In *Captives,* Linda Colley draws on "over a hundred printed and manuscript narratives written or dictated by Britons between 1600 and the mid-nineteenth century in response to captivity" in North Africa, North America, and Asia (13). Captivity did not necessarily lead to going native, but quite frequently captives changed their behavior, their language, their outward appearance, and even their political and religious allegiances. Often this occurred under duress and only temporarily; but in some cases it happened permanently and out of a measure of choice. Moreover, such adaptability to other cultures was never confined merely to captives.

In North America from the 1600s on, captivity narratives were common, but so were instances of white and black people voluntarily joining Indian tribes. "During the [French and Indian] War," writes Colley, "desertions from among the lower ranks of British regiments...to...indigenous communities proved so numerous that any redcoat discovered living alongside Indians and claiming to have been captured, risked being court-martialed" (195–96). Benjamin Franklin observed that whites who had been rescued from the Indians often took "the first opportunity of escaping again into the woods" to rejoin their captors, "from whence there is no redeeming them" (411); and Hector St. John Crèvecoeur declared that "there must be in [the Indians'] social bond something...far superior to anything to be boasted of among us; for thousands of Europeans are Indians" (214). These remarks have been confirmed by historian James Axtell, who documents that starting in the first days of colonization, hundreds of whites were assimilated into Indian families and societies. Escaped slaves also frequently joined the Indians, most famously in the case of the Seminoles.[3]

Related to going native is "indigenization," the term Terrie Goldie applies to a key way colonial societies sought to distinguish themselves as new and unique. The development of new, national literatures in the United States, Canada, Australia, and New Zealand led many writers, wishing to establish their or their texts' national, racial, or ethnic credentials, to confront what Goldie calls "the impossible necessity of becoming indigenous" (13). Even as the indigenous peoples in all of these places were being decimated, colonial and early nationalist literatures adopted "native" stories and themes. From the Indian getups worn by the Boston Tea Partiers to black Indians in Mardi Gras parades, there are countless North American examples of indigenization. In Australia, the Jindyworobaks—white poets in the 1930s and 1940s—sought to incorporate Aboriginal stories and motifs into Australian literature, a trend that continues today. And there are many instances of white writers who have pretended to be Aborigines or Native Americans. But writing as an Indian or an Aborigine is, after all, not the same as crossing the cultural divide and becoming, as nearly as possible, an Indian or Aborigine.

Pakeha Maoris and White Blackfellows

"White Indians" and "Pakeha" Maoris, writes Daniel Thorp, were "colonial officials' worst nightmare" (1). Among the first whites in New Zealand were escaped convicts from Australia who, if not killed and eaten, were often adopted by Maori tribes. Others were sailors who jumped ship, like Herman Melville in the Marquesas. An 1827 portrait of John Rutherford shows him with a complete facial tattoo or *moko,* which means that he had become a full-fledged Maori warrior.[4] There were perhaps two hundred Pakeha Maoris before midcentury, who ranged in status from slaves to chiefs. Jacky Marmon, for example, acquired mana, land, slaves, and several Maori wives. He came to be regarded in his *hapu,* or clan, as a shaman. He shot one wife whom he suspected of adultery. And he confessed to practicing cannibalism and to shooting another Pakeha Maori "in a dispute over a pig" (Bentley 44).[5]

At the end of his autobiography, another Pakeha Maori, Frederick Maning, predicted continuing warfare between the Maoris and the British colonists, while refusing to take sides: "I am a loyal subject to Queen Victoria, but I am also a member of a Maori tribe; and I hope I may never see [New Zealand] so enslaved and tamed that a single rascally policeman, with nothing but a bit of paper in his hand, can come and take a *rangatira* [chief] away from the middle of his *hapu,* and have him hanged for something of no consequence at all, except that it is against the law" (216). In 1865 Maning became a justice of the peace and a judge for the Native Lands Court; by all accounts he was an outstanding citizen of the colony.

In Australia, escaped convict William Buckley spent thirty-two years among the Aborigines. Calling himself "the real" Robinson Crusoe after having "lived for so many years among the savages," Buckley forgot, he declared, "the use of my own language, and [became] careless about every thing civilized, fancying I could never return to a better kind of existence, or to the intercourse of any other society than that of the tribes" (Morgan 87). Shipwrecked sailor James Morrill lived among the Aborigines of northern Queensland for seventeen years, while John Graham, the convict rescuer of Eliza Fraser, spent six years as a white blackfellow.[6]

Better known than these real-life characters is the 1845 novel *Ralph Rashleigh,* written by another runaway convict, James Tucker. In Tucker's probably autobiographical story, Rashleigh escapes from a penal colony and winds up living with a tribe of Aborigines for over four years. Rashleigh "was well content" with his lot, "convinced as he was that it was safer and better than what awaited him if he returned to live among white men" (Tucker 295). The head of the tribe, who treats him as his adopted son, gives Rashleigh a female Aborigine, who "was the first woman who had ever given him affection" (314). As do many other "native" women in colonial romances, she sacrifices herself to save her white lover from being killed by two renegade Aborigines. Nevertheless, "during the four years which he spent in this state of contented barbarism [Rashleigh's] life was steady and uneventful" (295). Like Tucker's novel, John Boyle O'Reilly's *Moondyne* (1878) features an escaped convict who becomes a white blackfellow. And in Rosa Praed's *Fugitive Anne* (1902), the title character, who has grown up in the outback in Queensland, escapes from her brutal husband to an Aboriginal tribe who worship her as a goddess, "Cloud Daughter." Anne is anxious to escape from the Aborigines, however, whom she—and Praed—view as untamable savages and cannibals.

If the white seal hunters and whalers along the coasts and islands of Australia who lived with Aboriginal women are included, white blackfellows may have been just as common as Pakeha Maoris. Despite the fact that the last full-blooded Tasmanian Aborigine died in 1876, sealers and Tasmanian women bred a mixed race that, as noted in chapter 2, finally received official recognition as an Aboriginal population in the 1970s. *Bringing Them Home,* the official report on the removal of half-caste Aboriginal children from their families, caused a major uproar when it appeared in 1997, in part because many white Australians did not want to acknowledge that their forebears had bred a sizable mixed-race population. Of course, white men having sexual relations with Aboriginal women did not necessarily mean that the men adopted Aboriginal customs and values; but there may have been quite a few who did, like Sretan Bozic, who, starting in 1973 with *The Track to Bralgu,* has written under the pen name "B. Wongar." Bozic was at first believed to be Aboriginal; he turned out to be a Serbian immigrant who married an Aboriginal woman and lived for a number of years among Aborigines in the Northern Territory.

White Nabobs and Rajahs

Throughout Asia before the Victorian period, many Britons and other Europeans acquired "Eastern" costumes, manners, languages, and sometimes religions. In the 1700s the white "nabobs" of the East India Company became notorious for going native. Like most early missionaries, Company employees often expected to live most of their adult lives in India, Ceylon, or elsewhere in Asia. The difficulty and time involved in travel necessitated lengthy stays abroad. Between 1770 and 1830, writes William Dalrymple in *White Mughals,* "there was wholesale interracial sexual exploration and surprisingly widespread cultural assimilation and hybridity: what Salman Rushdie...has called 'chutnification.' Virtually all Englishmen in India at this period Indianised themselves to some extent" (7). Earlier Job Charnock, the founder of Calcutta, "adopted the Bengali *lungi* and married a Hindu girl whom he allegedly saved from the funeral pyre of her first husband" (Dalrymple 17). According to Alexander Hamilton's *New Account of the East Indies,* "instead of [Charnock's] converting her to *Christianity,* she made him a Proselyte to *Paganism*" (quoted in Dalrymple 17). Although "chutnification" became less acceptable to the British in the 1800s, it did not stop. Throughout the history of British India, one result has been the creation of a large "Eurasian" population (see, e.g., Brendon).

Having gained fortunes, successful nabobs often returned to Britain, where they spent lavishly, gaining social and political influence. In 1773, in one of his many complaints about the pernicious impact of the nabobs, Horace Walpole lamented: "What is England now?—A sink of Indian wealth, filled by nabobs and emptied by Macaronis [Italian fops suspected of sodomy]! A senate sold and despised!" (quoted in James 47). According to Walpole, England itself was being Indianized, a conclusion also reached by Samuel Foote in his 1773 satiric play *The Nabob.* By 1790, the number of seats in Parliament purchased by nabobs reached 45, out of a total of 558 (James 48). By that time also, Robert Clive and Warren Hastings figured as the most notorious nabobs. But many other Anglo-Indians acquired Oriental tastes, customs, mistresses, and loot that made some of them fabulously wealthy. In his 1772 poem "Tea and Sugar...," Timothy Touchstone declared that the nabobs were his "country's shame and poor Hindustan's curse" (quoted in Juneja 185).

Especially because of the trial of Warren Hastings, pursued so vigorously by Edmund Burke in the 1790s, it became well known that at least some nabobs gained their power and wealth in India through devious, even criminal methods. In his 1840 essay on Clive, Macaulay treats him as a hero who, however, succeeded in conquering "an empire" in India by behaving like an Indian. Clive "knew that the standard of morality among the natives...differed widely from that...in England. He...had to deal with men destitute of...honour...who would unscrupulously employ corruption, perjury, forgery, to compass their ends." So Clive beat the Indians to the punch by employing corruption, perjury, and forgery. An "honourable English gentleman" at home, when "matched against an Indian intriguer," then Clive "became himself an Indian intriguer." (334). The trouble was, however, as Walpole, Foote, and Touchstone all complain, once back in Britain, the nabobs threatened to corrupt the entire nation. As Walpole's reference to "Macaronis" suggests, moreover, the corruption extended to sexual behavior. Foote's nabob, Sir Matthew Mite, threatens to set up a "seraglio" in London, and some of the nabobs did indeed bring their multiple Indian mistresses and their mixed-race children back to Britain (Brendon; Dalrymple).

Of course, most Britons in India were not so lucky or so rapacious as the nabobs. Kipling portrays various characters—the Irish father of Kim, for example, or McIntosh Jellaludin in the short story "To Be Filed for Reference"—for whom going native involves a metaphoric descent into hell like Kurtz's. Thus the Oxford-educated McIntosh has succumbed to alcoholism, converted to Islam, and married an Indian woman. The narrator of his story says, "In most big cities natives will tell you of two or three Sahibs, generally low-caste, who have turned Hindu or Mussulman" (*Plain Tales* 235). Then there are the two Irish ne'er-do-wells in "The Man Who Would Be King" who try to take over a small kingdom in the Himalayas; one of them gets beheaded for his trouble, while the other goes mad.

With reforms of the East India Company, however, the image of the corrupt and corrupting nabob gradually gave way to the supposedly self-less Anglo-Indian official, whom Kipling admired. The most important Anglo-Indian writer before Kipling, Philip Meadows Taylor, arrived in Bombay in 1824 at age fifteen. When his father's business in Liverpool failed, Taylor was apprenticed to a relative's firm in India. But that business also failed, so he became a military officer and policeman for the Nizam of Hyderabad, a quasi-independent "native territory." Taylor's 1839 best-seller *Confessions of a Thug* is based on interviews he conducted with jailed Thugs. While Taylor obviously didn't "go Thug" himself, he did become Indian enough—speaking several Indian languages, marrying the mixed-race daughter of an Indian princess, and working for a native prince rather than for the British—so that he was able to help capture some of the Thugs and then to write his authoritative novel about them.

There were white adventurers everywhere and of all sorts throughout the empire, and a few of them set up their own minor despotisms, as did "Rajah" James Brooke in Sarawak. Evidently Kipling had Brooke in mind in "The Man Who Would Be King": one of the Irish adventurers tells the narrator that they plan to "Sar-a-*whack*" in Kafiristan. Brooke was born in India and, after some education in England, saw service in the army of the East India Company. He then, on his private yacht *The Royalist,* pursued "geographical discovery." According to his Victorian biographer Spenser St. John, through exploration Brooke "could satisfy the yearning of his soul for the wildest liberty of action" (11). Part of that yearning for "liberty of action" may have been motivated by Brooke's attraction to boys and young men, a possibility St. John does not mention. In any event, once in Borneo, Brooke and his crew helped quell the "Dyak savages," who were "both pirates and head-hunters" (13). Brooke was rewarded by the Sultan of Brunei with the province of Sarawak, which he ruled as its "rajah."

Brooke's reign in Sarawak was celebrated by St. John, Charles Kingsley, and many other Victorians as an instance of British courage and justice bringing civilization to the savages. But his story is also one of going native. According to Kathryn Tidrick, under Brooke's rule and that of his heirs and successors as "white rajahs," the "administrative service [of Sarawak] became a sort of Lost Legion, gone permanently native." Brooke, his nephew, and grandnephew "took native mistresses, tattooed themselves *à la* Dyak...and avoided other Europeans" (*Empire* 39). Christopher Bayly calls Brooke "a colourful example of freelance imperialism" who "created his own kingdom from the fief of jungle and mangrove...which the Sultan of Brunei...assigned him in 1841, as recompense for help in the suppression" of Dyak piracy (104). By the end of the 1800s, as St. John admits, the progress of Sarawak toward civilization was slow. Concerning the "land Dyaks," he writes that "the missionaries appear to despair of making an impression on these poor savages," though the "sea Dyaks" were apparently somewhat more amenable to Christian instruction. St. John concludes his hero-worshipping biography with this comment: "It is a satisfaction, however, to know that, on the whole, the work of the old Rajah [James Brooke] is being so well carried on; that peace and security reign both in the exterior and interior; that piracy is a thing of the past; and that English influence is extending, however slowly" (378). But was Brooke's goal the taming of Sarawak, or was it to become its white rajah?

Lost Legions

Like Brooke and Philip Meadows Taylor, many British soldiers and sailors wound up in the service of non-British societies. The rank-and-file British soldiers serving in the army of the East India Company, poor at home and underpaid abroad, often decamped to join the armies of native princes, or else just decamped, merging into the local population wherever they found themselves (Dalrymple 19). Referring to Britons higher up the social ladder, military historian Byron Farwell writes that they "did not hesitate to exchange their bowlers for turbans, tarbushes or mandarin caps if only they were given men whom they could lead into battle. Lawrence of Arabia was a wonder...in [the twentieth] century, but there were hundreds of his countrymen...who performed similar exploits in the previous century." (3). It is men like these that Kipling had in mind when he wrote about "Gentlemen Rovers" in "The Lost Legion":

> Then a health (we must drink it in whispers)
> To our wholly unauthorised horde—
> To the line of our dusty foreloopers,
> The Gentlemen Rovers abroad. (Complete Verse 196)

Kipling does not ask how the most civilized men in the world—British "gentlemen"—could form an "unauthorised horde," much less go native, but that was often the case on all the frontiers of the empire.

One of the most famous "gentlemen rovers" was General Charles Gordon, martyr of Khartoum, who was called "Chinese" Gordon after leading the forces of the emperor of China against the Taiping rebels. He was one of many British gentlemen who seemed happier the farther away from Britain and civilization he could get. "I dwell on the joy of never seeing Great Britain again, with its horrid, wearisome dinner-parties and miseries," Gordon declared. "How we can put up with those things, passes my imagination! It is a perfect bondage....I would sooner live like a Dervish with the Mahdi, than go out to dinner every night in London" (quoted in Strachey 182). Gordon also declared, "I hate Her Majesty's Government for their leaving the Sudan after having caused all its troubles" (quoted in Strachey 183). Gordon himself disobeyed the order to leave the Sudan, which ironically led to his martyrdom and his acclaim by the British press as a hero of the empire after he was killed by the Mahdi's dervishes in 1885 (Strachey 192). He was an evangelical zealot, he was insubordinate, he caused a crisis in imperial affairs—in short, he might almost have been "a Dervish with the Mahdi" himself.[7]

Gordon's comments on the "perfect bondage" of civilized life make him sound like H. Rider Haggard's Allan Quatermain. In the introduction to the novel that bears his name, Quatermain asserts, "The thirst for the wilderness was on me; I could tolerate [England] no more; I would go and die as I had lived, among the wild game and the savages," adding:

> No man who has for forty years lived the life I have, can with impunity go coop himself in this prim English country, with its...stiff formal manners....He begins to long...for the keen breath of the desert air; he dreams of the sight of Zulu impis [regiments] breaking on their foes like surf upon the rocks, and his heart arises in rebellion against the strict limits of...civilised life. (Haggard, *She, King Solomon, Allan Quatermain* 419)

After all, Quatermain asks, what is civilization? It is "only savagery silver-gilt. A vainglory is it, and, like a northern light, comes but to fade and leave the sky more dark. Out of the soil of barbarism it has grown like a tree, and, as I believe, into the soil like a tree...it will once more fall" (420).

The desire to abandon "civilized life" to live "among the wild beasts and the savages" is a version of pastoral, as in Wordsworth. Tennyson, who succeeded Wordsworth as poet laureate, admonished his readers to "move

upward, working out the beast, / And let the ape and tiger die" (970).
But as Freud would argue in *Civilization and Its Discontents,* progress and
civilization are hard work: it is always possible to backslide. This is what
happens to some of Ulysses' followers in "The Lotos-Eaters," which recounts how the drug makes them wish to give up the struggle and dream
their lives away. Ulysses avoids their fate and returns home, but once he
gets there, he decides, as does Quatermain, that civilized life is too tame
for him. So in the dramatic monologue that bears his name, Ulysses an-
nounces he will set sail again "beyond the sunset, and the baths / Of all the
western stars, until I die" (565). Also, the disgruntled speaker of "Locksley
Hall" desires to burst "all links of habit [and] to wander far away, / On
from island unto island at the gateways of the day." On some island "of
Eden lying in dark-purple spheres of sea" he hopes to find happiness:

> There methinks would be enjoyment more than in this march of mind,
> In the steamship, in the railway, in the thoughts that shake mankind.
>
> There the passions cramped no longer shall have scope and breathing space;
> I will take some savage woman, she shall rear my dusky race.
>
> Iron jointed, supple-sinewed, they shall dive, and they shall run,
> Catch the wild goat by the hair, and hurl their lances in the sun;
>
> Whistle back the parrot's call, and leap the rainbows of the brooks,
> Not with blinded eyesight poring over miserable books.

Suddenly horrified, however, by the thought of betraying progress, civilization, and the white race, the speaker rejects his vision of going native:

> Fool, again the dream, the fancy! but I *know* my words are wild,
> But I count the gray barbarian lower than the Christian child.
>
> I, to herd with narrow foreheads, vacant of our glorious gains,
> Like a beast with lower pleasures, like a beast with lower pains!
>
> Mated with a squalid savage—?   (Tennyson 698–99)

Tennyson frequently writes about societal and individual progress and its
opposite, regression, one of whose forms is going native.

Another form of regression is hankering after the age of chivalry. In *Idylls of the King,* the knights of the Round Table carve a civilization out of the wilderness by defeating the "heathens." But Arthur and his knights are fallible. The knights go wild goose chasing after the Holy Grail, and Sir Lancelot commits adultery with Queen Guinevere. Thus does Camelot come toppling down. Even though Tennyson meant *Idylls* to celebrate Queen Victoria, Prince Albert, and the modern British Empire, he was better at doubt and pessimism than at optimism. Epics are supposed to be about the founding of civilizations, like Virgil's *Aeneid.* But Tennyson's strange "epic"—his "idylls"—shows how an entire civilization can go native or regress toward the beast.

Stories about humans turning into beasts are doppelgangers of those about going native. Werewolves, the frog prince, Spiderman, Lucifer turning into a serpent—regression from human or even archangel to animal is the stuff of mythology, of fairy tales, and nowadays of Marvel Comics. In the Victorian period, such stories had both Gothic and Darwinian overtones, as in *Dr. Jekyll and Mr. Hyde.* David Punter calls Hyde's behavior "an urban version of 'going native'" (241). When the good doctor turns into the evil Hyde, his description and actions match the stereotype of the Irish hooligan. Stevenson echoes the idea, expressed in much Victorian writing about urban poverty, that the street people of London and other cities were savages. These were the Magwitches, the criminally inclined denizens of "darkest England," like the savages of the so-called dark continent. In *London Labour and the London Poor,* Henry Mayhew claims that the "nomad" street people form a distinct, inferior race, yet he recognizes there are hundreds of Englishmen and women who have "lapsed" from the upper classes into "a nomad state." This is a "tendency [that] is by no means extraordinary; for ethnology teaches us, that whereas many abandon the habits of civilized life…few of the wandering tribes give up vagabondising and betake themselves to settled occupations" (1:214). As a "roving" reporter, Mayhew himself enjoyed, at least vicariously, life among the vagabond natives of London. At the opposite end of the social class spectrum, from John Polidori's "The Vampire" through Thomas Rymer's *Varney the Vampire* to Bram Stoker's *Dracula,* the standard bloodsucker is an aristocrat, though also a demonic beast, regressing nightly into a bloodthirsty and undying version of Batman—a bad Batman, of course, and well before Batman's time in the dark limelight of Gotham City.

As *Jekyll and Hyde* and *Dracula* suggest, by the end of the 1800s the threat of the biological degeneration even of "the imperial race" loomed large (Pick). Entire non-British races and populations had often been viewed as regressing to barbarism or even savagery. If the ancient Indians were civilized Aryans, today's Hindus were a sorry distance from the original (Ballantyne, *Orientalism*). In *A Simpleton* (1873), Charles Reade expresses a common British view that the Boers of southern Africa had "degenerated into white savages" and that the "Kaffirs" were "socially superior" to them (250–51). And it was often asserted that the Portuguese in Africa or in India had turned into Africans or Indians. There was always the troubling thought that if civilization could tame savagery, the entire process could be reversed in cultural but perhaps also in biological terms. And if it could happen to the Hindus, the Boers, or the Portuguese, it could even happen to the Anglo-Saxon race.

The idea was widely held that white people who resided for long in the tropics faced dire consequences, although medical authorities sometimes rebutted it.[8] Yet disease and death visited many Europeans in Africa, India, the West Indies, and elsewhere. Whites in the tropics might also acquire the seeds of racial degeneration, which could be passed on to their children. And they might go mad or, what was often thought to be the same thing, go native. Although something may have been defective about Kurtz before he came to the Congo, Marlow says that "the wilderness...had taken him, loved him, embraced him, got into his veins, consumed his flesh, and sealed his soul to its own by the inconceivable ceremonies of some devilish initiation" (Conrad, *Heart of Darkness* 48). Marlow is vague about what has driven Kurtz's "soul" over the brink, but in many accounts of the deleterious effects of the tropics on "the white race," a strain of Lamarckianism is evident—the idea that an organism forms characteristics as it adapts to an environment, which are then passed on to its offspring.[9]

In *Descent of Man,* Darwin demonstrated that heredity was much less subject to climate and environment than many had previously thought. Paradoxically, however, ideas about racial degeneration—including, most frighteningly, the degeneration of "the imperial race"—flourished in the last third of the nineteenth century and into the Edwardian period (Pick). The nabobs and later Anglo-Indians were perfect candidates for suspicions about racial regression. In *Semi-Detached Empire,* Todd Kuchta quotes the claim in an 1885 pamphlet, *Degeneration amongst Londoners,* that "a third generation of Anglo-Indians attaining adult years is impossible," though the author hastened to add that the British might "have the same non-continuance near home without our ever having given it a thought" (Kuchta 78). In Australia, too, anxiety about the degeneration of the Anglo-Saxon race was widespread. Charles Dilke, author of *Greater Britain,* was among those who believed "that a slender, effeminate, weak-voiced type was emerging in the antipodes" (Anderson, *Cultivation* 64). Warwick Anderson, who cites Dilke, also quotes an 1879 article, published in Adelaide in the *Victorian Review,* which predicts the "inevitable degeneration of the Anglo-Saxon stock" in Australia (64). Some Australian medical authorities even foresaw the time when that "stock" would become racially indistinguishable from the Aborigines, who were possibly an ancient, degenerate offshoot of the Aryan race (Anderson, *Cultivation* 182). In short, theories about racial degeneration suggested that entire populations, including those consisting of sturdy Anglo-Saxons, could go native or backslide toward the beast.

Not just falling away from civilization, however, but race suicide became a common theme in the 1880s and 1890s, especially among the advocates of eugenics. H. G. Wells's Time Traveller hypothesizes that the two species he encounters 800,000 years in the future, the Elois and the Morlocks, are the degenerate branches of the self-exterminating human species. What has brought about this tragic result? Perhaps, thinks the Time Traveller, too much progress, too much civilization—exactly what the eugenicists were arguing: civilization caused racial degeneration by encouraging the unfit to survive and multiply. Besides Wells's apocalyptic fantasy, as we'll see in chapter 8, there were many other late Victorian and Edwardian stories about how a weakened Britain or a weakened white race might be overrun by "the yellow peril," by aliens from outer space, or by vampires.

Colonial Desires

In *Heart of Darkness,* "Locksley Hall," and many other Victorian narratives, going native is both tempting and evil, like turning into a vampire. Again, however, some types of going native were, like Kim's, positive and beneficial. Kipling and Conrad understood that there were many degrees and varieties of going native. If in Kurtz's case going native means falling into an abyss of "horror," perhaps the opposite happens in *Lord Jim* (1900). The disgraced Jim finds a new life and even redemption in the remote Malaysian domain of Patusan. There, Jim's love for Jewel and his friendship with Dain Waris are not demoralizing but the reverse. All might end happily if it weren't for the intrusion of "latter-day buccaneer" Gentleman Brown (Conrad, *Lord Jim* 303), whom Marlow likens to "some man-beast of folk-lore" (318). Before Brown and his crew arrive, Jim has merged his life with the Patusans and become their "Tuan," their "Lord," like Sarawak's Rajah Brooke (Sherry 135–38). He regains a sense of honor by doing an honorable version of going native. Marlow comments:

> Three hundred miles beyond the end of telegraph cables and mail-boat lines, the haggard utilitarian lies of our civilisation wither and die, to be replaced by charm, and sometimes the deep hidden truthfulness, of works of art.... Romance had singled Jim out for its own—and that was the true part of the story, which otherwise was all wrong. (251)

Jim goes native, but he also dies for "a shadowy ideal of conduct" (351) which Conrad identifies as perhaps the only saving factor in Western imperialism and civilization.

Jim does not get the chance to start what would have been a mixed-race family. But in some of Conrad's other Malaysian stories, including *Almayer's Folly,* Western men and Oriental women produce half-caste children, as happens also in "The Beach of Falesá." At the end of Stevenson's story, Wiltshire doesn't know what to do with his mixed-race girls: "They're only half-castes, of course...and there's nobody thinks less of half-castes than I do; but they're mine, and about all I've got. I can't reconcile my mind to their taking up with Kanakas, and I'd like to know where I'm going to find the [white men to marry them]?" In Conrad's first novel, the Dutchman Almayer is similarly nonplussed about how to deal with his mixed-race daughter Nina, and is heartbroken when she chooses her native lover over his desire to take her to Europe and have her married there. Almost always in Victorian literature, even in Conrad, miscegenation is regarded as a mistake.

Yet races intermingled sexually as in many other ways in Africa, India, and everywhere else in the world. *Bringing Them Home* indicated some of the demographic results in Australia. According to Edward Long in his 1774 *History of Jamaica,* "so little restraint is laid on the passions, the Europeans...give a loose to every kind of sensual delight: on this account some black or yellow *quasheba* is sought for, by whom a tawney breed is produced" (quoted in Young 151). At the time of emancipation, "free people of colour" in some of the West Indies "outnumbered...whites" (Heuman 472). In 1917 J. C. Smuts declared that in South Africa there could be "no intermixture of blood between the two colours" (quoted in Reynolds, *Nowhere People* 7), but the newly formed Union had long been a racial rainbow. The Griquas, for example, were a so-called colored race that had sprung up since the early days of colonization by the Dutch. The British in India also bred a Eurasian population that was socially marginalized and virtually ignored in Victorian writing (Brendon). Kipling's "Without Benefit of Clergy" is an exception, although by conveniently dying, both the Indian mistress and the mixed-race baby pay the price for the white protagonist's indiscretion.

In *Empire and Sexuality,* Ronald Hyam contends that a key motivation in empire building was for European men to gain freedom from sexual repression at home. Racism may have acted as an ideological contraceptive against the sexual intermingling of whites with nonwhites, but it was a very weak contraceptive. Interracial sexual relations occurred everywhere, even at home. Apart from *Othello,* the most famous interracial love story in British literature is *Wuthering Heights.* Like most interracial romances, for the two main lovers it ends tragically. Heathcliff's racial origins are a mystery, but he is obviously not a white, thoroughbred Englishman. Plucked from the streets of Liverpool by Catherine's father, he is wild and dark-skinned, and is often called a "gipsy," which perhaps indicates his race. But he could also be an Irish castoff like Kim, or even partly African. Liverpool was Britain's major slave-trading port during the time frame of the novel; by the 1840s and the Famine, it was also the main port of entry for Irish immigrants.[10] Either way, Heathcliff is a version of the colonized native or the racially oppressed person in revolt. Certainly no characters in Victorian fiction better illustrate what Robert Young calls "colonial desire" than do Heathcliff and Catherine Earnshaw. Heathcliff may not be "a regular black," as Nelly Dean tells him, but he's "fit for a prince in disguise," she adds, telling him: "Who knows but your father was Emperor of China and your mother an Indian queen, each of them able to buy up...Wuthering

Heights and Thrushcross Grange together? And [maybe] you were kid-
napped by wicked sailors, and brought to England" (Brontë, *Wuthering
Heights* 54). And Nelly calls the young Catherine "a wild, hatless little
savage," whom the neighbors accuse of "scouring the countryside with a
gipsy" (49). In short, Catherine's passion for Heathcliff can be interpreted
as a version of going native and also of going for the native.

Jane Eyre also expresses colonial desire. Coming from the tropics, Rochester and Bertha Mason import excessive passion, violence, and sexuality.
They also bring with them a fortune extracted from slave labor. Although
Bertha comes from a slave-owning family, her "purple face" (328) and
Rochester's reference to her mother as "the Creole" (326) suggest racial hybridity. And her madness suggests a version of going native. Susan Meyer
notes that Bertha grows darker with each of her fleeting appearances, and
argues that "the Jamaican Bertha-become-black is the [novel's] incarnation
of the desire for revenge on the part of colonized peoples.... Brontë's language suggests that such a desire for revenge is not unwarranted" (69).

Jane sometimes speaks of her situation in terms of "slavery," as when
she likens her anger toward the Reeds to "the mood of the revolted slave"
(Brontë, *Jane Eyre* 22). Yet as a dark or darkening outsider, Bertha is to the
novel what Heathcliff is to *Wuthering Heights,* except that Heathcliff is able
to voice his passion and anger. Both characters are figures of destruction,
motivated by revenge, like rebellious slaves. Even more obviously than
Jane, the madwoman in the attic points to the analogy between the enslavement of Africans and the oppression of women under patriarchy—an
analogy employed by feminists from Mary Wollstonecraft to the suffrag-
ettes and beyond. Jane refuses to accompany St. John Rivers to India, but
she nevertheless undertakes, as Deirdre David puts it, the "reformation of
the colonizer rather than [of] the colonized" (85)—that is, the reformation
of Mr. Rochester. Jane as a "revolted slave," demanding greater freedom
for women, is a forerunner of the late Victorian "New Women," who were
often seen as threats to social stability and who were sometimes also called
barbarians or savages, as in Eliza Lynn Linton's 1891 article "The Wild
Women."[11] Perhaps Victorian feminism involved "renovating... Britannic
rule," as David contends (97), but its critics saw it as analogous to going
native.

And of course women as well as men could and occasionally did quite
literally go native. This was perhaps easy for the wealthy Lady Ann Blunt,

for example. A cousin of Lord Byron's, Lady Ann was the first Western woman to travel widely through the Arabian peninsula. After she and her husband, Wilfrid Scawen Blunt, separated, she chose to live the remainder of her life in Egypt, in the style of a rich Egyptian (Winstone). And then there was Annie Besant, who in her final avatars became a convert to Theosophy, emigrated to India, founded the Indian Home Rule League, served as president of the Indian National Congress, and befriended Gandhi.

Besant's conversion and adoption of an Indian identity were simultaneously religious and, like Theosophy itself, rooted in Darwinism and Victorian scientific racism, including Aryanism. Although she advocated independence for India, Besant also advocated turning the British Empire into a commonwealth of nations. Aryanism led her to believe that the British, including the Celtic "race," were a branch of the same racial family that had founded ancient Indian civilization. Drawing on both Theosophy and evolutionary theory, she contended that the British belonged to a "subrace" of "the Fifth Race," responsible for starting what would evolve into a worldwide empire, characterized by racial solidarity (though not equality) and leading to the emergence of a superhuman "Sixth Race."[12] As we shall see in chapter 8, hopes and fears about "the coming race" became a familiar theme in late Victorian and Edwardian culture.

Going native probably seemed as reasonable to Annie Besant as it did to Lady Ann Blunt. Going native was not easy for Maggie Tulliver, however. When at the start of *Mill on the Floss* Maggie runs away to live with the gypsies, she quickly changes her mind. The gypsies are rough, dirty, thievish, and speak a language she doesn't understand. "Her ideas about the gypsies [underwent] a rapid modification....From having considered them very respectful companions, amenable to instruction, she [began] to think that they meant perhaps to kill her as soon as it was dark, and cut up her body for gradual cooking" (Eliot, *Mill* 95). But the gypsies aren't cannibals, and one of them takes her safely home. Maggie abandons her dream of becoming the queen of the gypsies.

In general, for the Victorians to imitate the natives meant falling into the abyss that humanity was supposedly climbing out of, toward the light and toward perfection. And at the very bottom of that abyss gaped the horror of cannibalism, the threat Magwitch visits upon Pip and that Maggie Tulliver fears in the gypsies. In *Heart of Darkness,* however, Marlow turns the threat of cannibalism upside down. Steaming up the Congo with a crew of cannibals, Marlow wonders why, in their semi-starved condition, they do not make a meal of him and the other white men on the boat. Something restrains them, he thinks, perhaps some form of primitive honor. Marlow decides that his cannibal crew are not such bad fellows after all—definitely not so bad as supposedly civilized but hypocritical Europeans motivated only by greed. Even if you are a cannibal, you are probably better than a white man who goes native—who backslides down the slippery slope into the heart of darkness.

From Almayer to Kurtz to Lord Jim, Conrad's explorations of going native suggest the range and diversity of what that phrase signified. But as the Pakeha Maori, "Chinese" Gordon, and the Griquas suggest, history is even stranger and more diverse than fiction. Everywhere the boundaries of nations, races, religions, and cultures proved more "permeable" than most accounts acknowledge (Colley 195). Natives were expected to mimic the colonizers—that was the civilizing process—even though mimicry allegedly always fell short. But the colonizers weren't supposed to mimic the natives, and yet they did so in great numbers, motivated by everything from sheer survival to trade to sex to the many other attractions offered by non-Western cultures.

4

"God Works by Races"

Benjamin Disraeli's Caucasian Arabian Hebrew Tent

> But the question is, what is the Eastern question?
>
> Consul General Laurella in *Tancred*

As a "gentleman rover" like James Brooke or General Gordon, Richard Burton preferred adventuring abroad to stuffy, conventional life in England. He declared that in the desert "your *morale* improves...the hypocritical politeness and the slavery of Civilization are left behind you" (quoted in Burton, *Life* 104). He delighted in playing various "native" roles in which, he wrote, "I could revel in the utmost freedom of life and manners" (*Pilgrimage* 1:11). A founder of the Gypsy Lore Society, Burton was often called a gypsy. "The more I got to know" him, wrote his wife, "the more his strange likeness to the gypsies struck me" (Wilkins 54–55). Though a racist and an imperialist, Burton was closer to being an unorthodox Muslim than an orthodox Christian, and he acknowledged the cultural superiority of some non-Western peoples, particularly the "chivalrous" Bedouins of the desert, but also the Jews, who shared the Bedouins' "Semitic blood." He enjoyed as well the freedom to explore "native" sexual behaviors, including homosexual ones. Early in his career, his report on "lupanars" or male brothels in Karachi nearly cost him his officer's position in the Indian army. He claimed, however, that even his erotic explorations contributed to British power: "I...maintain that the free treatment of topics usually taboo'd...will be a national benefit to an 'Empire of Opinion,' whose very basis...[is] a thorough knowledge by the rulers of the ruled" (*Book* 10:301). Like Kim, Burton turned going native into a profession in the service of the mighty British Empire—one that often amounted to anthropological espionage.[1]

Famous after his "pilgrimage" to Medina and Mecca in 1853, during which he traveled in disguise as "Shayk Abdullah," an Afghan "Pathan," Burton became even better known as an explorer of central Africa. Sub-Saharan Africans were, Burton claimed, "inferior to the active-minded and objective...Europeans, and to the...subjective and reflective Asiatic" (*Lake Regions* 2:236). They were "unimprovable" savages. This was a common view among nineteenth-century Europeans. In contrast, Burton's respect for Islam and Islamic cultures was shared by various other British travelers to northern Africa and the Orient, including most famously Benjamin Disraeli. In her biography of Burton, Fawn Brodie writes that on his Eastern tour in the early 1830s, Disraeli "like Burton...shared the Arab tents and [became] enchanted with the nomadic Bedouin life" (135).

The Burtons admired Disraeli, with whom they occasionally socialized, although Isabel wrote that the great politician "never did anything for them," perhaps because of Richard's "strong anti-Semitic views" (Wilkins 614). Burton, however, usually expressed highly positive opinions about Jews and Judaism. On another occasion Isabel more accurately remarked, "I think nobody has more respect for the Jewish religion than my husband and myself, or of the Jews" (Wilkins 457). In *The Highlands of Brazil* (1869) Burton declared, "Had I a choice of race, there is none to which I would more willingly belong than the Jewish" (quoted in Brodie 265). And Disraeli topped the list of Jews the Burtons respected. Both Richard Burton and Disraeli found in Semitic cultures, Islamic and Judaic alike, support for their theories of race and their conservative ideologies.

The Burtons and Benjamin Disraeli

From Lord Byron and Edward Lane through William Palgrave and David Urquhart to Wilfrid Scawen Blunt and T. E. Lawrence, a number of Britons not only empathized with Islam and Turkish or Arabic ways but also adopted "Eastern" customs and costumes for extended periods (Nash).[2] While in Syria, both Richard and Isabel Burton "used to live a great deal with the native population, and as natives, in order to gain an insight into their lives. They wore European dress in Damascus and Beirut, and Eastern dress up-country or in the desert....If Isabel went to a harem, she often dressed like a Muslim woman with her face covered" (Godsall 285).[3] Burton served as British consul in Damascus from 1869 to 1871, a position that allowed him to mingle in disguise with the natives and yet, when he felt it necessary, to lord it over them. He ran into trouble by getting involved in various local fracases, including his interference with Jewish moneylenders who, he claimed, were bilking the peasantry. This was one of the reasons why he has sometimes been charged with anti-Semitism.

That behaving like Turks or Arabs and even converting to Islam contradicted the imperialist goal of dominating Turks and Arabs seems self-evident. On his Arabian "pilgrimage" and in Syria, however, Burton had it both ways. Through most of the 1800s, moreover, British foreign policy supported the Ottoman Empire with the aim of thwarting Russia's possible designs on India. Although the British navy demolished the Ottoman fleet in the battle of Navarino in 1827, Britain and France sided with the Ottomans in the Crimean War against Russia. In the aftermath of World War I, the victorious European powers divided the pieces of the defunct Turkish domains among themselves. But between 1827 and 1914 Britain had no intention of subverting Constantinople and thereby adding to its own already enormous burdens of governing the colonies and India (Bailey). The exception was Egypt, which had already parted ways with Constantinople; the British bombarded Alexandria in 1882 and then occupied Egypt in order to defeat Al Arabi's nationalist rebellion. The takeover of Egypt then led to Gordon's misadventures and martyrdom at Khartoum in 1885. Gordon asked Burton to join him in the Sudan, an offer Burton refused because, he said, "we were at once too like and too unlike to act together without jarring" (quoted in Godsall 330).

For Burton and many other Britons in the nineteenth century, "the East [was] a career." Quoting this epigram from Disraeli's *Tancred; or, The New Crusade* (1847), Edward Said adds, Disraeli "meant that to be interested in the East was something bright young Westerners would find to be an

all-consuming passion" (*Orientalism* 5). Furthermore, through such a career "one could remake and restore not only the Orient but also oneself"
(*Orientalism* 166), which is how Burton saw it. As Said indicates, Disraeli
also "remade and restored" his own career via the Orient, albeit in complicated, paradoxical ways. In any event, Isabel Burton was a great fan of
Tancred. She first read Disraeli's novel when she was fifteen, and it became, she said, "the book of my heart and taste," "my second bible." With
its "glamours of the East," *Tancred* whetted Isabel's enthusiasm for "gypsies, Bedawin Arabs, and everything Eastern and mystic, and especially
a wild and lawless life" (quoted in Rice 172). In one of her first meetings
with her future husband, she had Disraeli's novel with her, and Richard
"explained" it to her (Wilkins 81). When Disraeli died in 1881, Isabel's
journal, she recalled, was "four pages of lament.... As a Statesman I put
him on a pedestal as my political Chief and model. He had that peculiar
prescience and foresight belonging to his Semitic blood" (*Life* 417).

Despite Disraeli's doing nothing to advance her husband's career, Richard eventually wrote an unpublished, mostly appreciative pamphlet about
him. Richard also wrote three separate essays on the Jews, the gypsies, and
Islam, which William Wilkins assembled and published as a book in 1897.
In the section on the Jews, Burton quotes the first novel in Disraeli's Young
England trilogy, *Coningsby* (1844), as an authoritative source on why so
many Jews have been "illustrious [and occupy] the foremost rank in arts,
letters, statesmanship, and military science" (quoted in Burton, *The Jew* 17).
The character in Disraeli's novel who informs Coningsby about illustrious
Jews is the Jewish sage Sidonia. Much of what Burton says about "the
Hebrews" echoes Sidonia, who in turn echoes *The Genius of Judaism,* pub-
lished in 1833 by Isaac Disraeli, Benjamin's father.

Isaac writes of "the election" by "the Deity" of "a privileged race" who
have managed to survive dispersion and persecution through the ages (33).
Isaac uses the term "race" rather loosely, and inclines more to cultural than
to racial explanations of Jewish "genius"; biological difference is a matter
he leaves to the "anatomists" and "phrenologists" (114). But Isaac is certain
that there has to be some explanation for the survival of both the Jews and
Judaism. Nevertheless, he is less assertive about the racial basis of Jewish
superiority than his son, or for that matter than Richard Burton. The Jewish race, Burton contends, again echoing *Coningsby,* has shown through
its survival that it has an "indestructible and irrepressible life-power."

The secret lies in "the purity of their blood" (*The Jew* 5–6). In the colonies, Burton adds, Christian families eventually die out, while Jewish families thrive (13–14). "Physically and mentally the Jewish man and woman are equal in all respects to their Gentile neighbours, and in some particulars are superior to them" (7).

According to Sidonia, the Jews are a superior branch of the superior "Arabian" race, which is in turn the highest type among the various "Caucasian" peoples. As did his father, Benjamin Disraeli based his theory of races largely on Johann Friedrich Blumenbach, who is usually credited with inventing the "Caucasian" racial category, the highest and oldest of his five major races (Baum 73; Smith, introduction 12). Disraeli adds his own embellishment regarding the superiority of the "Semites" or the "Arabs of the desert," writing, "Sidonia was well aware that in the five great varieties into which Physiology has divided the human species: to wit, the Caucasian, the Mongolian, the Malayan, the American, the Ethiopian: the Arabian tribes rank in the first and superior class, together, among others, with the Saxon and the Greek" (*Coningsby* 241). The narrator of *Coningsby* attributes European civilization jointly to "the Mosaic and the Mohammedan Arabs" (235), with most of the credit going to the former "race." He continues:

> The overthrow of the Gothic kingdoms was as much achieved by the superior information which the Saracens received from their suffering kinsmen [the Jews], as by the resistless valour of the Desert. The Saracen kingdoms were established. That fair and unrivalled civilisation arose which preserved for Europe arts and letters when Christendom was plunged in darkness. The children of Ishmael rewarded the children of Israel with equal rights and privileges with themselves. During these halcyon centuries, it is difficult to distinguish the follower of Moses from the votary of Mahomet. (233)

All Europeans, along with all Semitic races, belong in the vast "Caucasian" tent. "But Sidonia and his brethren," the narrator declares, "could claim a distinction which the Saxon and the Greek, and the rest of the Caucasian nations, have forfeited. The Hebrew is an unmixed race" (242). Among the Arabian dwellers of the desert, there is "blood...as pure as" that of Abraham's descendants. "But the Mosaic Arabs are the most ancient, if not the only, unmixed blood that exists in cities." The narrator adds, "An unmixed race of a first-rate organisation are the aristocracy of Nature" (242). Just as

Disraeli liked to imagine himself, the wise Sidonia is a superior scion of a superior race. A sizable portion of Sidonia's wisdom, moreover, consists of his theory of human races and their impact on history.

Sidonia tells Coningsby everything the narrator asserts about race, with some refinements—for example, "the Jews...are essentially Tories. Toryism, indeed, is but copied from the mighty prototype which has fashioned Europe," that is, the Bible (271). Sidonia also says: "The fact is, you cannot destroy a pure race of the Caucasian organisation. It is a physiological fact.... The mixed persecuting races disappear; the pure persecuted race remains. And at this moment, the Jewish mind exercises a vast influence on the affairs of Europe" (271). If the great Caucasian race is superior to all the others, and if the "Semitic" or "Arabian" branch of that race is superior to the other branches, and if the Jewish race is the highest and purest of the Semites, then it follows that Jews are the most "aristocratic race." Sidonia is once more reiterating this message of Jewish superiority when he adds: "Pure races of Caucasus may be persecuted, but they cannot be despised, except by the brutal ignorance of some mongrel breed, that brandishes fagots [*sic*] and howls extermination, but is itself exterminated without persecution, by that irresistible law of Nature which is fatal to curs" (273). So much for anti-Semitism. That Sidonia's message to Coningsby about race is also Disraeli's is evident not only because the narrator makes the same assertions, but also because Disraeli repeated them both in *Tancred* and in the chapter on Jews and Judaism in his *Life of Lord George Bentinck* (1851). It is a message that both Richard and Isabel Burton accepted.

From Disraeli's Eastern Tour to Young England

The young Disraeli was not just an Oriental traveler and emulator of aspects of Eastern cultures; he also became a self-made English *and* Oriental aristocrat. The aspiring politician dreamed in at least two contrary ways about the Orient: in *Alroy, Contarini Fleming,* and *Tancred,* Disraeli fantasized about replacing Ottoman with British rule over the Near East; but even more significantly, he fantasized about himself as an Oriental— a Hebrew of aristocratic blood who, like Sidonia, was the equal of any Ottoman or, for that matter, of any British ruler. Traveling in the Middle East in 1830–31, Disraeli followed Byron's path while also admiring the

Ottoman dignitaries he encountered. Like both Byron and Burton, he took pleasure in "turning Turk" at least temporarily. As he traveled, he contemplated the mystery of heredity, having perhaps already concluded that he belonged to a "chosen" and "aristocratic" race. He did not, however, identify with the Jews he encountered; he identified instead with the Ottoman pashas and elites he delighted in meeting.

For the future conservative prime minister, fantasy had a way of becoming reality. Far more than with other, less imaginative statesmen, what Disraeli thought and felt about "the great Asian mystery" (*Tancred* 128) influenced modern history both in Britain and abroad, in the Orient itself. With Disraeli as his key example, Edward Said stresses that for the imperializing British, fantasizing about the Orient and ruling it were closely connected:

> To write about Egypt, Syria, or Turkey, as much as traveling in them, was a matter of touring the realm of political will, political management, political definition. The territorial imperative was extremely compelling, even for so unrestrained a writer as Disraeli, whose *Tancred* is not merely an Oriental lark but an exercise in the astute political management of actual forces on actual territories. (169)

Three qualifications of Said's argument seem necessary: first, Disraeli's Orientalism was less a unified ideology than a mixture of changing, often contradictory ideas, attitudes, and poses; second, it was mainly positive rather than negative (that is, it celebrated rather than denigrated things Eastern); and third, Disraeli was himself (as he insisted throughout his career) a hybrid character—both English and Jewish, and usually willing to play his Oriental cards.

Baptized when he was twelve, Disraeli self-consciously refashioned his own familial ties to Judaism into a more general Oriental persona, invested with the world-conquering "intellect of Arabia" (*Tancred* 299), which he saw as the more inclusive form of the world-dominating "Hebrew intellect" (*Coningsby* 264). Disraeli's Oriental self-fashioning was an aspect of his bold, aggressive defense against the anti-Semitism that he had to combat throughout his career. According to Paul Smith, "the readiness of opponents to exploit anti-Semitic feeling against him left him little option but to counter-attack in the most vigorous way possible." Smith adds that

Disraeli, after he entered the British political arena, "defied the prejudices of the bigoted Protestant party for which he spoke with an assertion
of Jewish racial pride rendered only slightly less risky by the unlikeli-
hood that it would catch the attention of many of his not very bookish
backbenchers" (10).

Various scholars have argued that Orientalism was never so monolithic
nor so uniformly negative as Said suggests. Adding a psychoanalytic di-
mension to Said's postcolonial critique, Homi Bhabha insists on the "over-
determined" quality of Orientalism (and colonial discourse in general),
such that "mastery and pleasure" are as much at work as "anxiety and
defence" (71–75). For a romantic Orientalizer like the young Disraeli, the
East evoked "fetishistic" fantasies based more on desire than on the "pho-
bic" responses evident in negative racist stereotyping as in, say, Thomas De
Quincey's *Confessions of an English Opium Eater* (Barrell, Infection). According to Nigel Leask, "the anxieties of empire" expressed in Oriental
tales from Samuel Johnson's *Rasselas* to John Keats's *Endymion* and beyond
were "more various than Said's thesis will allow" (2), an observation that
applies also to *Tancred*. Similarly, in her reading of a number of British
and French writers, Lisa Lowe stresses the heterogeneity of "orientalizing
formations" even for a single author. Thus for Flaubert, Eastern themes
and motifs "are divided and polyvocal, containing orientalist postures as
well as critiques of those postures" (80). Much the same can be said of Eastern themes and motifs in Disraeli's writings and speeches throughout his
career, with the added difference that Disraeli's Orientalism was centered
on his own family history and personal experience in relation to Judaism,
anti-Semitism, and what he saw as the virtues and weaknesses of Islam
and the Ottoman Empire.

Despite Disraeli's general "enthusiasm for the Orient," Said claims that
Tancred "is steeped in racial and geographical platitudes; everything is a
matter of race, Sidonia states, so much so that salvation can only be found
in the Orient and amongst its races" (*Orientalism* 102). Nevertheless, Said
too quickly characterizes the notion of "salvation" via "the Orient" and its
"races" as just more of the same, basically negative ideology. Embedded
in that notion of "salvation" is Disraeli's linking of the concept of racial
"genius" or uniqueness to religion. For Disraeli, it was the specifically racial "genius" of the "Semites" or "Arabians" (terms he uses interchangeably) that had created the world's great religions. And the "Hebrew race"

was the leading branch of the "Semites," which made them also the superiors of their racial next of kin the Europeans, an opinion that Disraeli
bravely—his opponents thought, brazenly—voiced throughout his career,
as in his chapter on the "Jewish question" in *Lord George Bentinck*. Furthermore, Said does not explore Disraeli's emphasis on the positive effects
of the mingling of races in imperial sites far removed from London such
as Constantinople. Said suggests that Disraeli's racial platitudes simply
reproduce the negative stereotyping they were intended, at least in part,
to counteract. But both Disraeli's insistence on the racial supremacy of
the Hebrews and his youthful self-fashioning along Oriental lines expressed a philo-Semitism that was at once a form of romantic racism akin
to nationalism and a direct response to anti-Semitism. As to nationalism,
Disraeli advocated returning "the Hebrews" to their "homeland" in Palestine, though he did little or nothing politically to advance that cause
(Endelmann 124).

One obvious ingredient in Disraeli's early self-fashioning was his family's Jewish roots, reinforced by his reading about Judaism and Jewish
history—reading that informed his historical romance *Alroy* (1832), based
on the life and legend of Menahem ben Solomon al-Ruhi, who in the 1100s
led a revolt of the Jews in Azerbaijan against their Muslim overlords. *Alroy*
is Disraeli's least ironic early novel, and also an Oriental fantasy belonging
to the genre of Eastern tales that were partly inspired by the first European
translation (into French) of the *Arabian Nights* (1704–12), but were also
reflections of Britain's and Europe's increasing commercial, military, and
imperial involvement in India and the Ottoman Empire.

From the 1300s to the Enlightenment, the rise, power, and splendor of
the Ottoman Empire inspired both fear and "imperial envy" in the West
(MacLean). The Levant Company was formed in 1581 to carry on trade
with Constantinople. Numerous plays on the seventeenth-century stage
featured sultans and Turks who were both terrible and lustful (Wheatcroft, *The Ottomans*). Even as Ottoman power began to decline in the
1700s, similar portrayals evoked both fear and fascination. Disraeli was
enamored of the *Arabian Nights* and of other Oriental tales like William
Beckford's *Vathek* (1786). Shortly after his Eastern tour, he proposed to at
least one publisher that he translate the *Nights,* no doubt from the French,
in monthly installments, to which he would add his own editorial comments and imitations.[4] But the most direct models for his own Eastern

narratives—*Alroy, Tancred,* and parts of his other novels, including *Contarini Fleming* and *Lothair*—were undoubtedly furnished by Byron.

That Disraeli interpreted much of what he encountered during his Eastern travels in terms of literary, Orientalist preconceptions—part biblical, part *Arabian Nights,* part Byronic—is evident throughout his letters and novels. "I longed to write an Eastern tale," Contarini Fleming declares in the midst of his own Eastern tale (*Contarini Fleming* 307). Contarini travels through such colorfully exotic scenes that, despite the desolation of recent warfare, he is enchanted by "the now almost obsolete magnificence of oriental life.... It seemed to me that my first day in a Turkish city [Yanina in Albania] brought before me all the popular characteristics *of which I had read....* I gazed about me with a mingled feeling of delight and wonder" (307; my emphasis). It is a "delight and wonder," both in the "infinite novelty" (324) that Contarini discovers especially in Constantinople and in a thoroughly conventional, stereotypic sense of pastoral ahistoricity that fits neither the changing scenery nor the warfare in which Contarini participates. In the following passage Disraeli resorts to platitudes that can be found in numerous Eastern tales:

> There is a charm in oriental life, and it is Repose. Upon me, who had been bred in the artificial circles of corrupt civilisation...this character made a forcible impression. Wandering over those plains and deserts, and sojourning in those silent and beautiful cities, I experienced all the serenity of mind which I can conceive to be the enviable portion of the old age of a virtuous life. The memory of the wearing cares...and vaunted excitement of European life, filled me with pain.... Truly may I say that on the plains of Syria I parted for ever with my ambition. (335)

Before we dismiss such a passage as trite pastoral with an Eastern flavor, it is worth comparing it to the similar but less conventional celebration of "Arabian" life that Contarini offers when he sojourns among the Bedouins of Syria: "This singular people, who combined primitive simplicity of habits with the refined feelings of civilisation[,]...appeared to me to offer an evidence of that community of property and that equality of condition, which have hitherto proved the despair of European sages, and fed only the visions of their fanciful Utopias" (342). Yet in celebrating "primitive simplicity," Disraeli's Eastern tales themselves express a pastoral utopianism.

Although Disraeli adopted fashionably Byronic poses both during and after his Eastern tour, some of the political opinions he already held were decidedly different from Byron's. In his letters home from "the East" and in *Contarini Fleming,* Disraeli expresses sympathy for the Ottoman Empire rather than for Greek nationalism. He opposed the British destruction of the Turkish fleet at the battle of Navarino (Richmond 27). Yet in *The Rise of Iskander,* the hero-liberator is a Greek fighting against Muslim domination, perhaps suggesting that Disraeli, like Byron and Shelley, was more interested in heroism, rebellion, and liberation in general than in particular racial, cultural, or national identities. During his stay at Malta, however, Disraeli considered participating in the Ottoman campaign against the rebel Albanians, expressing a desire to see the military action in Greece at first hand—a desire that Contarini Fleming fulfills (*Letters: 1815–1834* 173; Blake29). To side with the Turks against the Greeks was, for a young British Radical and Byronian, strangely un-radical and un-Byronic. "Disraeli, for whatever reason," writes Robert Blake, "took the view that the polyglot empire of the Sultan was a barrier against anarchy and barbarism. He was [also], all his life, totally unsympathetic to the spirit of nationalism which was the dominating force in his time" (30).

Disraeli's attitudes toward nationalism were, however, more complicated than Blake allows, in two ways. First, nationalism and imperialism are not antithetical. (Once they have broken free from older dominations and established independent nation-states, nationalisms often turn into new versions of imperialism.) Disraeli is regarded today as one of Victorian Britain's leading imperialist statesmen and patriots. And second, Disraeli's philo-Semitism was also a proto-Zionism that can be construed as a kind of higher nationalism in contrast to the narrow-minded nationalisms, racisms, and religious prejudices that plagued him throughout his career. Already in *Alroy,* the hero's attempt to liberate the Jews from their Muslim overlords is couched in nationalistic terms that foreshadow Zionism:

> Empires and dynasties flourish and pass away; the proud metropolis becomes a solitude, the conquering kingdom even a desert; but Israel still remains, still a descendant of the most ancient kings breathed amid these royal ruins, and still the eternal sun could never rise without gilding the towers of living Jerusalem. A word, a deed, a single day, a single man, and we might be a nation. (40)[5]

The "we" in this passage is inclusive: this is the narrator (or Disraeli) rather than Alroy meditating on the restoration of Israel. But for the modern narrator-author, the chief obstacle to that restoration was apparently not the Ottoman Empire.

Certainly in regard to the question of Greek nationalism versus Ottoman imperialism, the young Disraeli took the exact opposite position from that of his hero Byron (whose life he celebrated, along with Shelley's, in *Venetia* [1837]). Throughout his letters from Greece and Turkey, Disraeli expresses much sympathy for the Turks, little for the Greeks. "I confess...that my Turkish prejudices," he wrote to Edward Bulwer-Lytton, "are very much confirmed by my residence in Turkey" (*Letters: 1815–1834* 179). Disraeli was fascinated by Muslim customs and costumes. I add "costumes" because as a young dandy, Disraeli saw the world, *pace* Carlyle's Teufelsdröckh, very much in terms of clothes. That "the Turks indulge[d] in all combinations of costume" was not the least of their charms; "the meanest merchant in the Bazaar looks like a Sultan in an Eastern fairy tale" (*Letters: 1815–1834* 183). Moreover, the effects of his own wardrobe on the Turks was not lost upon Disraeli. About his experiences in Navarino in Greece he wrote:

> I am quite a Turk, wear a turban, smoke a pipe six feet long, and squat on a Divan....I find the habits of this calm and luxurious people [the Turks] entirely agree with my own preconceived opinions of propriety and enjoyment, and I detest the Greeks more than ever. I do not find mere Travelling on the whole very expensive, but I am ruined by my wardrobe....When I was presented to the Grand Vizier I made up such a costume from my heterogeneous wardrobe, that the Turks, who are mad on the subject of dress, were utterly astounded....Nothing wo[ul]d persuade the Greeks that we were not come about the new King and I really believe that if I had 25,000£ to throw away I might increase my headache by wearing a crown. (*Letters: 1815–1834* 174)

While this sartorial fantasy is playful, and it invites the very critiques of superficiality and inauthenticity that Carlyle, for one, would later make of Disraeli (the Jewish "old clothes dealer"), it nevertheless expresses a political pragmatism that recognizes the importance of image making, symbolism, and credit or belief in the forging of status and power.

"There is only one way to travel in the East with ease, and that is with an appearance of pomp," Contarini Fleming declares. "The Turks are much influenced by the exterior, and although they are not mercenary, a well-dressed and well-attended infidel will command respect" (344). Similar statements about the political importance of image making are frequent in Western travelogues and exploration journals throughout the nineteenth century; keeping up appearances, even if that meant temporarily going native, was seen as at least as important for pacifying restless natives as gun-boats and artillery.[6] Disraeli's letter about his Eastern "wardrobe" expresses his belief that belief is the basis of power. At the same time, the letter contains a considerable dose of ironic egocentrism. If only, Disraeli speculates, he had been able to complement his exotic but elegant dress with a crown, the Greeks might have taken him for their new king. But "Disraeli was no doubt joking" (Blake 47).[7] He was already, however, a man who would be king, or at least prime minister.

Tancred's "New Crusade"

That Disraeli's early sympathy for the Ottoman Empire is related to his later imperialistic policies is suggested by the theme of empire in his novels from *Alroy* to *Tancred*.[8] In the earliest of Disraeli's Oriental romances, Alroy is an empire builder on a grand scale, a Jewish Napoleon, attempting to transform the dispersed, invisible empire of the Jews into a real, "restored" empire. Throughout his career, Disraeli thought of the Jews as forming an invisible empire, the spiritual power behind the earthly powers that governed the European nation-states and much of the rest of the world. Thus Sidonia can tell Coningsby that "at this moment, in spite of centuries, of tens of centuries, of degradation, the Jewish mind exercises a vast influence on the affairs of Europe. I speak not of their laws, which you still obey; of their literature, with which your minds are saturated; but of the living Hebrew intellect" (*Coningsby* 263–64). And in *Tancred,* Sidonia speaks of "the spiritual hold which Asia has always had upon the North" (127). Why, Disraeli/Sidonia wonders, do the "Saxon and Celtic societies persecute an Arabian race" to whom they owe so much? "Vast as the obligations of the whole human family are to the Hebrew race, there is no portion of the modern population so much indebted to them as the British people" (*Tancred* 274). In this passage it is evident that "Arabian race" and "Hebrew race" are identical.

Tancred, however, appears to abandon the specifically Jewish identity of the fantasy of spiritual empire basic to *Alroy.* The last novel in Disraeli's Young England trilogy is a tale of the empire-building aspirations of its "crusading" Christian hero and his Oriental ally, the young Syrian emir Fakredeen. Yet it would be more accurate to say that *Tancred* enlarges Disraeli's personal identification with Jewish history to incorporate a general "Arabian" or "Semitic" identity. While *Tancred,* like *Alroy,* is an "Oriental fantasia" whose main theme "is the essential aristocracy of the Jewish people" (Roth, *Disraeli* 66), Disraeli's racial and religious categories were flexible enough, or perhaps inconsistent enough, to involve some curious forms of cultural hybridity. In *Alroy,* the hero is inspired by a vision of the ghost of King Solomon, who comes to him in the Tombs of the Kings at Jerusalem. In *Tancred,* the hero is inspired by a vision (or is it just a dream?) of "the Angel of Arabia," who visits him on Mount Sinai and who, among other higher truths, informs him that Christianity, Judaism, and Islam alike are only alternative versions of "theocratic equality" provided to the world at large by "the Most High" through "the intellect of Arabia." Tancred learns that Christendom itself is just "the intellectual colony of Arabia" (299). Given the decrepitude of the Ottoman Empire in the 1800s (it was "the sick man of Europe"), it seems unlikely that this "intellectual colony" could have been Turkish. Disraeli's use of "Arabian," however, covers just about all Middle Eastern and North African bases.

Disraeli often insisted that God had chosen to reveal His truths in just one part of the world and to just one race: the Arabian race, to which the Hebrews belonged. Christianity is simply the consummation of Judaism, a fulfillment accomplished by a superior minority of Jews. "The first preachers of the gospel were Jews, and none else; the historians of the gospel were Jews, and none else. No one has ever been permitted to write under the inspiration of the Holy Spirit, except a Jew" (Disraeli, *Bentinck* 348). Disraeli does not go as far as Turkophile David Urquhart, however, who viewed the Koran as the ultimate revelation in what he saw as the progressive series from Judaism to Christianity to Islam. In any event, what Tancred learns about "the Arabian race" is an extension of what Sidonia tells Coningsby about the "Hebrew intellect," which continues to hold invisible sway over Europe because of its racial superiority and purity. It helped politically to know, moreover, that the Jews were the preservers of an ancient religious tradition that they had maintained throughout centuries of persecution and diaspora: that is the primary reason why the Jews, according to Sidonia, "are essentially Tories" (*Coningsby* 263).

Through his philo-Semitism, Disraeli outflanks the Anglo-Saxonism or Teutonism that underwrote British or, more specifically, English nationalism in the Victorian period. Disraeli doesn't reject Anglo-Saxonism but revises it partly by adopting Blumenbach's racial classification, which included both European and Semitic groups under the Caucasian rubric. Beyond the Anglo-Saxons' seemingly ancient racial roots lies an even older, more inclusive and influential racial configuration. As Michael Ragussis puts it, Disraeli "looks beyond not only the Norman invasion but the celebrated Saxon institutions themselves to find in Hebrew culture the most profound basis of English national life" (187).[9] In short, Disraeli accepted Anglo-Saxonist racial and nationalist categories only to supplement them through the claims of his philo-Semitism. These claims, moreover, were no more logical or illogical than Anglo-Saxonism. A brilliant *bricoleur* of the racial ideas of his era, Disraeli constructed an intellectual arsenal that, while according his Jewish origins both racial and religious primacy and dignity, suited him well as a politician climbing "the greasy pole."

Disraeli/Sidonia insists on the religious basis of all principled politics. Economic self-interest or narrow utilitarian aims are completely inadequate to explain collective behavior. World history is in the first instance the history of the world's great religions, and of the empires founded and destroyed by faith. The place of origin of all visionary empires as of all religions, moreover, has been the Orient (or, more specifically, the Middle East). Sidonia himself, scion of the "pure" race of the Sephardic Jews of Spain (*Tancred* 129), exemplifies the spiritual genius of the Hebrews, which is also the world-conquering genius par excellence. As the narrator of *Coningsby* says of Sidonia:

> Such a temperament, though rare, is peculiar to the East. It inspired the founders of the great monarchies of antiquity, the prophets that the Desert has sent forth, the Tartar chiefs who have overrun the world: it might be observed in the great Corsican, who, like most of the inhabitants of the Mediterranean isles, had probably Arab blood in his veins. It is a temperament that befits conquerors and legislators, but, in ordinary times and ordinary

situations, entails on its possessor only eccentric aberrations or profound melancholy. (230)

On this account, Napoleon is as much an "Arab" as a Corsican—like both Sidonia and Disraeli, simultaneously Oriental and European. Napoleon's "Arab blood" explains his world-conquering talent, but the racial explanation is simultaneously a spiritual explanation.

"Man is only truly great when he acts from the passions," Sidonia tells Coningsby, "never irresistible but when he appeals to the imagination. Even Mormon counts more votaries than Bentham" (*Coningsby* 253). In *Tancred,* the Angel of Arabia delivers the same message to the "crusading" English hero: empires (indeed, all successful polities and politics) are based on "the passions," on "imagination," and ultimately on faith. It does not seem to matter what that faith is; a great religion, faithfully adhered to by leaders and masses alike, will translate into the conquest and rule of great empires. The Ottoman Empire, though in decline, is one example; the British Empire is another, albeit also threatened by decline because its Whiggish rulers are neglecting its "visionary" or religious basis for mere material, utilitarian profit-and-loss concerns.

The lessons that he learns from the Angel of Arabia Tancred teaches to Fakredeen, who aspires to be a Syrian Napoleon and to conquer the world. Even before his encounter with the Angel, Tancred teaches Fakredeen that "the world was never conquered by intrigue: it was conquered by faith" (267). Once Fakredeen accepts this "Arabian principle" (299) that the Western Tancred knows better than he does, the two young aristocrats join forces, more visionary than actual, in a scheme to overthrow Ottoman rule and to conquer most of Asia, possibly for the British Empire. Indeed, despite his earlier desire to join the Ottomans in their struggle against the Greek rebellion, Disraeli in *Tancred* treats Fakredeen's Syria as an ideal domain where "we find several human races, several forms of government, and several schemes of religion, yet everywhere liberty," free from "the tyranny of the Turk" and also "from Arabian rapine" (348).[10] The last phrase contradicts Disraeli's positive uses of "Arabian," but never mind. "We wish to conquer [the] world, with angels at our head," Tancred tells the Queen of the Ansaray (434). Perhaps this was the sort of misty-eyed notion of imperial rule that helped Disraeli persuade Queen Victoria to accept the title of "Empress of India" in 1876. Such heroic idealism is appealing: even if he and Fakredeen do not conquer Asia, Tancred conquers the eastern queen's heart. Disraeli, no doubt, was as much amused as he was serious about Tancred's quixotic escapades. The political machinations that he and Fakredeen become embroiled in continue to seem more like "intrigue" than religious inspiration. Nevertheless, Disraeli clearly believed that world conquest depended on "faith" at least as much as on "intrigue." Furthermore, he also believed that nationalisms turn into imperialisms. As Napoleon demonstrated, a militant nationalism can become an attempt at world conquest. And Disraeli maintained, both in *Tancred* and in his other writings and speeches, that the Middle East (and more specifically the "Semitic" or "Arabian" race, including "the Hebrews") was the source of the "visionary" principles necessary for the forging and rule of all great empires, including the British Empire.

"All is race; there is no other truth," Sidonia declares (*Tancred* 153), a theory that Disraeli often reiterated in later texts and contexts. Disraeli's insistence that race was *the* central category of politics and history led a few of his Victorian critics to consider his views outlandish.[11] But more often than not, the critics also viewed race as the central category of politics and history; they objected only to Disraeli's philo-Semitism or positive Orientalism (and perhaps to his Jewish origins). The numerous intellectuals and politicians who believed that the Anglo-Saxon or, more generally, the Germanic or Teutonic race was supreme and destined to rule the rest of the world had perforce to believe Jews and all other non-Germanic peoples inferior. Anglo-Saxon supremacy was the positive side of a coin whose reverse included anti-Semitism, negative Orientalism, and other forms of the stereotypic denigration of the non-Western races of the world. Anglo-Saxon supremacists such as Dr. Thomas Arnold, E. A. Freeman, and Charles Kingsley, in common with "Aryanists" like the artist Mr. Phoebus in Disraeli's novel *Lothair,* were perforce to some degree or in some manner anti-Semitic (though, as with all ideologies, there were shades and degrees of anti-Semitism then as now).[12]

From Young England to the "Bulgarian Horrors"

In *Lothair* (1870), Disraeli's Oriental self-fashioning comes full circle. Once again, Disraeli sends a youthful protagonist with both a political and a religious vocation on an Eastern journey, culminating in Jerusalem. Once

again, the young hero learns about the intellectual and spiritual supremacy of Orientals and, more specifically, of the Jews. More clearly than in the
earlier novels, however, the opinions of the Aryanist Mr. Phoebus help to
contextualize Disraeli's philo-Semitism in relation to its racist antitheses.
According to Phoebus:

> The fate of a nation will ultimately depend upon the strength and health of
> the population.... As for our mighty engines of war in the hands of a puny
> race, it will be the old story of the lower empire and the Greek fire. Laws
> should be passed to secure all this, and some day they will be. But nothing
> can be done until the Aryan races are extricated from Semitism. (134)

Phoebus means that "Semitism"—Jewishness, Judaism, Christianity, and
perhaps Islam—should give way to Aryanism and Western, classical
values.

"Welcome, my friend!" says Phoebus to Lothair as they disembark on
the former's Aegean island. "Welcome to an Aryan clime, an Aryan land-
scape, and an Aryan race. It will do you good after your Semitic hallucina-
tions" (*Lothair* 371). From Disraeli's perspective, however, it is Phoebus
who hallucinates, along with Aryanism in general, which has lost sight of
the true racial basis of both civilization and religion. Later, near Jerusalem,
Lothair learns the truth about these racial matters from Paraclete, the Syrian who plays Sidonia's role of speaking racial wisdom to the protagonist.
Paraclete tells Lothair:

> "In My Father's house are many mansions," and by the various families of
> nations the designs of the Creator are accomplished. God works by races,
> and one was appointed in due season...to reveal and expound in this land
> the spiritual nature of man. The Aryan and the Semite are of the same blood
> and origin, but when they quitted their central land they were ordained to
> follow opposite courses. Each division of the great race has developed one
> portion of the double nature of humanity, till after all their wanderings they
> met again, and, represented by their two choicest families, the Hellenes and
> the Hebrews, brought together the treasures of their accumulated wisdom
> and secured the civilisation of man. (396–97)

Here Disraeli is responding especially to Matthew Arnold's argument in
Culture and Anarchy that Victorian society has become overly "Hebraic"—
that it needs to correct the imbalance by "Hellenizing." Arnold himself

may have been partly responding to Disraeli's frequent reiterations of the debts that modern British and European civilization owed to the ancient (and modern) Hebrews. Both Arnold and Disraeli accepted the general idea that "God works by races," though both attempted to revise the standard racial theories of their time in anti-stereotypic directions. Moreover, it is not always clear how far their racial ideas are to be understood in strictly biological terms. Both were master ironists, capable simultaneously of self-mockery and mockery of the foibles, contradictions, and irrationalities of their age (Ragussis 211–27; Young).

Just how seriously did Disraeli take his philo-Semitism? It is certainly one of the most consistent, clearly articulated features of his ideas throughout his career. Through his positive Orientalism, Disraeli cannily positioned himself to criticize his political adversaries on religious grounds that were simultaneously racial grounds. The neglect of religious ideals by worldly politicians is a neglect of what the "Hebrew intellect" taught wiser politicians in the past. This must have seemed to Disraeli an especially powerful argument because coming from a "Hebrew" rather than from an evangelical Christian—the very type that Arnold accused of too much "Hebraizing."

For both Arnold and Disraeli, the issue of irony is difficult to resolve. While Disraeli seems to express some of his most serious, consistent ideas through Sidonia and Paraclete, how is the reader to react to the Angel of Arabia in *Tancred*? Disraeli's amusement over Tancred's quixotic excesses verges on satire, and hence on self-mockery. One way that Disraeli echoes Byron is through his combination of romantic flights of imagination with irony and satire: stories of idealistic young adventurers and lovers recounted by presumably mature, wise, disillusioned narrators. Especially in the early novels (with the exception of the comparatively solemn, over-written *Alroy*), the clashes between romance and ironic deflations of romance produce an ambivalence that was part of Disraeli's intellectual and emotional armor.

Despite his philo-Semitism, Disraeli also, according to Said, agrees with other Orientalists that "an Oriental lives in the Orient, he lives a life of Oriental ease, in a state of Oriental despotism and sensuality, imbued with a feeling of Oriental fatalism" (*Orientalism* 102). But while all of these traits fit some of the Oriental characters whom Disraeli portrays in his novels and letters, they do not fit the heroic protagonist of *Alroy*, and in *Tancred* they do not fit Fakredeen, the beautiful Jewess Eva (with whom Tancred falls in love), or for that matter the half-Orientalized Tancred himself, who matures into a hybrid figure in some ways like Disraeli. Although the racial traits that Disraeli ascribes to Fakredeen are "all the qualities of the genuine Syrian character in excess" (*Tancred* 219), these traits read like a critical self-portrait of the artist as a young man (a more realistic self-portrait, at least, than the obviously idealized ones of Sidonia and Tancred). Disraeli may be reproducing Orientalist stereotyping, but he is surely also half-mocking himself when he writes that "the genuine Syrian character in excess" is "vain, susceptible, endowed with a brilliant though frothy imagination, and a love of action so unrestrained that restlessness deprived it of energy, with so fine a taste that he [Fakredeen] was always capricious, and so ingenious that he seemed ever inconsistent" (*Tancred* 219). Perhaps here the "ingenious" Disraeli beats his anti-Semitic critics to the punch by caricaturing himself. Shorn of their "excess," however, several of these racial traits (sensitivity, imaginative brilliance, love of action, taste, ingenuity) also fit Sidonia.

"Orientalism was ultimately a political vision of reality whose structure promoted the difference between the familiar (Europe, the West, 'us') and the strange (the Orient, the East, 'them')" (Said, *Orientalism* 43). This "vision" involved racial and cultural stereotyping of the sort evident in James Mill's *History of British India* (1819), with its claims of European superiority and of the inability of Indians to achieve civilization without British intervention. From start to finish of his career, Disraeli contested negative Orientalism with the weapons of his positive version of that ideology. In the case of the Jews, their very survival in the face of centuries-long hostility from other races was a sign of their racial purity and superiority: "The degradation of the Jewish race is alone a striking evidence of its excellence, for none but one of the great races could have survived the trials which it has endured" (*Bentinck* 352). To quote his chapter on "The Jewish Question" in his life of Bentinck once more:

The Saxon, the Sclave, and the Celt, have adopted most of the laws and many of the customs of these Arabian tribes, all their literature and all their religion. They are therefore indebted to them for much that regulates, much that charms, and much that solaces existence. The toiling multitude rest every seventh day by virtue of a Jewish law; they are perpetually reading, "for their example," the records of Jewish history, and singing the odes and elegies of Jewish poets; and they daily acknowledge on their knees, with reverent gratitude, that the only medium of communication between the Creator and themselves is the Jewish race. Yet they treat that race as the vilest of generations; and instead of logically looking upon them as the human family that has contributed most to human happiness, they extend to them every term of obloquy and every form of persecution. (346)

Disraeli's early self-fashioning, involving his Byronism and his Eastern travels, also involved his celebrations of Turkish, Syrian, Jewish, and more generally Oriental customs, costumes, and cultures. While, with the exception of Judaism and Christianity, his knowledge of any of the cultures and societies of the Orient may never have been much more than touristic, in *Alroy, Contarini Fleming,* and elsewhere he was already situating the "Hebrew race" in the context of the larger categories of the "Semitic," "Arabian," and ultimately "Caucasian" races. These Oriental—and European—races formed a hierarchy of empires, religions, and cultures at the apex of which (could good British Christians, no matter how anti-Semitic, deny it?) were the Jews, the chosen race through which God revealed His everlasting truths to mankind. Such a theory allowed Disraeli not just to agree with both his friends and his enemies that, despite his conversion to Christianity, he remained Jewish and to some degree Oriental, but to assert his Jewish and Oriental affiliations with pride. As Robert Blake puts it in his account of the young Disraeli's Eastern travels, "the identity which Disraeli sought was found on his tour of the Near East. He was a member of a great race" (128)—Caucasian, Semitic, Arabian, but above all, Jewish.

Disraeli and the Bulgarian Crisis

Disraeli's purchase of the Suez Canal in 1875 did not mean that he advocated British imperial expansion in Egypt or the Middle East. As prime minister from 1874 to 1880, he faced his greatest foreign policy crisis in the midst of widespread protest against the massacres of Serbians and Bulgarians committed by Ottoman troops in the mid-1870s. For the protesters, whose most prominent leader was Disraeli's perennial adversary William Ewart Gladstone, the massacres proved the validity of the ancient stereotype of the terrible Turk. "There was nothing new or unusual in the fact either of insurrection or of massacre," writes Richard Shannon. "Both were endemic features of Ottoman administration. The massacres in Bulgaria were not unusually extensive, and there is no reason to assume that they were unusually atrocious" (22).

Why, then, did "the Bulgarian horrors" arouse such moral condemnation in Britain? Part of the answer is that they allowed Liberal dissenters to forge an anti-Islamic crusade that repudiated what was widely seen as the lack of moral principle in the Conservative Party in general and in Disraeli in particular. The crusade sought to elevate British foreign policy from what the protestors perceived as mere expediency to the moral high ground. Gladstone and his followers did not stop to ask how many massacres and atrocities British forces had committed over the centuries in Ireland, India, and elsewhere. Against Ottoman corruption and evil, with the racist stereotype of the terrible Turk as its incarnation, British imperial rectitude shone forth in brilliant contrast.

Adding fuel to the anti-Turkish fire, the bankruptcy of the Ottoman treasury by 1875 left British and French creditors in the lurch. By the 1870s, writes Sina Akşin, the Ottoman Empire

> had become financially bankrupt and more dependent on European good-will than ever before. The bond-holders' 50% loss of revenue led to furious protests from British and French creditors.... Public opinion in Europe now turned against the Ottomans. Until the Reduction of Interest Decision [in 1875], there had been sympathy for their plight and a belief that they were doing their best to make progress. This was now reversed and the Ottoman state was viewed [once again] as sunk in barbarism. (38)

From June 1876, revelations of atrocities in Bulgaria, including rape and the slaughter of Christian women and children, led to the agitation that propelled Gladstone back into the political spotlight. His pamphlet *Bulgarian Horrors and the Question of the East* expresses his moral outrage that Britain should continue to support the Ottoman Empire when it was ruled by a "race" of Turkish "savages." Indeed, "there is not a criminal in an European gaol, there is not a cannibal in the South Sea Islands," Gladstone declared, "whose indignation would not rise and overboil at the recital of that which has been done" in Bulgaria by Turkish forces, "but which remains unavenged" (62). The bloodthirsty Turks have perpetrated a "murderous harvest," which today would be called "ethnic cleansing" or even "genocide." Unlike Gladstone's South Sea cannibals, however, Turkish leaders and forces were not whom Disraeli blamed for the atrocities. He continued to support the Ottomans throughout his last premiership, even though doing so diminished his popularity.

Gladstone's speeches, articles, and pamphlets on Bulgaria drew a huge following, including many Victorian writers, artists, and intellectuals. The "Eastern question" brought William Morris into his first public engagement with politics; he became treasurer of the Eastern Association. Most of the Pre-Raphaelite Brotherhood also joined the association. Figures as diverse as Anthony Trollope, Thomas Carlyle, and Charles Algernon Swinburne supported the anti-Turkish cause. Far to the political right of Morris, Alfred Tennyson penned his sonnet "Montenegro" at Gladstone's behest, publishing it in *The Nineteenth-Century* as a preface to an anti-Ottoman article by Gladstone. (But because of the old fear of Russia, Tennyson soon changed his mind.) Like Morris and Swinburne, many of the supporters of the Eastern Association saw it as a way not just of condemning the Ottomans but also of condemning Disraeli and the Conservative Party.

Through his anti-Turkish campaigning, Gladstone was propelled back into the political spotlight, succeeding Disraeli as prime minister in 1880. But the old policy of propping up the Ottomans as a foil to Russian aggression continued. And Gladstone also found himself towed into the British takeover in Egypt in 1882, a move that led to further imperial expansion in East Africa (the Sudan, Uganda, Kenya). Both a decrepit Ottoman Empire and the British presence at Cairo seemed to ensure the security of India until World War I, after which Britain, France, and Russia carved up the carcass of the Orient—that is, the Middle East—among them. By that time, the racism and Anglo-Saxonism that supported the British Empire had reached a crescendo that resonated with the beginnings of European (including British) fascism. By that time, too, no one any longer paid any attention to Disraeli's philo-Semitism, much less to his theory of the superiority and vast influence of "the Hebrew intellect."

Part III

The 1860s: The Decade after Darwin's *Origin*

5

Race and Class in the 1860s

The aim of the Saxon man is the extermination of the dark races.

DR. ROBERT KNOX, *The Races of Men*

Comparing attitudes toward urban poverty in both Britain and British India, John Marriott treats the 1860s as a "watershed" for explanations of social phenomena in terms of race, ranging from poverty and the urban underclass to the evolution of the human species. So, too, in his study of attitudes toward "the Negro" in nineteenth-century Britain, Douglas Lorimer writes, "After the mid-century, and especially from the 1860s onwards, English spokesmen adopted a more stridently racist stance" (16). And Alastair Bonnett contends that, starting in the 1860s, "the use of the language of race" to describe the urban working class "became so commonplace that it...formed a new and distinctive kind of racialized discourse" (326).[1] Prior to mid-century, Chartism, trade union agitation, the Irish Famine, and the continental revolutions of 1848 seemed to corroborate the assertion in *The Communist Manifesto* that "all history has been a history of class struggles" (Marx and Engels, *The Marx-Engels Reader* 472). But over the next two decades many naturalists, historians, social scientists, politicians, and literary intellectuals emphasized race rather than class conflict. Why did race acquire such significance in Victorian culture from about 1860 forward?[2]

Versions of negative racial stereotyping and positive Anglo-Saxonism arose earlier than the 1860s, but in that decade the conjunction of six major factors brought race to the fore in many arenas and genres, from novels and melodramas to histories and scientific treatises.[3] These factors include debates over evolution, the Indian Rebellion of 1857–58, the American Civil War, the 1865 Jamaica uprising, parliamentary reform, and Fenianism. On many occasions these and various other factors, such as the exploration of central Africa and the second Maori War, were interwoven in complex ways. Underlying them all seems to have been the unacknowledged desire to downplay class conflict and inequality or, when class was an unavoidable issue, to treat it in terms of race—in short, to translate the politics of class into biological necessity.

Though it was often overshadowed by race, class after mid-century remained a crucial issue. Thus, reactions to Fenianism frequently expressed a racism that compared the Irish to black slaves, African savages, and chimpanzees (Curtis). Moreover, the controversy over the Second Reform Bill of 1867 concerned how the different social classes should be represented in Parliament. Should some portion of the working class be granted the vote or not? Pro-reform demonstrations in Trafalgar Square and Hyde Park in 1866 were sometimes compared to the Jamaican uprising while also evoking memories of the Indian Rebellion (Semmel 19). Julie Evans notes that Edward Eyre, governor of Jamaica, had himself spoken about "freedpeople as a peasant *class*—with potential to be included in the colonial polity," but "when resistance and repression spiralled out of control as social conditions worsened in Jamaica and rebellion approached, he spoke of them as a *race* of people whose inclusion was simply inconceivable" (13). And in the 1860s many explorations of urban poverty and slums, like Henry Mayhew's *London Labour and the London Poor* (1861–62), invoked race to help explain their discoveries. Biological rather than social inequalities could not be altered by revolution, by the abolition of slavery, by parliamentary reform, or by granting home rule to Ireland. This fact made race an attractive alternative to class.[4] Sidonia's assertion in Disraeli's *Coningsby* that "all is race" anticipated the frequent substitution of racial for social class discourse that emerged in the 1860s.

Race and Science

After the failed revolutions of 1848, in France Count Arthur de Gobineau contended that history was the outcome of "the inequality among the
races." So he declared in his multivolume work of that title (1853–1855).
Gobineau argued that there were, throughout history and everywhere in
the world, three races that formed the "three original classes": these were
"the nobility, a more or less accurate reflection of the conquering race;
the bourgeoisie composed of mixed stock coming close to the chief race;
and the common people who lived in servitude or at least in a very de-
pressed position." The third group constituted a "lower race," which in
Europe "came about in the south through miscegenation with the negroes
and in the north with Finns" (120). Race determined the class hierarchy
over the ages, with the vast majority of people belonging to the "lower
race" of slaves, serfs, peasants, workers, and paupers. Paradoxically, however, Gobineau also argued that progress occurred when a superior race
conquered an inferior one and assimilated the survivors. But the reverse
happened when the inferior race, or the mixed race that assimilation produced, outpopulated the superior race. Gobineau simultaneously affirmed
miscegenation as the source of progress and claimed that it caused racial
degeneration and the subversion of civilization (Biddiss; Banton, *Racial
Theories* 43–52).

   In contrast to Gobineau, Marx argued that "the central ideological supports for continued bourgeois dominance were divisive ideas of racial or
ethnic inferiority," or in other words racism. The antipathy and competition between English and Irish workers, Marx observed, was similar to that
between poor whites and blacks in the American South. Concerning the
split between English and Irish workers, Marx wrote to two veterans of
the 1848 revolutions, "This antagonism is the secret of the impotence of the
English working class, despite its organization[,]...the secret which enables
the capitalist class to maintain its power." He recognized that anti-Irish racism was "intensified by the press, the pulpit, the comic papers, in short by all
the means at the disposal of the ruling classes" (quoted in Miller, "Social and
Political Theory" 78). After the demise of Chartism in 1848 and the catastrophe of the Irish Famine (1845–1850), racist attitudes toward the Irish and
the more general imperialist discourse of racial conflict began to be widely
applied to domestic affairs.

In Britain and North America a number of authorities from the 1850s on espoused views similar to Gobineau's. A major influence on later discussions of race was James Cowles Prichard, whose *Natural History of Man* appeared in 1843. Charles Hamilton Smith published *The Natural History of the Human Species* in 1848, while *The Natural History of the Varieties of Man,* by Robert Latham, followed in 1850. Also in that year, in *The Races of Men,* Dr. Robert Knox announced that "race is everything: literature, science, art, in a word, civilisation, depend on it" (90).⁵ Because there were so many versions of this claim, it seems unlikely that Knox had Disraeli in mind. And in the United States, Josiah Nott and George Gliddon produced *Types of Mankind; or Ethnological Researches* (1854), which Young calls "the founding textbook of the new racialist American anthropology" (66)—an anthropology in the service of the slave economy of the southern states. Among Nott and Gliddon's conclusions were that the races were separate species or "types" and that these "types have been permanent through all recorded time." The "higher castes of what are termed the Caucasian races [have] the largest brains and the most powerful intellect; *theirs* is the mission of extending and perfecting civilization." The superior Caucasians "have in all ages been the rulers," while the dark races are "only fit for military governments" (quoted in Banton, *Racial Theories* 42–43).

For the scientific or pseudoscientific racism that began to gain wider currency in the 1850s, Darwin's *Origin of Species* in 1859 served as an anticlimactic climax.⁶ It was anticlimactic because Darwin postponed discussing how *Homo sapiens* and its different races had evolved until 1871, when he published *The Descent of Man.* To both his followers and opponents in the 1860s, however, that controversial topic was unavoidable. Thomas Henry Huxley's *Man's Place in Nature* and Charles Lyell's *Antiquity of Man* both appeared in 1863, followed by Alfred Russel Wallace's essay "The Origin of Human Races and the Antiquity of Man Deduced from the Theory of 'Natural Selection'" in 1864. When in 1863 Disraeli was asked whether he sided with the apes or the angels, he famously replied, "My Lord, I am on the side of the angels"—a dramatic response which hardly gibes with his own emphasis on the historical significance of race (quoted in Blake 486).

From Knox's *Races of Men* to Darwin's *Origin,* arguments about whether the races had a single beginning (monogenesis) or different ones (polygenesis) and were therefore distinct species were inconclusive, and continued to be so for several more years. In 1861 Thomas Hunt formed the

Anthropological Society, which counted Richard Burton among its most prominent members. It espoused a polygenist version of the differences among the races, in contrast to the earlier, monogenist Ethnological Society, whose members typically echoed Prichard. In 1863 Hunt published "On the Negro's Place in Nature," a proslavery riposte to Huxley's *Man's Place in Nature*. As George Stocking puts it in his history of Victorian anthropology, Hunt expressed "the traditional racist view of blacks." He claimed that "Negroes were a different species, closer to the ape than to the European," and that they were "incapable of civilization, either on their own or through the influence of others" (251).

Hunt and most of the other "Anthropologicals," whose leaders formed a clique they dubbed "The Cannibal Club" (Stocking 252), were opposed to Darwinism as well as to political liberalism, including those liberals who, like Darwin and Huxley, advocated the criminal prosecution of Governor Eyre after his brutal suppression of the Jamaican uprising. Darwin, Huxley, and others who espoused monogenism and the abolition of slavery favored the Ethnological Society. Stocking writes that many members of Hunt's Anthropological Society were, in contrast, opposed "to all who would not see basic issues of politics, economics, and philanthropy in racial terms." Hunt thought that liberals, humanitarians, and abolitionists "were simply people of 'arrested brain growth' and 'deficient reasoning power' who suffered respectively from 'the religious mania, and the rights-of-man mania'" (Stocking 252).

By the end of the 1860s, Huxley managed to effect a merger between the Anthropological and the Ethnological Societies. Perhaps the end of the American Civil War and the passage of the Second Reform Bill tempered Hunt's extreme racism. Certain it is that Darwinism provided a bridge between monogenism and polygenism. The Reverend Frederick Farrar, whom Darwin nominated for a fellowship in the Royal Society on the basis of his essay on the origin of language, opined in an 1867 article that there were "three distinct and different *strata or stages of humanity*." In "Aptitudes of Races," published by the journal of the Ethnological Society, Farrar wrote that these three "strata" are "the Savage races, the Semi-civilised races, and finally the two Civilised races," (116) Caucasian and Semitic. There was no such thing as a noble savage; all savages were "irreclaimable," stuck in "the lowest mud of barbarism" (118). All savages were apparently also cannibals. As to the African "negro," no Europeans "have weaned him, on his native continent from his cannibalism, his rain-doctors, his medicine-men, his mumbo-jumbo" (122). And the "aborigines of Victoria, among whom new-born babes are, when convenient, killed and eaten by their parents and brothers" (118), are equally uncivilizable. Besides cannibalism, for Farrar a proof that savages cannot be improved is that, "so far from being influenced by civilisation, they disappear from before the face of it as surely and as perceptibly as the snow retreats before the advancing line of sunbeams" (120). Yet even cannibal savages are humans, Farrar concludes in monogenist fashion, and therefore equal in the eyes of God. Like Darwin and Huxley, Farrar was an abolitionist.

"Evolutionary theory swept away the creationist rug that had supported the intense debate between monogenists and polygenists," writes Stephen Jay Gould; "but it satisfied both sides by presenting an even better rationale for their shared racism." He explains: "The monogenists continued to construct linear hierarchies of races according to mental and moral worth; the polygenists now admitted a common ancestry in the prehistoric mists, but affirmed that races had been separate long enough to evolve major inherited differences in talent and intelligence" (73). In *Man's Place in Nature,* Huxley sought to prove that between "man" and the "higher apes"—gorillas and chimpanzees—there was more physiological similarity than between the higher apes and the lower ones, including monkeys and lemurs (144). Although he did not directly address differences among human races, he nevertheless asserted that there was a greater biological distance between the higher, "civilized" races and the "lower races" than between humans in general and gorillas. This was a point that Hunt agreed with.

Discussing "cranial capacities," Huxley claims that "the difference in the volume of the cranial cavity of different races of mankind is far greater, absolutely, than that between the lowest Man and the highest Ape" (107). He also compares "the civilized great toe" with the toes of races he considers closer to the apes: "The Chinese boatmen are said to be able to pull an oar; the artisans of Bengal to weave, and the Carajas to steal fishhooks" by using their opposable (hence, apelike) big toes (119). And when Huxley mentions "savages," he suggests that to believe humans evolved from apes is no more difficult or degrading than to believe civilized humans developed from some primitive or savage condition:

Is it, indeed, true, that the Poet, or the Philosopher, or the Artist whose genius is the glory of his age, is degraded from his high estate by the undoubted historical probability, not to say certainty, that he is the direct descendant of some naked and bestial savage, whose intelligence was just sufficient to make him a little more cunning than the Fox, and by so much more danger-ous than the Tiger? (154)

For Huxley, the answer is a resounding "No!" But meanwhile his argu-ment leaves "savages" and "the lower races of mankind" (188) far behind in what he and many other Victorians, whether or not they accepted Dar-win's ideas, saw as progress. Huxley had no doubt that the British, in con-trast to present-day savages, not to mention gorillas, were in the vanguard of "Nature's great progression, from the formless to the formed—from the inorganic to the organic—from blind force to conscious intellect and will" (151).

For Huxley and other evolutionary thinkers, the races may have had a single origin, and therefore all humans belonged to the same species. Yet history—including the many thousands of years of "prehistory"—was characterized by "the struggle for existence," not only among species but also among races.[7] The "fittest" races triumphed; the weaker ones per-ished. All of history could be explained in terms of clashes and competition among races. In his 1865 essay "On the Methods and Results of Ethnol-ogy," Huxley writes that the human species had evolved into a number of "persistent modifications" or "stocks," terms he prefers to "varieties," "races," and also "species" because of the ambiguity of the last three terms. (Elsewhere, Huxley nevertheless employs the term "race.") In distinguish-ing among races, he rejects linguistic and other forms of cultural evidence in favor of morphology, or more or less permanent physical characteristics, on the basis of which he asserts that there are eleven different "persistent modifications" among humans.[8] Only two, the "Xanthochroi" (white peo-ple) and the "Melanchroi" (Semites), have fully entered history, in the sense of founding progressive civilizations, and only the "Xanthochroi" are still progressing.

The details of Huxley's taxonomy of racial "stocks" did not become or-thodoxy, but its hierarchy from savage to civilized was virtually axiomatic from Enlightenment natural history to Victorian race science. As we have seen, Huxley's claim that the driving force of history is the "struggle for survival" among races was also widely shared by 1863. And although Hux-ley, like Darwin, abhorred slavery, in "Emancipation Black and White" Huxley declared: "It is simply incredible that, when all his disabilities are removed, and our prognathous [black, ape-like] relative has a fair field and no favour, as well as no oppressor, he will be able to compete successfully with his bigger-brained and smaller-jawed rival, in a contest which is to be carried on by thoughts and not by bites" ("Emancipation" 67). In contrast, with the white race "has originated everything that is highest in science, in art, in law, in politics, and in mechanical inventions. In their hands, at the present moment, lies the order of the social world, and to them its progress is committed" ("Methods," in *Man's Place* 232).

Huxley also tackled the subject of the "ethnology" of the races inhabiting Britain. In the 1860s a number of other writers dealt with that topic, or else more generally with the Celts, the Anglo-Saxons, the Teutons, or the Aryans.[9] Luke Owen Pike published *The English and Their Origins* in 1866, in which he critiqued the Anglo-Saxonist orthodoxy on that topic. And Joseph Davis and Joseph Thurnam took up the subject of skull measurement or craniometry, which had become a key method of race science (partly owing to Paul Broca's publications starting in the 1860s), in their 1865 *Crania Britannia: Delineations and Descriptions of the Skulls of the Aboriginal and Early Inhabitants of the British Islands*. To be English was, according to most authors, to belong to the highest, most successful British race—which also happened to be the highest, most successful race in history. It was, then, not easy to understand why white savages, or worse than savages, starved in Ireland and prowled the streets of Britain's major cities.

Henry Mayhew's Nomads

Complementing scientific approaches to race in the 1860s, a historiography that stressed "England's" Anglo-Saxon or Germanic roots, and the unparalleled greatness that sprang from those roots, emerged in the works of William Stubbs, E. A. Freeman, James Anthony Froude, and J. R. Green. Froude's twelve-volume *History of England* (1865–1870) was exemplary in narrating "the Anglo-Saxons' triumph" against all other races, including the Celts (in his later work on Ireland, Froude called the Celts an "ignorant," "selfish," and naturally weak race that needed to be ruled by the English) (MacDougall 99). "Aryanism" broadened but also still racialized ideas about the origins of civilization by incorporating all speakers of Indo-European languages, including Indian speakers of Sanskrit-based tongues, into a single, civilizing ur-race, as in Sir Henry Maine's *Ancient Law* (1861). Charles Kingsley published his Cambridge history lectures as *The Roman and the Teuton* in 1864, in which he proclaimed that "the welfare of the Teutonic race is the welfare of the world" (338). And a new emphasis on colonial affairs was marked by Charles Dilke's *Greater Britain: A Record of Travel in English-Speaking Countries during 1866 and 1867* (1868), which looked forward to the establishment of a "commonwealth" of British colonies and former colonies, including the United States, based on the Anglo-Saxon roots of the colonizers. "These contexts, though apparently distant from the political conflicts of the 1860s, provided a series of shared reference points for all members of the political classes who read or contributed to the major periodicals of the day" (Hall, McClelland, and Rendall 26).

Underlying the race science and racial chauvinism of the 1860s are many worries, some of which involved the threat of class conflict. What would the effect of the newly emancipated African Americans be on America's social order? What if the "freedpeople" of Jamaica seized control of that colony? Suppose the Indian Rebellion had succeeded? What would become of Ireland if the Fenians had their way? And was passage of the Second Reform Bill in 1867 like "shooting Niagara," as Carlyle claimed? The protesters who trampled flowerbeds and knocked hats off the heads of bourgeois citizens in Hyde Park in 1866, while the Reform League tried to rally support for the enfranchisement of "respectable workingmen," were deemed savages or worse by much of the press. Writing about white working-class rioters in 1866, the *Daily Telegraph* stated, "There are a good many negroes in Southampton, who have the taste of their tribe for any disturbance that appears safe, and who are probably imbued with the conviction that it is the proper thing to hoot and yell at a number of gentlemen going to a dinner party" (quoted in Bonnett 323).

Also distressing to the British middle and upper classes was the renewed publicity given to urban poverty. The genre of travelers into "the undiscovered country of the poor" (Mayhew 1:xv) was an old one, extending back at least to the 1820s, but it flourished in the 1850s and 1860s. The metaphor of exploration, which likened slumming in London or Manchester to exploring "the dark continent," is one way that writers on urban conditions treated the poor as though they were a separate, nonwhite or non-English race (Nord; Herbert). This is evident, for example, in the title of Phillips Watts's *Wild Tribes of London* (1855), as later and more famously in William Booth's *In Darkest England* (1890).[10] And it is a central theme in Mayhew's *London Labour and the London Poor* (1861–62).

Based on interviews he and his team of journalists conducted in the 1850s and first published in the *Morning Chronicle,* Mayhew's multivolume project opens with his claim that mankind is split into "the wanderers and the civilized tribes" and that these are two distinct "races" (1:1). He supports this claim by referring to the "ethnologists," in the second paragraph quoting James Cowles Prichard at length on the "three varieties" of mankind, distinguished by "the form of the head and other physical characters." For Prichard, these three "varieties" or, as Mayhew puts it, "three forms of head" (1:1) correspond to the three standard social formations: savagery, barbarism, and civilization. Mayhew proceeds, without giving a reason, to reduce these three "varieties" to "two broadly-marked varieties," the brutish "wandering tribes" and the settled denizens of "civilization." Given his obvious sympathy for the street people, why did Mayhew portray them as totally antithetical to civilization? The wish to create a journalistic sensation may be part of the answer.

Mayhew also claims that every settled, civilized society has a wandering "horde" attached to it parasitically. Even "the Kafirs" [*sic*] of Africa "have their Bushmen as well as the Hottentots—these are called *Fingoes*—a word signifying wanderers, beggars, or outcasts" (1:1). What makes the "nomads" of London "outcasts" seems on one level to be biologically determined: "wandering" or "roving" is the result of their racial inferiority. This racial component includes their volition; even though many of them are following their parents' mode of getting a living, and even though many others are victims of circumstance, Mayhew suggests that they have in some sense chosen to be street people:

> Strange to say, despite its privations, its dangers, and its hardships, those who have once adopted the savage and wandering mode of life rarely abandon it. There are countless examples of white men adopting all the usages of the Indian hunter, but there is scarcely one example of the Indian hunter or trapper adopting the steady and regular habits of civilized life; indeed, the various missionaries who have visited nomade [*sic*] races have found their labours utterly unavailing. (1:2)

Going native, in other words, was far more common than natives becoming civilized. As Mayhew and his team of interviewers proceed, however, they elicit from the street people dozens of stories of misfortune and involuntary deprivation. For example, speaking of coffee stall vendors, Mayhew writes, "Many have been bred to dealing in the streets...but many have taken to the business owing to the difficulty of obtaining work at their own trade" (1:185). Mayhew is also well aware that the "street Irish" have been driven from Ireland by famine and evictions. So, too, among the prostitutes interviewed in the fourth volume are many "fallen" women who were seduced and abandoned by their lovers, and who turned to prostitution to avoid starvation. Nevertheless, Mayhew elicits stories from former members of the upper classes who have chosen the "nomadic" street life, like the "countless...white men" who have chosen to become Indians. He claims that "ethnology" has demonstrated this phenomenon. But how to explain it when members of the higher race choose to behave like members of the lower one, even though their jaws and cheekbones do not brutishly protrude, their heads are elliptical, and they have been well educated?

What prompted Mayhew to use the language of race is unclear, although one reason was the influx of the Irish into England, especially during and after the Famine: "At the time of the famine in Ireland...the number of Irish obtaining a living in the London streets must have been at least doubled" (1:5). As the citations from Prichard and other "ethnologists" suggest, Mayhew was also impressed by what seemed to him to be their scientific rigor about the racial basis of many or perhaps all social phenomena. And besides the Irish, many of the street people belonged to other non-English races. Mayhew devotes a chapter of the second volume to "the street Jews" (2:115–32). The seller of rhubarb and spice identifies himself as a "native of Mogadore in Morocco," adding, "I am an Arab" (1:452). Furthermore, over "half of the tract sellers are foreigners, such as Malays, Hindoos, and Negroes. Of them, some cannot speak English, and some—who earn a spare subsistence by selling Christian tracts—are Mahometans, or worshippers of Bramah!" (1:242).

Most of Mayhew's subjects have homes, even if they are rented hovels in the slums. Mayhew and his team of interviewers frequently visit the homes of, say, the costermongers. They qualify as "nomadic," however, by making their living on the streets. The nomadic "race" to which the street people belong have characteristics diametrically opposed to "settled," bourgeois types. A "wanderer" (though he may be working in specific places in the streets) is characterized by

> his repugnance to regular and continuous labour—by his want of providence in laying up store for the future...by his passion for stupefying herbs and roots, and...intoxicating...liquors...by his love of libidinous dances...by the looseness of his notion as to property—by the absence of chastity among his women, and his disregard of female honour—and lastly, by his vague sense of religion. (1:2)

These stereotypic traits are, according to Mayhew, shared by all savages. "The costermongers strongly resemble the North American Indians in their conduct to their wives," for example (1:43). Apparently Mayhew did not know much about North American Indians.

Related to the supposedly nonmetaphoric equation between the street people and savages are two metaphors that unmistakably cast them as the absolute nadir of the social class pyramid: they are like rats or cockroaches, and they are also like sewage. Even though most of them are making their living by honest means, the street people are London's parasites. At the start of the third volume, Mayhew interviews various pest controllers, including Jack Black, who bills himself as "Her Majesty's Ratcatcher" (3:11), and also an anonymous "Bug Destroyer to Her Majesty" (3:36). These interviews are wedged between ones with other rat catchers, cockroach hunters, and boys who sell flypapers. All of these characters, even those who claim to serve the queen, are, so to speak, parasites of parasites. In presenting them and many similar figures (mudlarks, sewermen, dog-shit "finders," and so on), Mayhew goes into lengthy detail about the lives and deaths of rats, bedbugs, and other pests. Thus, he quotes various experts on rats (3:3–5), flies (3:24–28), and other vermin, including Charles Fothergill's Malthusian observations from his 1813 *Natural History* on overpopulation and cannibalism among rats: "The rat is amazingly prolific, usually producing from twelve to eighteen young ones at one time. Their numbers would soon increase beyond all power of restraint, were it not for an insatiable appetite, that impels them to destroy and devour each other. The weaker always fall a prey to the stronger" (quoted in Mayhew 3:3). Fothergill offers the extreme Malthusian nightmare when he says that if rats were allowed to multiply without any natural "checks," then "the whole surface of the earth in a very few years would be rendered a barren and hideous waste, covered with myriad of famished grey rats, against which man himself would contend in vain." Fortunately, however, among other "checks" is the fact that "the male rat has an insatiable thirst for the blood of his own offspring" (3:4).

Citing these passages in his chapter on Mayhew's "Cockney Polynesia," Christopher Herbert remarks, "Thus the cannibalism and infanticide practiced with fiendish avidity in Polynesia, as early ethnographers reported, have their London equivalents also, even though the human street folk are guilty of these crimes only by metaphorical association." Mayhew goes about his reporting on rats, rat catchers, and other parasites very matter-of-factly, so that the nightmarish apocalypse of a world overrun by rats does not sound totally outlandish. All the more reason why the first readers of *London Labour* "preyed on by deep-running fears of 'the dangerous classes,' could hardly have missed the sociological import of this imagery" (Herbert 212).

The same is true of Mayhew's treatment of the sewers and those who make their living from them. Of course, the subject of sewers brings up rats again. And these again are linked, at least metaphorically, to the population or overpopulation of street people. One sewerman relates, "I've sometimes heerd the rats fighting and squeaking" in the sewers "like a parcel of drunken Irishmen" (2:432). All of the sewermen have stories to relate about their subterranean battles with rats. Just as Mayhew goes into overwhelming, meticulous detail about all of the commodities exchanged on the streets, so he goes into similar detail about everything that winds up in the sewers, including both the sewermen and corpses. The sewers contain

> all the ingredients from the breweries, the gas-works, and the several chemical and mineral manufactories; dead dogs, cats, kittens, and rats; offal from slaughter-houses...street pavement dirt...vegetable refuse; stable-dung; the refuse of pig-styes; night-soil; ashes; tin kettles and pans....Our criminal annals...show that often enough the bodies of murdered men were thrown into the Fleet and other ditches, then the open sewers of the metropolis. (2:394)

In *The Politics and Poetics of Transgression,* Peter Stallybrass and Allon White cite Mayhew as an example of "the semantics of the sewer" (140). They also cite Victor Hugo, who in *Les Misérables* calls the Parisian sewer "the conscience of the town...the ditch of truth" (quoted in Stallybrass and White 141). The idea that truth lies beneath appearances, in the lower depths, is central to Mayhew's enterprise, as well as to nineteenth-century novelistic realism. It is also central to Malthusian political economy. And it suggests evolution—progress upward from the apes or the lower depths, meeting savages and London's street people along the way.

Between sections on rubbish carters, street sweepers, chimneysweeps, and various scavengers, leading to his main discussion of sewers, Mayhew offers statistical tables showing the "increase of population" of England and Wales, of Scotland, of Ireland (in 1851 registering a catastrophic decline due to the Famine), and of the United Kingdom as a whole (2:317–18). Next comes a table "showing the increase in the productions and commerce of the United Kingdom, from 1801–1850," and then a table "showing the number of paupers in England and Wales" and a second one "showing the increase in the number of criminals in England and Wales from 1805–1850." Overpopulation and lack of work are the chief causes of these problems (3:319–22). Mayhew then returns to "rubbish-carters," followed by sections on chimney sweeping, "house-drainage," and the sewers. At this point in volume three, his statistics "on the quantity of metropolitan sewage" seem also to signify excess population and both nonproductive and productive "waste" of all kinds. (Sewage is productive, after all, for the sewermen and scavengers who make their living from it.)

Mayhew does not explicitly equate the sewermen or his other street people with excrement. On the contrary, he admires many of those he interviews for their resourcefulness, courage, and amazing productivity despite their impoverished circumstances. But the metaphor of human waste was basic to Malthus's central idea of overpopulation. Mayhew's parasitic hordes of street people, and especially the criminals and prostitutes whose stories fill volume four, are understood by him and his readers as, at least on one level, of no more value than the contents of the sewers of London. They are, in the words of the Reverend Sidney Godolphin Osborne, writing with the Irish Famine in mind, "immortal sewerage." Conscious of the "garroting panic," a writer in the *Saturday Review* for 1862 declared: "We have not yet found out what to do with our criminals.... Our moral sewage... remains in the midst of us polluting and poisoning our air" (quoted in Pick 178). Earlier Malthusian economist J. R. McCulloch did not bother with the adjective "immortal" when he wrote of the "half-famished hordes" of Irish who were "inundating" England in the 1820s; he called

Ireland itself a sewer (quoted in Brantlinger, *Dark Vanishings* 104; see also Greenslade 36).

Unlike Mayhew, Thomas Archer, in *The Pauper, the Thief, and the Convict* (1865), does not try to explain poverty and crime in racial terms. Nevertheless, he employs many of the same racial metaphors—and clichés—that can be found in Mayhew and in earlier writers such as Phillips Watts. The Irish are, of course, omnipresent in the slums, workhouses, and prisons he visits. For Archer, the criminal "type" is also often discernible in physical features, as with the baby of a deceased "coiner" or counterfeiter, "the overhanging brow and large lower jaw showing even in infancy the type from which it came" (78). The thieves, prostitutes, and even legitimate shopkeepers who prey upon British "Jack Tars" are no better than "land rats" (89), and Tiger Bay near the London docks, where sailors are often preyed upon, is inhabited by human "tigers…slinking, watchful, crouching, cruel beasts, who wait there, sharpening their claws" (128). In Victorian discourse after the Indian Rebellion, the tiger metaphor evokes that catastrophe. Tiger Bay is also inhabited by many impoverished foreigners including Chinese. There one can find opium dens

> where yellow Chinese sit in the midst of filth…and stupefy themselves with opium, while their two or three wives quarrel or fight…or themselves lie in blank indifference on the floor, overcome by the heavy fumes which are even more sickening than the foul air of the reeking hovels where Sin-Yang or How-Chi sit looking at intruders with an imbecile expression of surprise on their dirty gamboge faces. (Archer 134).[11]

For Archer, child beggars and thieves form a "horde of lawless young Arabs who infest the streets" (163), while the slums of London in general manifest "the savage wretchedness which cowers behind the ramparts of civilization" (93).

While Archer does not try to explain the "savage wretchedness" of the London slums in racial terms, neither does he try to explain it in social class terms. He is no Marxist. That is true also of John Hollingshead in his *Ragged London in 1861*. Like both Archer and Mayhew, Hollingshead is a sympathetic chronicler of the poor. And yet he can also write that the denizens of Seven Dials and other slums are "human rats" and a "refuse population" (130); those who live in the "huts" of Agar Town lead a "swinish life" (136). Hollingshead also uses Mayhew's phrase "the wandering tribes" (240), though he does not cite Mayhew and has no special theory about nomadic versus civilized "races."

Hollingshead and all of the other writers about London's poor in the 1850s and 1860s seem to be Malthusians: the poor are a "refuse population" that society does not know how to deal with. No matter how sympathetic the bourgeois observers, the frequent comparison of slum dwellers to "human rats" suggests extermination as a possible solution. And they all offer or at least imply comparisons to "savage" peoples in the far reaches of the empire. A wishful aspect of this comparison may have been that those "savages" who were supposedly uncivilizable were also held to be doomed to extinction by the laws of nature. In any case, Archer says that life in the slums is worse than "savage"; describing poverty in Shoreditch he writes, "Savage life has nothing to compare to it" (10). Many other middle-class explorers of the slums also indicate that life in them is worse than "savage," as does anthropologist Edward Burnett Tylor in his major work, *Primitive Culture* (1871): "In our great cities, the so-called 'dangerous classes' are sunk in hideous misery and depravity. If we have to strike a balance between the Papuans of New Caledonia and the communities of European beggars and thieves, we may sadly acknowledge that we have in our midst something worse than savagery" (1:42–43).

In his 1865 *London Vestries and their Sanitary Work*, William Rendle criticized investing in foreign missions for savages when there was so much work to do in the slums at home. This was an old theme, evident in Dickens's portrayal of Mrs. Jellyby in *Bleak House* and Carlyle's fulminations against evangelical missionaries and abolitionists. In *The Mysteries of London* (1845–1848), G. W. M. Reynolds writes, "There is no barbarism in the whole world so truly horrific and ferocious—so obscene and shameless—as that which is found in the poor districts of London!" This observation then leads him to declaim, "How detestable it is for philanthropy to be exercised in clothing negroes or Red Men thousands of miles distant, while our own poor are cold and naked at our very door" (quoted in Himmelfarb 446).[12] Rendle spruces up the Mrs. Jellyby theme by presenting a fictional dialogue between a missionary and a "savage." The missionary acknowledges that, while he is attempting to convert the savage, thousands of poor people in England live in poverty, squalor, and heathenism. The savage is "increasingly astounded," while the missionary grows "increasingly remorseful" (Wohl 51).

A related irony, stressed by Malthus in his *Essay on Population,* was that charity to the poor did nothing to eradicate poverty; on the contrary, it encouraged its spread.[13] According to Malthus, the chief effect of unregulated charity to the poor was their multiplication. The specter of overpopulation by the poor which had haunted the 1800s from their outset provided a key explanation for the economic woes of Ireland and also for poverty in England and Scotland. In the second, 1803 edition of his *Essay,* moreover, Malthus provided an elaborate comparison between the poor at home and savages abroad. Unlike the poor in Britain, savages keep their populations in check through such savage measures as infanticide, cannibalism, and widow strangulation. As is well known, Malthus had a profound influence on Darwin, whose theory of evolution is based on population dynamics in the struggle for existence within and between species.

Degeneration

Malthus also profoundly influenced social and economic thought in general in the 1860s, when upper-class anxiety about the slums and "the residuum," a term John Bright coined in 1867 during debates on the Second Reform Bill, became linked to the fear of racial degeneration. By "residuum," Bright was referring to the most impoverished of Britain's "lower orders." Just as it had seemed necessary at the time of the New Poor Law of 1834 to distinguish between the "deserving" and the "undeserving" poor, so in the 1860s it seemed necessary to distinguish between those members of the working class who were solid citizens and could vote responsibly, and those who were not and could not. Along with "the residuum" emerged the concept of a "labour aristocracy" (see Hobsbawm; Hall, McClelland, and Rendall 18–20; Smith, *Making* 8–14). These were primarily skilled artisans with some education. In a chapter of *Our New Masters* (1868) titled "The Two Races of Poor," Thomas Wright, "the Journeyman Engineer," sought to distinguish in near-absolute terms between the "industrious" working classes and the parasites who lived by begging and charity (359–92). His "industrious" category included more than skilled artisans, however; he meant everyone willing to work, whether they could find employment or not.

An often cited example were the factory workers of Lancashire, deemed long-suffering patriots at the time of the "cotton famine," during the American Civil War. In *Progress of the Working Class* (1867), J. M. Ludlow and Lloyd Jones write that "the working men of Lancashire stood firm and fast to the holy principle of human freedom," despite their distress. Ludlow and Jones cite Abraham Lincoln on the "sublime Christian heroism" of the English textile mill workers (99). But Robert Lowe declaimed in Parliament that to find "venality...ignorance...drunkenness" and "impulsive, unreflecting and violent people," one should look to "the bottom" of the class hierarchy (quoted in Smith, *Making* 81). Thomas Carlyle racialized this opinion by declaring that "Manhood Suffrage" meant "the equality of men" and, hence, equating "Quashee Nigger to Socrates or Shakespeare" (quoted in Smith, *Making* 242). But even the Hyde Park "roughs" who especially bothered Matthew Arnold were not so downtrodden and "ragged" as many of the paupers and slum dwellers whom Mayhew interviewed. Unlike middle- and upper-class Victorians, Mayhew's poorest of the poor seemed to have no stake in the British constitution. And it was these so-called bottom dwellers who most aroused fears concerning racial degeneration, as in Dr. John Edward Morgan's 1866 article for the Social Science Society, "The Danger of Deterioration of Race from the Rapid Increase of Great Cities."

Worries about the poor overpopulating and about the fitness of workers to vote cannot by themselves explain the specific anxiety about racial degeneration that sprang up in the 1860s. That anxiety derived increasingly from the idea that progress and civilization worked to counteract "natural selection." In a civilized condition, the effectiveness of Darwin's evolutionary mechanism diminished or perhaps ceased to operate altogether. Savages in Australia or North America might become extinct before they could be tamed or civilized. But savage costermongers and paupers within the gates of civilization threatened to overrun it. This happened because civilization reversed the formula of "survival of the fittest": it encouraged the unfit to overpopulate, while it did nothing to encourage the fit to keep pace. Francis Galton, Darwin's cousin, thought that the key to the progress of any race was to preserve "the desirables" and eliminate "the undesirables." Galton "first published his eugenic ideas in 1865—well before he coined the word [eugenics] itself—in a two-part article for *Macmillan's Magazine* which he subsequently expanded into a book, *Hereditary Genius,* published in 1869" (Kevles 3). According to Daniel Pick, Galton's "long inquiry into heredity was perhaps the most striking example of the re-direction of questions of economic and social progress to the evolution-ary problem of the body's reproduction" (197). Galton's travels in Africa "confirmed his standard views of 'inferior races,'" though he was more concerned about such "races" at home than abroad. How could the "unfit" be kept from breeding in the slums of British cities? Conversely, how could the "hereditary aristocracy" be prevented from undermining the biologi-cal progress of "our valuable race'"? (quoted in Kevles 8–9). What Galton feared was not class conflict in the economic and political sense but racial degeneration, with Britain swamped by the biologically inferior, rat-like specimens who made up the residuum and who lived in the slums, if not quite the sewers (Pick 199).

Even before Galton broached the worrisome theme of racial degen-eration, the apparent unfitness of many of the troops sent to fight in the Crimean War (1853–1856) raised the concern, expressed in the *City Press* in 1857, that the government "has a direct interest in guarding against a deterioration of our race" (quoted in Wohl 68). In 1860 psychologist Henry Maudsley optimistically identified evolution with progress (Pick 201). But by the end of that decade, Maudsley had decided that there is "truly a brute brain within the man's," and that civilization was threatened by regression because it bred "a distinct criminal class of beings who herd together in our large cities…propagating a criminal population of de-generate beings" (quoted in Pick 208–9). In Britain in the 1860s, Cesare Lombroso's criminology was still on the horizon. But his general thesis of the criminal as "an atavistic being who reproduces in his person the fero-cious instincts of primitive humanity and the inferior animals" was already being advanced by Mayhew, Maudsley, and other British social investiga-tors. Lombroso would declare that "criminals, savages and apes" shared a "craving of evil for its own sake, the desire not only to extinguish life in the victim, but to mutilate the corpse, tear its flesh and drink its blood" (quoted in MacMaster 36). *London Labour,* however, did not go so far as to attribute vampiric or cannibalistic bloodthirstiness to British criminals, and the hour of Jack the Ripper was yet to strike (but of course Jack may have been an upper-class gentleman).

Besides the profligacy of the unfit, a second source of racial degen-eration, it was commonly believed, was miscegenation.[14] While this was not a major concern in Britain itself, it was in the Australian colonies, in India, and in America. Slavery and the American Civil War brought this issue into intense focus even in Britain, and a number of British novels and melodramas in the 1850s and 1860s featured tragic mulattas, as in Dion Boucicault's play *The Octoroon*. (In contrast to Boucicault's heroine, the mixed-race Cora in Mary Elizabeth Braddon's 1861–62 novel *The Octoroon; or, The Lily of Louisiana* is not doomed. Beautiful and well educated, Cora, after many trials and tribulations meant to show both slavery and racism in a bad light, happily marries the stalwart English hero.) The Indian Rebellion, too, aroused fears about lustful sepoys and rajahs, and, at least implicitly, about the bourgeoning Eurasian population of the subcontinent. Although it was widely acknowledged that the English, in common with other European races and nationalities, were the result of interracial minglings and assimilations throughout history, Victorian authorities typically viewed miscegenation as a cause of the weakening or even extinction of races.

The growing population most feared in 1860s writing about "the condition of England question" was the white "residuum" in London, Manchester, and other British cities. Again, despite Mayhew's sympathy with many of those he interviewed, his treatment of the street people as savages operates as a sort of rhetorical miscegenation, mixing and mingling those of English and Irish descent with all those uncivilized types who have "nothing but their appetites, instincts, and passions to move them." The street people of London are

> made up of the same crude combination of virtue and vice—the same generosity combined with the same predatory tendencies as the Bedouins of the desert—the same love of revenge and disregard of pain, and often the same gratitude and susceptibility to kindness as the Red Indian—and furthermore, the same insensibility to female honour and abuse of female weakness, and the same utter ignorance of the Divine nature of the Godhead as marks either Bosjesman, Carib, or Thug. (Mayhew 1:213)

Though he may not have intended it, one effect of Mayhew's racialization of the poor is that it reduces or eliminates the possibility of reform, which was predicated on the notion of taming the poor by getting them to adopt bourgeois values and behaviors. For Galton, population control—eugenics—was the main reform needed: correct breeding in the biological sense.

In Mayhew's case, however, the language of race perhaps expresses his own bohemian preference to let the street people always be street people, or in other words, not to interfere with their lives. As Seth Koven remarks in his history of slumming, just as did the far reaches of the empire, so the slums of London and other major cities "functioned as sites of personal liberation and self-realization—social, spiritual, and sexual—for several generations of educated men and women" like Mayhew (5). You could go native in the slums as well as in the desert or jungle.[15]

In any event, as their interviews with the street people proceed, Mayhew and his team of slumming journalists rarely override the voices of the poor with bourgeois preaching. In this regard, *London Labour* seems qualitatively different from many other works in the 1850s and 1860s that also naturalize class distinctions by treating them as racial distinctions. Any race-based explanation of social inequality and poverty is a version of blaming the victim because it suggests that class relations are inalterably rooted in biological factors, which were, in the nineteenth century, often summed up by the term "blood": the rulers and the rich had good "blood"; the dominated and the poor had racially inferior "blood." This seemed to be explicitly the case with the Irish poor, who, especially after the Famine, flocked to Liverpool, London, and other English and Scottish cities. In *Ragged London in 1861,* John Hollingshead declared, "The Irish have a marvellous power of lowering the standard of comfort and cleanliness in any court, street, or colony in which they appear" (quoted in Wohl 9). According to Anthony Wohl, "to his English host the Irish immigrant served as an outstanding example of how slums were formed by slum dwellers" (10). Except perhaps for its intensification, however, there was nothing new in this attitude toward the Irish in the 1860s; it was the same view that had been expressed by Thomas Carlyle, Friedrich Engels, and many other writers in the 1830s and 1840s. Among British statesmen, Benjamin Disraeli knew better. At the time of the Famine he wrote, "The Irish peasant had to choose between starving and assassination" (*Bentinck* 81)—although immigration offered a third possibility.

To what extent the growing numbers of nonwhite immigrants to Britain fueled the racialization of the poor in the 1850s and 1860s is unclear, but in those decades "epithets such as 'wild tribes,' 'wandering tribes,' 'savage races' and 'nomad races' were invoked by Henry Mayhew, Phillips Watts and James Greenwood," among many others (Marriott 152).

Emigration out of Britain to the colonies and the United States by starving Irish, Scottish, and English workers was regarded as a key means of alleviating poverty at home. Obviously immigration into England from Ireland or Jamaica or India counteracted that alleviation, and also posed the menace of various forms of cultural and racial degeneration, including through miscegenation. As John Marriott puts it, "the racialization of the poor...which began in mid century and intensified during the 1860s" was "so similar to constructions of colonial others that they can be seen as shared and mutually reinforcing responses to deep anxieties about the future of the imperial race" (42).

Darwin abhorred slavery, believed that humans belong to a single species, and rejected James Hunt's strident racism. In *Descent,* he argued that the traits that distinguish the races from one another are insignificant compared to the similarities among all humans. Differences of race such as skin color and hair texture, moreover, could not be explained by natural selection, which was a key reason why he developed his theory of sexual selection (Stepan 63–65). Yet in his journals, in *The Voyage of the Beagle,* and even in *Descent,* Darwin accepted the view that the human races formed a hierarchy from lower to higher in both intelligence and morality and that present-day "savages" were closer to the animals and mankind's primeval ancestors than were civilized people (Stepan 57). Darwin also believed on the one hand that a main element of both history and prehistory had been struggle among races in the competition for survival. Just as he had emphasized the extinction of species in *The Origin,* as evident in the fossil record, so in *Descent* Darwin emphasized the extinction of "primitive races" by their civilized superiors. On the other hand, he agreed with Galton that civilization tended to reverse natural selection by preserving the weak and allowing them to multiply, while the fittest civilized individuals failed to keep pace. "Thus the weak members of civilized societies propagate their kind" at a greater rate than do the fit ones, a formula that readily translates into both class and racial terms: the "lower classes," the Irish (*Descent* 188).

During the 1860s, the debate about the origins of the human species and the different races was joined by speculations about the origins and evolution of society. Among the numerous authorities Darwin cites is Walter Bagehot, whose *Physics and Politics* (1872) was first published as a series of essays in the *Fortnightly Review* in the late 1860s. "As Mr. Bagehot has remarked," Darwin says, "we are apt to look at progress as normal in human society; but history refutes this." On the contrary, "many savages are in the same condition as when first discovered several centuries ago" (*Descent* 137). Darwin then also quotes "another high authority," Sir Henry Maine: "The greatest part of mankind has never shown a particle of desire that its civil institutions should be improved" (quoted in *Descent* 137). How, then, does progress occur? Darwin does not simply turn to race as the answer; far more "complex" factors seem to be at work when one society progresses and another fails to progress. Darwin, however, seems in general to agree with Bagehot, who argues that competition and warfare among "tribes," "races," or "nations"—Bagehot uses these terms almost interchangeably—is the main source of progress.

"Man, being the strongest of all animals, differs from the rest," writes Bagehot; man "was obliged to be his own domesticator; he had to tame himself" (49). Paradoxically, it turns out that the taming or civilizing process comes about through violence and warfare; among savages, "the most obedient, the tamest tribes are, at the first stage in the real struggle of life, the strongest and the conquerors." In short, the winners win because they practice violence the most violently. At the most primitive level, the "tribe" or "race" that first learns to cooperate among themselves have an advantage in "the struggle for existence." In warfare, "the compact tribes win, and the compact tribes are the tamest. Civilisation begins, because the beginning of civilisation is a military advantage" (50–51).

Bagehot says that his focus is on "nations" rather than "races," but he views nations as relatively recent offshoots of races—they are sub-races, so to speak. And even though, during prehistory and in the state of savagery, progress toward civilization was made by "the military races," once civilization is achieved, progress still occurs in the same manner: through the struggle for existence among nations—economic competition and warfare. Inequality among the races, meanwhile, is a permanent fixture of history and prehistory:

If we look at the earliest monuments of the human race, we find these race-characters as decided as the race-characters now. The earliest paintings or sculptures we anywhere have, give us the present contrasts of dissimilar types as strongly as present observation. Within historical memory no such differences have been created as those between Negro and Greek, between

Papuan and Red Indian, between Esquimaux and Goth. We start with car-
dinal diversities; we trace only minor modifications, and we only see minor
modifications. (108)

Nevertheless, Bagehot agrees with almost all nineteenth-century authorities that, while a few races (white) manage to tame themselves and achieve
civilization, more races (yellow, brown) progress up to a certain point and
then fail to continue, while others (red, brown, black) make no progress
whatsoever. And many races—he does not speculate on the number—
have fallen by the wayside like the dinosaurs, failing to survive in the great
battle of life. Races can, of course, also regress or degenerate. For Bagehot, "the Hindoos" are an example of a race that has progressed only so
far toward civilization, and then fallen prey to "the despotism of custom"
(156–57). Among degenerative races or nations, he counts the French and
the Irish—that is, the Celtic race.

> We see frequently in states what physiologists call "Atavism"—the return,
> in part, to the unstable nature of their barbarous ancestors. Such scenes of
> cruelty and horror as happened in the great French Revolution, and as hap-
> pen, more or less, in every great riot, have always been said to bring out a se-
> cret and suppressed side of human nature; and we now see that they were
> the outbreak of inherited passions long repressed by fixed custom, but start-
> ing into life as soon as that repression was catastrophically removed, and
> when sudden choice was given.

The "original savage nature," it appears, is likely to erupt "even [among]
some very high races, as the French and the Irish" (155).

One of the authors in the 1860s who agreed with Bagehot about the
"instability" of the Celtic race was Matthew Arnold, who, as Robert Young
contends in *Colonial Desire,* made "ethnology" or race science the center-
piece of his theory of culture. In regard to *Culture and Anarchy* (1867), Young
writes, "The highly influential, virtual founding document of English culture, locates that culture's energy and history" as racially determined (141).
"Science has now made visible to everybody," Arnold declares, "the great
and pregnant elements of difference which lie in race, and in how signal
a manner they make the genius of an Indo-European people vary from
those of a Semitic people" (quoted in Young 141). If "the State" for Arnold "becomes a work of art [and] the nation its culture," Young argues,

"anarchy"—class conflict and rebelliousness—"becomes explicable as the workings of a permanent racial difference" (60–61). Both *Culture and Anarchy* and Arnold's "On the Study of Celtic Literature" (1867) express the race-based thinking and race science that flourished in the 1860s. For many Victorian intellectuals, including Bagehot and Arnold, race conflict rather than class struggle explained the major developments of prehistory and history. If antagonisms between social classes at home could be interpreted racially, as outcomes of nature, then middle- and upper-class consciences were assuaged and the inequities of wealth and poverty justified. Race explained the social class hierarchy as readily as it explained the expansion and power of an empire "on which the sun never set."

6

The Unbearable Lightness
of Being Irish

> Out of every corner of the woods and glynnes they came creeping forth
> upon their hands...they did eate the dead carrions.
>
> Edmund Spenser, *A View of the State of Ireland*

The main factors that produced the nineteenth-century racial stereotype of "the Celt," as well as the equally stereotypic notion of "the Anglo-Saxon," were economic, political, military, religious, and institutional rather than biological. Yet Irish attitudes and behavior were typically attributed to race. The centuries-long conquest and exploitation of Ireland by England produced many varieties of blaming the victim, all stereotypic. By the Victorian era these had led to a widespread view in England of the Irish or Celtic "race" as brutes, savages, degenerates, white apes, noxious weeds, overpopulating rabbits, drunken beggars, and so on. Wales and Scotland were the other "Celtic fringe" areas that had been gradually incorporated into Great Britain, and by the 1800s these areas were largely tame. After the final defeat of the Jacobites in 1745, Scottish honesty, bravery, thrift, diligence, and lawfulness were often contrasted to their supposed antitheses in Ireland. Those virtues the English also attributed to themselves.[1]

Many studies have shown that the systemic stereotyping of Ireland began in the Middle Ages and has had persistent features ever since. Luke

Gibbons notes that "Giraldus's broadside against the Irish [*Topographia Hibernia*, 1187] coincides with the moment when purgatory was given its earthly co-ordinates in the northeast corner of Ireland, and indeed Lough Derg features in its bestiary of wonders, along with gold-toothed fish, bearded women, and other less heavenly creatures" (34). The "gold-toothed fish" and "bearded women" did not persist, but Ireland continued well into the 1800s to be a "site of borderline human beings"—particularly apelike savages. "Much of the early colonial stereotyping in Giraldus's text—depictions of Irish life steeped in blood-drinking, cannibalism, or incest, or of Irish people at the mercy of unbridled lust, superstition, and endemic violence—was carried over into the discourses of race and the Gothic that emerged in the modern period, and given a new, biological underpinning," writes Gibbons (34–35). Gothic fiction, with its racial themes and implications (Malchow), had its Irish or Anglo-Irish contributors, from Robert Maturin through Sheridan Le Fanu and on to Bram Stoker at the end of the 1800s.

Starting in the 1700s, various positive albeit also stereotypic features seemed to counter the wild or savage features attributed to the Irish. They were now said to be generous, good-humored, imaginative. They may not have been rational (they were Roman Catholics, and they believed in fairies), but they were emotional, sentimental, poetical, and musical. To these traits, whether viewed as virtuous or not, a number of Victorians, Matthew Arnold prominent among them, would add another trait that Arnold interprets positively: the Irish were not a "hefty" people; they weighed comparatively little. This lightness, Arnold suggested, corresponded to their spirituality. Racist stereotypes, no matter how illogical or inaccurate, often have some basis in material reality. This chapter examines several of the stereotypic traits applied to the Irish, including the notions that they were savage and naturally rebellious and also that they were both lightweights and spiritual in the context of the general tragedy of English-Irish relations.

Savages and Rebels

The positive traits of the Irish were sometimes embellished by Aryanism. The general idea was that the Celts had come from the East, and shared in the world's earliest civilization—that is, the civilization of the Aryas of ancient India. In 1797 Charles Vallencey published *The Ancient History of Ireland, Proved from the Sanscrit Books of the Bramins of India.* In 1831 James Cowles Prichard published *The Eastern Origins of the Celtic Nations,* and in 1875 Ulick Bourke produced *Aryan Origin of the Gaelic Race and Language* (Ballantyne, *Orientalism* 36–40; Lennon). This Aryan and apparently pro-Celtic line of argument, however, seems to have had little impact on Arnold's 1867 defense of Celtic literature, much less on the anti-Irish racism that was widespread in Victorian culture.

Immediately after the disastrous United Irishmen's rebellion of 1798, without taming Ireland, the Act of Union officially joined it to Great Britain. How could Irish rebelliousness be explained? For many English commentators, it was a matter of Irish character—or lack of character. "The real ultimate seat of Irish misfortune is in Irish character," proclaimed the evangelical *Record* in 1867. "It is not the character of an imperial race" (quoted in de Nie 178). It was declared ad nauseam in tautological versions of stating what seemed to be glaringly obvious: rebelliousness was an Irish character flaw. Nature, or perhaps Providence for some mysterious reason, had made the Irish "race" prone to anti-landlord and antigovernmental violence. The Whiteboys and Ribbonmen, the United Irishmen, the repeal of the Union "mobs," the Young Irelanders, the Fenians, the Land Leaguers, and the IRA provided the material reality that apparently validated the stereotype. But underlying the material reality of rebellion were oppression, poverty, and starvation, as Marx and Engels understood. The Irish reliance on potatoes for food, Engels commented in 1844, just before the potato blight brought on the Great Famine of 1845–1850, "gives the people about half the nourishment that they would obtain from a really adequate diet.... They are as poor as church mice; they go about in rags.... In short the Irish can be regarded as a half-civilized people" (307).

Rebelliousness as a racially determined character flaw of the Irish can be traced back much further than 1844 to depictions of "the wild Irish" by Edmund Spenser and other early writers. From Spenser until the era of the Fenians and the Land War, Irish rebelliousness was often linked to savagery and sometimes to cannibalism. In the 1790s British journalists and politicians frequently tarred the United Irishmen with the same brush they applied to French revolutionaries. According to Michael de Nie, "cannibalism was a common theme in numerous descriptions and cartoons of the [French] *sans-culottes,* the crazed revolutionaries who tore apart and devoured the body politic" (54). In 1798, after Irish rebels had massacred a group of Protestants at Wexford, the *Times* of London proclaimed that "carnage and desolation were the main objects of the rebellion, for wherever it obtained the upper hand, murder and devastation went hand in hand. To say nothing of the diabolical cruelties practiced at Wexford, in which if the rebels did not eat the flesh of the loyalists, in the thirst of cannibals they licked their blood" (quoted in de Nie 61).[2] The reduction of rebellion to savagery and savagery to cannibalism obfuscated the possibility that English misrule had fueled the rebellion and that the massacre at Wexford was retributive.

Improvidence was another Irish flaw, though the Irish had little to be improvident with except having too many children. Before the Famine, the Irish peasantry was often accused of the Malthusian sin of overpopulation. Even after the Famine, when they were commonly declared to be a dying race, they were also often accused of mindless multiplication. In an 1868 article for *Fraser's* that Darwin cites in *Descent of Man,* W. R. Greg writes:

> The careless, squalid, unaspiring Irishman, fed on potatoes, living in a pigstye, multiplies like rabbits or ephemera....Given a land originally peopled by a thousand Saxons and a thousand Celts,—and in a dozen generations five sixths of the population would be Celts, but five sixths of the property, of the power, of the intellect, would belong to the one sixth of Saxons that remained. In the eternal "struggle for existence," it would be the inferior and *less* favored race that had prevailed—and prevailed by virtue not of its good qualities but of its faults. (Greg 361)

Greg's eugenic view is that the more civilized "man" becomes, the more he will be swamped by the weak and uncivilized specimens that civilization protects, including the Irish. In 1868 Greg's fantasy of an overpopulating Ireland was, to say the least, counterintuitive: by the end of the 1800s, Ireland had lost half of its pre-Famine population. But many Irish had fled to England, Canada, the United States, and Australia, where they were growing in numbers.

James Anthony Froude insisted that the main mission of his countrymen in Ireland had always been taming its Celtic savages, but taming them wasn't easy. According to Gary Peating, "perhaps the most notorious passage in [Froude's] *The English in Ireland* was entitled 'Irish ideas' and depicted forms of crime, banditry, and barbarity in eighteenth-century Ireland." The purpose of Froude's book was "to expose the perceived dangers of the latest…effort to govern Ireland according to Irish ideas—namely, the effort initiated by William Gladstone's government in 1869–70, notably with its disestablishment of the Irish Episcopal church." According to Froude, "the national sentiments of the Irish people were the antithesis of civilization" (Peating 167). In short, there were no genuine "Irish ideas," just savagery. Froude makes the hero of his 1889 "Irish romance" *The Two Chiefs of Dunboy* remark: "What were we when we had the island to ourselves? If you can believe those glorious ballad singers and annalists of ours, we were no better than the cannibals of the Pacific. If we were again free, we should cut one another's throats in the old style" (371). Soon after this, Englishman Dick Traherne declares that it is impossible to make the Irish "mend their ways. I'd as soon think to make a nigger into a white man, or one of those cannibals that the voyagers write of, into a Christian" (386).

Froude's personal hero Thomas Carlyle had no doubt that most of the Irish were savages. In his essay opposing repeal of the Union, Carlyle wrote:

> The Celt of Connemara, and other repealing peasantry, are white and not black; but it is not the colour of his skin that determines the savagery of a man. He is a savage who in his sullen stupidity, in his chronic rage and misery, cannot know the facts of the world when he sees them; whom suffering does not teach but only madden[;]…[who] brandishes his tomahawk against the laws of nature. (quoted in Gibbons 33)

Although not with tomahawks, Irish rebels were forced to fight with the weapons of the weak, often resorting to acts of terrorism. But this then gave rise to the additional stereotypic notions that the Irish were cowardly and treacherous. Furthermore, as Luke Gibbons remarks, "the retreat from visibility," as in phantom-like "Captain Moonlight," became another "marker of the Celtic race" and one of the sources of the many Gothic treatments of them in literature (41). "Paddy's cowardly habit of assassinating landlords under cover of night or from behind hedgerows had been well noted during the famine," writes de Nie, "but under the influence of the Fenians the Irish...degenerated even further. This would be further evidenced in the various agrarian atrocities of the Land War, British reports on which consistently contrasted the manly English ways with those of the cowardly Irish" (161).

Irish rebelliousness usually ended in defeat, so it was not just savage, cowardly, and secretive, but also ineffective, yet somehow natural—the outcome of inferior race and character—and therefore to be expected despite the good intentions and generosity of the English. The Irish rebelled because they were Irish. Because they weren't civilized, they might inflict a good deal of violence on Protestants, on landlords and their agents, and on one another, but they had been no match for Cromwell's revolutionary army in the 1640s. When the English rebelled, they knew how to do so effectively and for just, righteous reasons. They supposedly sealed the deal with the Glorious Revolution of 1688, guaranteeing liberty and justice for all English citizens. In contrast, the Irish failed all the tests of history. To the victors go the virtues.

If rebelliousness was a trait that could be simply explained in terms of material reality (the Irish rebelled), so was Irish poverty caused by the racial character flaws of laziness and improvidence. Ireland itself, it was often asserted, was "a nation of beggars."[3] Throughout the eighteenth and nineteenth centuries, English travelers to Ireland produced accounts that, no matter how sympathetic or understanding of the causes of Irish poverty, were versions of slumming. In his *Irish Sketchbook* (1842), for example, William Makepeace Thackeray compares a scene in Waterford to slums in London: "We ascended to the court-house through a steep street, a sort of rag-fair, but more villainous and miserable than any rag-fair in St. Giles's: the houses and stock of the Seven Dials look as if they belonged to capitalists when compared with the scarecrow wretchedness of the goods here hung out for sale" (51).

Writing several years before the Famine, Thackeray encounters in every town "the same squalid congregation of beggarly loungers" (46), adding: "The traveller is haunted by the face of the popular starvation. It is not the exception, it is the condition of the people. In this fairest and richest of countries, men are suffering and starving by millions" (86). Thackeray believes several factors account for "the popular starvation," including Catholicism and absentee landlordism, but a key factor is the great Irish character flaw of indolence (139). He repeatedly suggests that the Irish are "content" with their poverty, rags, and starvation. From accounts like Thackeray's emerge other stereotypic negatives, as when Carlyle in *Chartism* (1839) quotes an Irish "lady" who says that, apart from their "two faults" of lying and stealing, a "finer people" than the Irish never existed. "Such people works no longer on Nature and Reality," Carlyle declares; "works now on Phantasm, Simulation, Nonentity; the result it arrives at is naturally not a thing but no-thing,—defect even of potatoes" (181).

Some of the other stereotypic traits attached to the Irish, however, either were positive or could be construed that way: they were sociable, generous, sentimental, imaginative, poetic. The peasantry might be ignorant and superstitious, but they wove wonderful stories out of their impoverished circumstances. They were also musical. In "The Bard," Thomas Gray had written about "the tuneful race of Erin," a phrase cited by Sydney Owenson (Lady Morgan) in *The Wild Irish Girl* (1806). The English narrator of Owenson's "national tale," son of an absentee landlord, engages in an exploration of Irish "national character" which rids him of his "confirmed prejudice" about "Irish ferocity," a prejudice that includes a hint of cannibalism (Owenson 107). His main guide and teacher is the lovely Glorvina who, instead of the negative traits of wildness and barbarity, exhibits the positive, aesthetic traits that Gray, Thomas Moore, John Keats, and other Romantic writers stressed. Through her singing and harp playing, Glorvina exemplifies the meaning of "the tuneful race of Erin" (124). Music is in turn connected to sentimentality. "Our national music," Glorvina tells the English protagonist, "like our national character, admits of no medium in sentiment: it either sinks our spirit to despondency by its heart-breaking pathos, or elevates it to wildness by its exhilarating animation" (167). And music, of course, accompanied conviviality as well as sentimentality.

In "The Good-Natured Gael," Eagleton writes that the Celts in general and the Irish in particular were affirmatively stereotyped (and often self-stereotyped) as a "genial," friendly people. He argues that this caricature, like many others, has some grounding in fact. "Stereotypes are not to be confused with reality, and many of them are simply baseless," Eagleton declares; "but they may occasionally provide clues to specific social conditions" (*Crazy John* 68). How was a trait like geniality related to Irish "social conditions"? Eagleton continues:

> It is not...that Gaels are necessarily more genial than the English....It is rather that they have been on the whole more *con*genial. They have been, as

the etymological root of that term suggests, more of the *gens* or clan, members
of societies in which the ideology of possessive individualism arrived rather
later than in England, and which, when it emerged, found itself at odds
with some still-powerful residues of clannish custom and tradition. (70)

Eagleton proceeds to link Gaelic congeniality with the eighteenth-
century literary and artistic emphasis on sentimentalism as expressed by
writers with Irish roots: Richard Steele, Laurence Sterne, Richard Sheridan, Oliver Goldsmith, Henry Brooke, Edmund Burke, and others. He
cites Charles Kingsley's 1859 preface to Brooke's *Fool of Quality,* "a novel
which," Eagleton notes, "runs to five volumes of swooning and snivel-
ling" (72). According to Kingsley, who championed the "Teutonic race,"
Brooke's "characters are gifted with a passionate and tearful sensibility,
which is rather French or Irish than English, and which will irritate, if not
disgust, many whose Teutonic temperament leads them to pride themselves rather on the repression than the expression of emotion" (quoted
in Eagleton, *Crazy John* 72). From Eagleton's cultural-materialist perspective, "the convivial yet melancholic Celt" was the product not of nature or
race but of a set of premodern, preindustrial societal circumstances: "It is a
question of the way in which, in family-based agrarian communities, personal and social relationships are less easily separable than they are in the
market-places or political institutions of modernity" (73).

Eagleton might have added that other, perhaps premodern traits attributed to the Irish and, more generally, to the Celts in Wales, Scotland,
and also France were, like rebelliousness, far less positive than congeniality: laziness, alcoholism, superstitiousness, irrationality. Irish ignorance
had obvious material causes in poverty and illiteracy—a version of Marx's
"idiocy of rural life." In his study of the Victorian stereotyping of the Irish,
L. P. Curtis notes that a common feature of anti-Irish bigotry was to accuse the Irish of being childish (and not just childlike). In *Tales of Irish
Life and Character* (ca. 1840), Mrs. S. C. Hall says that the Irish are "the
children of impulse: a single idea fixes itself upon their imaginations and
from that they act" (quoted in Curtis 55). Childishness means emotional
instability; Curtis also quotes Tennyson's remark about "the blind hysterics
of the Celt" (54).

The Celts' positive aesthetic attributes, corresponding to their "good-
natured" sentimentality, are stressed by Arnold in "On the Study of Celtic
Literature" (1867): "If the Celtic nature is to be characterised by a single

term, [sentimental] is the best term to take." He then defines sentimentality as "always ready to react against the despotism of fact" (343–44), a phrase that he borrows from Ernest Renan's "Poetry of the Celtic Races" (1854). Arnold follows Renan closely, because he views him as informed by the latest discoveries in ethnology or "the science of origins" (301)—specifically racial origins. In his biography of Arnold, Lionel Trilling notes:

> Arnold embraced the whole of the racial assumption and was at pains to show that the English are an amalgam of several "bloods"—German, Norman, Celtic. Each blood, he believed, carried specific constant qualities, each quality preserved in the mixture of all. It was his task to make the English understand the existence and nature of the mixture that they might give proportionate play to each distinct component. (213)

Trilling immediately adds that Arnold's version of race science was, like all versions, contradictory, in part because Arnold insisted that individuals could choose which aspect of their racial inheritance to emphasize. Even though race supposedly determined "specific constant qualities" of temperament and character that could not be altered, the overly "Hebraic" English, for example, could choose to "Hellenize" a little more.

Trilling also points out that Arnold seeks to use ethnology to offset earlier stereotypic notions, including his father's, of an unbridgeable gulf between "Saxons" and "Celts." Ethnology has discovered, Arnold says, "a great Indo-European unity, comprising Hindoos, Persians, Greeks, Latins, Celts, Teutons, Slavonians." Unlike Disraeli's Caucasian category, however, the Aryan or "Indo-European unity" excludes the "Semitic unity" as well as the "Mongolian unity" (Arnold, "On the Study" 300–301). Furthermore, Arnold contends that the Saxons never completely exterminated the Celts in England proper, so the remnants of that conquered race were biologically and culturally assimilated. It turns out that for his "buried self" (see Arnold's poem of that title), every Englishman has an internal leprechaun (337–38). Arnold wishes to overcome or at least balance the sluggish Philistinism of the dominant Saxon or English self by familiarizing it with its submerged twin, even though the second, Celtic self is only a minor, repressed aspect of Englishness.

With the Celtic revival of the 1880s and 1890s in mind, Seamus Deane declares, "Even now it is difficult to overestimate the importance of

Arnold's Oxford Lectures" on the resurrection and understanding of Celtic literature. "Published in 1867, the year of the Fenian Rising and of Gladstone's speech at Wigan [advocating the end of the Protestant Ascendancy in Ireland], they depict the nineteenth-century idea of the Celt with a clarity outstripping even Renan" (*Celtic Revivals* 25). In 1927 Wyndham Lewis declared that "Arnold's contrast of the Celt and the Saxon" was "ethnologically...worthless: he was not even a great student of celtic literature. He only went to the 'Celt' hurriedly, on a political mission, to get ammunition for his war with the 'creeping Saxon'" (quoted in Young 86). Perhaps so, but by 1927 Victorian "ethnology" in general, involving stereotypic depictions of racial differences, was considered almost obsolete. In any event, Arnold's position is a compound of liberalism, influenced by Edmund Burke's writings on Ireland, and a racism that attributes to the Celts a number of fixed, biologically determined, yet sometimes positive stereotypic traits. He assigns various negative traits to the English, moreover. Deane argues that, echoing Burke, Arnold contends that "the dull and hard English could not, by virtue of their blighted middle-class nature, legislate effectively for the sanguine, vivacious and overly imaginative Irish." Deane adds, "Although the argument for a separation between the two countries" is implicit in the essay, "Arnold refused it as vigorously as Burke would have done." Arnold was decidedly pro-Union. "Instead, he pleaded for a change in the English middle classes which would enable them to win over the Irish" (Deane, *Celtic Revivals* 22), as he would later do in another major essay on Irish affairs, "The Incompatibles" (1881).

Heft versus No Heft

In his essay on Celtic literature, Arnold writes that the Celtic Gauls "had a rule inflicting a fine on every warrior who, when he appeared on parade, was found to stick out too much in front,—to be corpulent, in short." Arnold suggests that such a rule must have seemed bizarre to a carnivorous race like the Saxons. But, Arnold asks, "has [the rule] not an audacious, sparkling, immaterial manner with it, which lifts one out of routine, and sets one's spirits in a glow?" ("On the Study" 348). Arnold's argument boils down to the "immaterial," "sentimental," feminine, and ineffectual Celt versus the material, practical, masculine, and Philistine Saxon. The Celt's immateriality and comparative weightlessness have reduced his race to near extinction; the Saxon's "heft" has conquered and tamed all of Britain except for Ireland.

Arnold was not alone in attributing in quite literal terms greater heft to the Anglo-Saxons and less corporeality to the Celts. In *Friedrich II,* for example, Carlyle had expressed "a strong anti-Saxon bias, treating all Saxons comprehensively as drunkards 'lumbering about in pot-bellied equanimity'" (Briggs 3), while his standard Irishman was a scrawny ragamuffin. In *The English and Their Origin* (1866), Luke Owen Pike cites Dr. Robert Knox's *Races of Men* (1850), which claims that the Celt "in stature and in weight [is] a race inferior to the Saxon" (Pike 50). A *Saturday Review* article on archaeology also noted the discovery of the site of "an ancient battle, and when the skeletons were removed from the barrow [in Somersetshire], it was seen that they were evidently of two different races. In one group, indeed, a man of giant stature had fallen in a hand-to-hand fight with two comparative pigmies: a conquering Teuton beside two conquered Britons" (Faverty 27). The "Britons" may or may not have been Celts, but measured against a "conquering Teuton" of "giant stature," just about anyone of any non-Teutonic race might have seemed a "comparative pigmy." Pike, however, debunks the idea that the Celts were small and the Teutons or Anglo-Saxons strapping. He even rejects others' physiological and philological arguments that the English were a Teutonic people— they were as much Celtic or Cymric as anything else—only to argue that the contemporary English, via the Cymric connection, were very similar to the ancient Greeks, especially in "energy" and other positive mental and emotional characteristics. Pike's argument seems to have had little influence. In any event, in Britain, he contended, the Celts and the English were already unified, and this single race could trace its roots and its virtues back to the ancient Greeks.

Arnold wanted the English to be more Greek in cultural terms—to "Hellenize" more and "Hebraize" less—though for him these were also racial terms. Whether or not he was aware of Pike's work, he also argued that the Saxon was more of a racially mixed-up fellow than the Saxon knew—a bit Celtic as well as Hebraic and Hellenic. And if the hefty Saxon could only get to know the immaterial Celt within, that would help overcome Saxon Philistinism, which for Arnold meant something like crass materialism. As a "people to whom nature has assigned a large volume of intestines" (Arnold, "On the Study" 348), the Saxons need to lighten up both spiritually and physically. Their potbelliedness bespeaks a race who both eat too much beef and conquer everyone in their path. Arnold hints at an equation between imperialism and cannibalism: the Saxons, he says, "have plenty of strength for swallowing up and absorbing as much as we choose," including the weak remnants of the Celtic race (298).

The "Celtic genius" is a childlike, lightweight, irrational, but home-grown version of Hellenism. The ethereal or frothy Celt, whom many Saxon Englishmen believe to be good for nothing, turns out to be good for something. Yet when Arnold writes that the Celt is "undisciplinable, anarchical, and turbulent by nature" (347), he echoes the standard negative stereotype of the rebellious Irish, a stereotype that he criticizes only by giving it a positive spin. Arnold says that the "sensuousness of the Greek made...Corinth," that of "the Latin made Rome," and that of "the La-tinised Frenchman made Paris" (345–46). But what did "the sensuousness of the Celt proper" make? It "made Ireland," and we're all supposed to know what that means. "Arnold used his theory of Celticism to attack the dullness and stolidity he saw in the Saxon temperament," writes Richard Fallis, "though it could be argued that he saw in the Celts an imaginative and inept people who needed to be ruled by sturdy Saxons" (60).

In Arnold's claims about Greek, Roman, French, and Celtic "sensuous-ness," that term sounds bodily, but it means aesthetic taste and is another way of saying that the "genius" of a "race" produces the history it deserves. When it comes to poetry and music, the Celt has plenty of "sensuousness," but not in regard to architecture, sculpture, painting, science, economics, politics, or anything else substantial. Arnold's ideal Celt is itself a poetical apparition, belonging to the romantic past; the real Celt of the present is a troublemaker and probably a Fenian. It is a help to Arnold's argument that, throughout most of Britain and western Europe, the Celt supposedly belongs to a dying race, who beyond Ireland has almost ceased to exist in any pure form (ignoring Boston and other Irish enclaves in North Amer-ica and Australia). During the Famine of 1845–1850, the Celt had almost ceased to exist in Ireland, too. Over Arnold's physiological and philological notions of race, and over other studies of the "genius" of the Celtic "race," hovers the immaterial phantom of the famished Celt who was also, how-ever, a quite material reality. Arnold transforms this emaciated figure into a "sentimental," "spiritual" principle, "always ready to react against the despotism of fact" (77). The scrawny, starving Celt is either dead or dying; but as an immaterial, ghostly potentiality, he can help to render the Saxon a bit less intestinal and somewhat more poetical.

As does Arnold, Renan treats the Celts as a poetic but childish race. "The charm of the *Mabinogion*," Renan writes, derives from its seeming to be "the simple recital of a child" (14). Moreover, "no race has so delicately understood the charm of littleness, none has placed the simple creature, the innocent, nearer God" (45). Although this does not exactly mean that the Celts are physically little, they are nevertheless more delicate and more feminine than the "sturdy ancestors" of the "pure Teutonists" (56). Indeed, "if it be permitted us to assign sex to nations as to individuals," writes Renan, "we should have to say without hesitance that the Celtic race, especially with regard to its Cymric or Breton branch, is an essentially feminine race" (7). It is to the Celts, moreover, that Europe owes the invention of chivalry and the idealization of woman (7–8).

A romantic race, the Celts, Renan claims, live in an ideal world of natural magic, which is simultaneously realistic and unreal or counterfactual. This is the realm of faery as well as of chivalry. The unworldliness of Celtic literature is connected, for both Renan and Arnold, to the notions that the Celtic race is misplaced in time, locked in the past, and that its imaginative creations are essentially elegiac, ghostly:

> The Celtic race has worn itself out in resistance to its time, and in the defence of desperate causes. It does not seem as though in any epoch it had any aptitude for political life. The spirit of family stifled within it all attempts at more extended organisation. Moreover, it does not appear that the peoples which form it are by themselves susceptible of progress. (Renan 7)

For Renan and Arnold, it seemed self-evident that ghosts and other elegiac apparitions should haunt the imagination of the Celtic race. It had been defeated in the past by the Saxons and other invaders of France and Britain, and in the present it is a vanishing race, subjugated in Britain by the Anglo-Saxons and on its way to extinction. "Alas! it too is doomed to disappear," writes Renan, "this emerald set in the Western seas. Arthur will return no more from his isle of faery" (2). Conquered by stronger, progressive races, the Celts have grown sad over the ages. "Take the songs of its bards of the sixth century," Renan declares; "they weep more defeats than they sing victories. Its history is itself only one long lament....Its songs of joy end as elegies; there is nothing to equal the delicious sadness of its national melodies" (7). Many of their poems read like "memories of another world," too. "The soul's peregrinations after death are...the favourite theme of the most ancient Armorican poetry. Among the features by which the Celtic races most impressed the Romans were the precision of their ideas upon the future life, their inclination to suicide" (56).

Thus the Celt, as imagined by Renan and Arnold, is more apparitional than real, more lost in a romantic past than alive in the present, more child-like than adult, and more lightweight—both physically emaciated and ideal—than sturdy, masculine, and intestinal. In terms of intestines, one difference between the two accounts is Renan's defense of Celtic inebriation, which Arnold does not emphasize. The Celts are a drinking race, says Renan, not because of physical addiction or any bodily craving for booze, but because of their "invincible need of illusion." He goes on: "This race desires the infinite, it thirsts for it, and pursues it at all costs, beyond the tomb, beyond hell itself....Do not say that [drinking] is an appetite for gross enjoyment; never has there been a people more sober and more alien to all sensuality" (9). Yet in "On the Study of Celtic Literature," when Arnold is commending the lack of "heft" of the Celts, it isn't just their spirituality he has in mind. It is also their tendency to starve. It is this quite apparent material reality that prompted Engels to write, "The language and customs of the Celt are rapidly vanishing before the triumphant march of English civilisation" (22).

Because he is operating as a literary critic rather than an expert ethnologist, Arnold through much of his essay seeks to show the Celtic "note" in much of the greatest English literature. He claims that Shakespeare, Milton, Byron, and many other great English writers achieve their greatness through combining Celtic and Greek with Saxon and Norman elements. Just how he knows that a particular phrase or theme in a poem is Celtic is unclear, although he attaches that adjective to passages that express "aërialness and magic" as opposed, for example, to "Greek clearness and brightness" (379).

The airy magic of Celtic "romance" is, moreover, feminine—"a mistress" (374), just like the Celtic race itself. "Some people have found in the Celtic nature and its sensibility the main root out of which chivalry and romance and the glorification of a feminine ideal spring," he writes;

indeed, "the Celt is thus peculiarly disposed to feel the spell of the feminine idiosyncrasy," whatever that means (347). But this effeminacy hardly accords with what Arnold calls the "Titanism" of "the Celt," although that Titanism has long since been defeated. (It persists, however, in the poetry of Milton and Byron.) The Celt has proven himself "ineffectual" both in "material civilisation" and in "politics." But he was once Titanic: "This colossal, impetuous, adventurous wanderer, the Titan of the early world, who in primitive times fills so large a place on earth's scene, dwindles and dwindles as history goes on, and at last is shrunk to what we now see him" (346). Here is another way the Celt has ceased to be weighty, or of any consequence in the modern world: yesterday's giant is today's pygmy. These pygmies, Arnold goes on to say, mostly belong to "us"—that is, to the British Empire—and we ought to make the best of them:

> Let us consider that of the shrunken and diminished remains of this great primitive race, all, with one insignificant exception, belongs to the English empire; only Brittany is not ours; we have Ireland, the Scotch Highlands, Wales, the Isle of Man, Cornwall. They are a part of ourselves, we are deeply interested in knowing them, they are deeply interested in being known by us. (384)

Needless to say, Arnold's "us" versus "them" rhetoric, along with his various attributions of unweightiness, femininity, rebelliousness, irrationality, and worldly ineptitude to the Celtic race, do not seem to advance his arguments for unity across racial and cultural boundaries or even for the acknowledgment of the diminutive Irishman within each substantial Englishman.

From the Famine to the Celtic Revival—or Twilight

The positive aesthetic traits that Arnold identifies in Celtic literature were central to the Victorian Celtic revival, commencing with Young Irelanders such as Thomas Davis and James Clarence Mangan in the 1840s and culminating with Yeats. A key aim of Arnold's lectures on Celtic literature was to advance its academic study, and in this he was successful. A chair of Celtic studies was created at Oxford in 1877. Through this means, writes Robert Young, Celtic languages and literature became "the museum relic[s] of an extinct culture" (71). The mutual understanding between England and Ireland for which Arnold hoped did not come about in his lifetime. Arnold himself had no difficulty in opposing Home Rule: the Irish were incapable of self-government. Though he held England responsible for much of Ireland's misery, "it was one thing to appreciate Celtic genius," as L. P. Curtis puts it, "and quite another matter to surrender the Act of Union to the demands of a ravenous Irish party led by Parnell in the House of Commons" (45). In "The Incompatibles" (1881), Arnold criticizes "English opinion" for attributing "Irish misery to the faults of the Irish themselves," and yet in the same breath he declares, "Undoubtedly, the native Irish have the faults which we commonly attribute to them" (244–45). Arnold also states that he is in favor of "coercion" to quell Irish "turbulence" over land, religion, or any other issue (250). Yet once again his aim is more to critique English than Irish faults: the English are too bogged down by bourgeois narrow-mindedness, and so have failed to "attach" Ireland to England. As to Irish "turbulence," however, Arnold knew that the Irish peasantry had been literally and not just metaphorically starving and were therefore rebellious.

From the 1860s into the 1900s, other accounts of the Celtic race and its differences from the Teutonic or Saxon or English race contain stereotypic motifs similar to those in Arnold's essays. The heyday of the lightweight Irishman, however, came with the Famine of 1845–1850. The iconography of the Famine in both English and Irish novels, paintings, and the press stressed figures of starvation, disease, hopelessness, death, the afterlife, and, as in Edmund Spenser, even cannibalism. The *Times* in 1849 "reported alleged cases of cannibalism in Clifden in County Mayo" (Kinealy 29). In Skibbereen in 1846, a Cork magistrate, Nicholas Cummins, entered a cottage and was confronted by "six famished and ghastly skeletons, to all appearances dead." Outside, he reports, "I was surrounded by at least 200 such phantoms, such frightful spectres as no words can describe" (quoted in Fallis 15–16). G. F. Watts's painting *The Irish Famine* depicts an emaciated Irish couple with grim expressions, the mother holding a dying or dead baby—Madonna and corpse? James Mahony's horrific pictures for the *Illustrated London News* include a ragged, emaciated boy and girl scouring the ground searching for the last few, rotten potatoes. A pamphlet titled *The Phantom* portrays the Famine itself as just that—a gigantic, nebulous emblem of death hovering over Ireland—though it also features a narrative in which Ireland recovers, so the final image is of Ireland herself as an angel in a clearing sky.[4]

In "On the Study of Celtic Literature," Arnold does not mention the Famine, Fenianism, or other unpleasant facts about Ireland, no doubt because his central topic is Welsh poetry. Nevertheless, the longest quotation that Arnold offers from any Celtic poet comes from Llywarch Hen, illustrating "the Celtic melancholy." The poet "in old age" addresses "his crutch":

> O my crutch! stand straight, thou wilt support me better; it is very long
>   since I was Llywarch.
> Behold old age, which makes sport of me.   (quoted 118)

And so on. Although Llywarch is Welsh, not Irish, he nevertheless seems to stand in for that post-Famine staple of representations of the Irish: a dying old man with his crutch.

During the fin-de-siècle Celtic Revival, it wasn't the population of Ireland that Yeats, Lady Gregory, Douglas Hyde, AE (George Russell), and others sought to revive but a dying language and culture. As in many other nationalist revival movements, the intellectuals who participated in the Irish one from the 1840s to 1922 accepted the racial categories imposed on them by the colonizers, the English, while revaluing them in positive terms. Celts were fundamentally, racially distinct from the English; they were in many ways, however, the superior race. Richard Fallis points out that "neither Yeats nor Douglas Hyde nor AE was a Celt by birth, but for all three the notion of Celticism became a fundamental way of defining Irishness. Nationalist theories of ineradicable racial differences between Celt and Saxon went back at least as far as Thomas Davis in the 1840s, but for many of the younger writers it was enough to have been born Irish, even Anglo-Irish, to qualify them as spokesmen for Celtic Ireland" (Fallis 60).

In *The Nation* in the late 1840s, during the Famine, Young Irelanders analyzed Irish history and culture in elegiac, ghostly terms similar to those employed by Sydney Owenson, Thomas Moore, and other writers during the first Celtic Revival and later employed by Renan and Arnold. Writing about the chiefs of "ancient Ireland," Thomas Davis declares that they "had around their board harpers and bards who sang poetry as gallant and fiery, though not so grand as the Homeric ballad-singers, and flung off a music which Greece never rivalled.... Their music lives in the traditional airs of every valley" (41). Poverty, rags, and starvation enter the picture when Davis considers the modern condition of the peasants (205–7), declaring that "the puff of the landlord's breath may blow [them] off the land where [they have] lived... till the strong wings of Death... bear them away" (206). Extolling "the long, long patience of the People" and their "virtues," Davis avers that "these truths" of their oppression "must cry day and night. Oh! how they cross us like *Banshees* when we would range free on the mountain" (206). The "banshees" themselves, however, like the ancient "harpers and bards," are passing away: "the Fairies and the Banshees... are vanishing into history" (209). According to Davis, "no conceivable effort will get the people, twenty years hence, to regard the Fairies but as a beautiful fiction to be cherished, not believed in, and not a few real and human characters are perishing as fast as the Fairies" (208).

Davis, Gavan Duffy, James Clarence Mangan, and other writers for *The Nation* were prelude to the Celtic Revival that helped usher in British literary modernism. It is symptomatic, however, that this turn-of-the-century revival was not a "dawn" but rather "the Celtic twilight," to adopt Yeats's title. The "twilight" consists of tales about fairies, leprechauns, and apparitions—in general, the "Celtic longing for infinite things the world has never seen," and "infinite things" moreover that modernity has left behind (Yeats, *Celtic Twilight* 37). This is Carlyle's Irishman all over again, who "works now on Phantasm, Simulation, Nonentity; the result it arrives at is naturally not a thing but no-thing,—defect even of potatoes" (*Chartism* 181).

In *The Celtic Twilight,* Yeats declares, "Across the villages of fishermen and turners of the earth, so different are these from us, we can write but one line that is certain, 'Here are ghosts'" (40). At the outset of his career, at least, Yeats populated, or perhaps overpopulated, the west of Ireland with "ghosts" and imaginary little people, the fairies. Whatever else Celtic culture consists of, it is insubstantial, ephemeral, lightweight because spiritual or haunted, woven from "the sorrow of beauty and... the magnificence and penury of dreams" (51). In "To Ireland in the Coming Times," Yeats claimed that he sympathized with Fenianism, but he also associated that revolutionary movement with "the hosting of the Sidhe," or the fairies: "all are a portion of that great Celtic phantasmagoria whose meaning no man has discovered, nor any angel revealed" (39).

In "The Celtic Element in Literature," Yeats restates Arnold and Renan. He does so mainly by insisting that the "Celtic element" is universal, no different from what at one time "every people in the world believed." They believed "that trees were divine, and could take a human or grotesque shape and dance among the shadows.... They saw in the rainbow the still bent bow of a god thrown down in his negligence.... All old literatures are full of these or of like imaginations" (174–75). He agrees in part with Arnold's assessment of the "natural magic" of the old Irish and Welsh bards, but for Arnold "it was not easy to know as much as we know now of folk-song and folk-belief, and I do not think he understood that our 'natural magic' is but the ancient religion of the world" (176). The Celts, Yeats argues, are closer to the source of all art, mystery, beauty than are any other European people: "Of all the fountains of the passions and beliefs of ancient times in Europe, the Slavonic, the Finnish, the Scandinavian, and the Celtic, the Celtic alone has been for centuries close to the main river of European literature" (185). Yeats wants to claim for Celtic folklore the same depth and universality that Madame Blavatsky claimed for her supposed ur-religion at the heart of Theosophy and that Sir James Frazer sought in *The Golden Bough.*[5]

From James Macpherson on, Celtic revivalists were generally melancholic and crepuscular. Many authors mourned the loss or the passing of the oral, folk traditions of Ireland, Scotland, and Wales. Moore's *Irish Melodies* are often laments, as in "The Harp That Once through Tara's Halls," in which the harp "Now hangs as mute on Tara's walls, / As if that soul were fled" (Moore 182). And then there is Sir Walter Scott's "last minstrel," who used to sing "light as a lark at morn" his "unpremeditated lay" (Scott 3–4). A phantom today, of course. Katie Trumpener quotes Robert Fergusson's "Elegy, on the Death of Scots Music" (1772):

> On Scotia's plains, in days of yore,
> When lads and lasses tartan wore,
> Saft Music rang on ilka shore,
> In hamely weid;
> But harmony is no more,
> And Music dead.   (74)

What is past or passing is an entire culture, and with it "music." "Revival" can never be more, perhaps, than a faint imitation of the distant music of the ancient bards. In these romantic poems, as in Arnold's essay on Celtic literature, Irish and Scottish poetry and music are vanishing, which is why they need to be preserved and revived. Although people of Irish and Scottish descent were far from dying out, the stereotype—and mystique—of a vanishing race whose ancient bards had once tapped into the sources of universal spirituality and the afterlife would have its own afterlives in Celtic revivalism and a literary modernism that itself has had seemingly universal appeal.

If Yeats was an enthusiastic revivalist, James Joyce was at best an equivocal one. He was skeptical about the attempts by Yeats and Lady Gregory to express "the soul of Ireland" through collecting the rambling, "senile" stories told by old people "in the West of Ireland" (Joyce, *Critical Writings* 103). But the early Joyce nevertheless indulged in romantic poetry about "the wise choirs of faery" (*Collected Poems* 23). As early as *Dubliners,* however, he parodies several of the themes and stereotypes of the Celtic Revival, seeing it as an elitist attempt to reverse the demise of the Gaelic language. Ireland consists of a diminished and insular population, stymied by a "paralysis" that undermines Irish nationalism, as in "Ivy Day in the Committee Room." In "The Dead," the final story in the volume, the present itself is trapped and diminished by the past. As Gretta tells her husband about the boy from the west of Ireland who had stood in the rain and, she believes, died for her, Gabriel Conroy feels both dwarfed and haunted by her memory of lost love. All of "old Ireland," as Gabriel falls asleep, seems to be passing away, souls corresponding to "the snow falling faintly through the universe and faintly falling, like the descent of their last end, upon all the living and the dead" (124).

Joyce may not have had Arnold in mind, but paralysis and death in *Dubliners* are matched by a sense of pettiness and littleness concerning Irish politics and, in "A Little Cloud," Irish poetry. In that story the aspiring poet "Little Chandler" tries "to weigh his soul to see if it [is] a poet's soul" (*Dubliners* 73). For better or worse, his is not a weighty "soul." Little Chandler knows he will never be "popular," but wishes at least to "appeal to a little circle of kindred minds" (74). He imagines a reviewer writing that his book of poems expresses "a wistful sadness.... The Celtic note" (74), perhaps like the poems in Joyce's *Chamber Music.* But "his own sober inartistic life," henpecked and stuck with a wailing baby, is thoroughly disillusioning and reduces Little Chandler to tears. By 1914 Joyce believed that "old Ireland," if it had ever been more than romantic illusion, was beyond resuscitation.

The unhefty Celt, then, starving to the point of spirituality, or at least sentimentality, is a stereotype vividly and quite literally presented by Arnold in "On the Study of Celtic Literature." It is a stereotype that has had many permutations. Like Eagleton's "good-natured Gael," however, it stems not from race but from history. In the Victorian period the most glaring form of such historical reality, producing the emaciated, phantasmal Celt, was the Famine. That catastrophe resulted in an Ireland greatly diminished in many respects—most obviously in population. A catastrophe that cut a population of 8 million people in half by the end of the 1800s was indeed a "Celtic twilight."

Summing up Arnold's race thinking, Lionel Trilling says that even though Arnold intended to use his version of ethnology "for liberalizing purposes," his ideas on this topic "cannot wholly be dissociated from the...dangerous lucubrations of Houston Stewart Chamberlain...and the whole of official German thought in the present day." Trilling was writing in 1939. "It is not, after all, a very great step from Arnold's telling us that the Celt is by 'blood' gay, sensual, anarchic, to Treitschke's telling us that Germans excel Latins in artistic appreciation because when a Latin reposes in the woods he crassly lies on his stomach whereas 'blood' dictates to the German that he lie, aesthetically, on his back" (215).

Part IV

ANCIENT AND FUTURE RACES

7

Mummy Love

H. Rider Haggard and Racial Archaeology

There is…a growing passion for mummies among Nile travellers.

Amelia Edwards, *A Thousand Miles up the Nile*

Although he was neither an explorer nor an archaeologist, H. Rider Haggard penned adventure stories that helped set the pattern for fiction combining geographical with archaeological discovery. Including the racist stereotyping of Africans and Middle Easterners, the pattern is alive and well in such action-adventure films as the *Indiana Jones* and *Lara Croft Tomb Raider* series. Haggard's three best-known novels—*King Solomon's Mines* (1885), *She* (1887), and *Allan Quatermain* (1887)—feature British heroes discovering the remnants of ancient civilizations in southeastern Africa. Each of these "lost" civilizations was the work of a white or light-skinned race. In the 1880s, when Haggard published these adventure stories, most of Africa had been explored, mapped, and, after the Berlin Conference of 1884–85, claimed as colonies by the European empires. By that decade, too, archaeology had emerged as a modern social science. The period between 1850 and 1900, writes Glyn Daniel, "saw the birth of archaeology from antiquarianism, history and geology." Among its leading results were "the discovery of the proofs of man's antiquity and of the ancient civilisations of

Egypt, Assyria and Sumeria, and the creation of a complicated 'sequence' of man's prehistoric cultures." Daniel adds that "it also saw…the beginnings of systematic archaeological techniques of excavation, field survey, conservation and protection" (152).[1]

Archaeology informs many of Haggard's romances, including *She,* whose antique aspects involve Egypt and southeastern Africa. Throughout his career Haggard took a special interest in ancient Egypt. The Egypt Exploration Society was established in 1883, with Sir Flinders Petrie as field director and the novelist and Egyptologist Amelia Edwards as secretary. Another Egyptologist, Georg Ebers, had begun to publish historical romances based on life in ancient Egypt, including his popular novel *An Egyptian Princess,* first published in German in 1864 and translated into English in 1868. Starting with *Cleopatra* in 1889, Haggard wrote a number of novels, short stories, and articles featuring ancient Egypt.[2] He traveled to Egypt four times beginning in 1887, and he collected Egyptian antiquities, even though he worried about tomb robbery and, according to Shirley Addy, "spoke out against the desecration of the mummies" (35). He also "met and befriended many of the luminaries of the Egyptological world; [and] was shown round 'The Tomb' [of Tutankhamen] by Howard Carter," its discoverer (Addy 35).

Lilias Haggard writes that her father "felt…completely at home" in Egypt, "knowing as he himself said, more of its civilization and history than he did that of his own country" (183). She means, of course, the civilization of ancient Egypt, not the modern version, which Haggard and many other Westerners considered less than civilized, petrified in Islamic barbarism (see Barrell, "Death on the Nile"). In *The Days of My Life,* Haggard himself confessed, "Whatever the reason, I seem to myself to understand the Norse folk of anywhere about 800 A.D., and the Egyptians from Menes down to the Ptolemaic period, much better than I understand the people of the age in which I live" (*Days* 1:255).

Haggard's claim that, starting in boyhood, he avidly read all he could find about ancient Egypt (*Days* 1:254) means he likely was familiar with everything from Giovanni Belzoni's *Narrative of the Operations and Recent Discoveries within the Pyramids* (1820) and Thomas Pettigrew's *History of Egyptian Mummies* (1834) to Ebers's *Egyptian Princess* and Théophile Gautier's *Roman de la momie* (1857; first translated into English in 1863). Though

he learned much about Egyptian archaeology, however, his interest was always far more romantic than scientific. He even liked to imagine that he
might have been, in two previous incarnations, ancient Egyptians, while in
a third incarnation he might have been an ancient Norseman who sailed up
the Nile (*Days* 1:254).

Two aspects of Haggard's interest in archaeology in regard to *She* and
his other novels are especially noteworthy. The first is obviously political: Haggard's portrayals of Kôr, Egypt, and other ancient civilizations,
whether wholly imaginary or having some basis in reality, express a reac-
tionary utopianism that buttresses his versions of political authoritarianism
and imperialism. This backward-looking utopianism also has racist implications, reflected in his views about modern Egyptians, about the Zulus
and other sub-Saharan Africans, and about the origins of Great Zimbabwe and the other ruins in southeastern Africa. Second, central to many of
Haggard's fictional archaic realms are powerful women—princesses and
queens who are also femmes fatales: Ayesha in *She* and its sequels, but also
Cleopatra, Sheba, Helen of Troy, Nefra in *Queen of the Dawn*—and who
give his romances what Anne McClintock calls a "porno-tropic" dimen-
sion (22). These portrayals also carry political implications, connected to
Haggard's misogyny. Fatal women are, well, fatal. Most obviously in *She*
and in "Smith and the Pharaohs," the figure of the femme fatale turns archaeological fascination with the past into necrophilia.

In his imperial Gothic romances, Haggard mummified his erotic fears and
desires in unattainable but porno-tropic white or light-skinned queens, while
also constructing a version of African history that was the exact opposite of
European progress and civilization. The ancient Egyptians had created an archaic civilization and had erected enduring monuments to immortality. But
that civilization, along with its colonial remnants in southeastern Africa, had
passed away. It had been wiped out by waves of savages, climaxed by the Zulu
mfecane and its black kingdom or empire. There were aspects of the Zulu race
and its history that Haggard admired and wrote about in several novels, but
he believed that there was a nearly unbridgeable gulf between savagery and
civilization. The Zulus might or might not be civilizable—Haggard contradicts himself on this score—but Africa had devolved from the civilization on the Nile to noble savagery, the exact opposite of civilization, on the
Zambesi.

Imperial Pasts and Present

Deciphered by Jean-François Champollion in 1822, the Rosetta stone served as a model for the sherd of Amenartas in *She* (Mally 281). Haggard and his sister-in-law manufactured the sherd, and he called on various experts to help him with ancient languages for inscribing on it the story of Amenartas, Kallikrates, and Ayesha. Haggard hoped to fool the "antiquarians," but except for the Egyptian cartouche on the sherd, the languages are ancient Greek, Latin, and an antiquated version of English, which would not have deceived anyone with even a modicum of archaeological expertise. But the creation of a faux-archaeological object signals Haggard's desire to fabricate a romantic version of antiquity that would be, unlike reality, adaptable to his daydreams.

On his first journey to Egypt in 1887, Haggard "had an introduction to Brugsch Bey, who was then...the head of the Boulak Museum." Haggard recalls: "He took me round that heavenly place. He showed me the mummies of Seti, Rameses, and the rest, and oh! with what veneration did I look upon them" (*Days* 1:256). At the prompting of archaeologist Gaston Maspero, in 1881 Emil Brugsch had discovered numerous pharaohs' mummies "in a lonely spot in the most desolate and unfrequented part of the great Necropolis," in the Valley of the Kings near Luxor (Edwards 113). The site had earlier been discovered by an Egyptian, whose family cautiously set about tomb robbing, so the removal of the mummies and other treasures to the Boulak Museum and later to the Cairo Museum was, in theory at least, tomb robbing to prevent more tomb robbing. This was the general justification given by Western archaeologists for the removal of Egyptian antiquities altogether from Egypt to Western museums.[3]

Haggard was also well aware of archaeological discoveries in other parts of the world. Between 1845 and 1847, Sir Austen Henry Layard's excavations led to his publication of *The Monuments of Nineveh* (1849) and the popular *Nineveh and Its Remains* (1848–49). The "priceless treasures" Layard sent to the British Museum "included the huge winged bulls, the Black Obelisk of Shalmaneser III, and the sculptures of Ashur-nasir-pal, which are among the Museum's most valued possessions" (Daniel 72). Earlier in the 1840s, John Lloyd Stephens had come upon the ruined cities of southern Mexico and Guatemala (Daniel 271). Stephens published *Incidents of Travel in Central America, Chiapas, and Yucatan* in 1841 and

Incidents of Travel in Yucatan two years later. In 1890 Haggard journeyed to Mexico at the behest of J. Gladwyn Jebb, a trip that inspired him to pen *Montezuma's Daughter* (1893). Haggard writes, "The original cause of my visit to Mexico was the tale of a certain hidden treasure which appealed to all my romantic instincts." He and Jebb went on an unsuccessful treasure hunt for "eighteen large jars of gold" and "the golden head of Montezuma" (*Days* 2:51–53).

As in *King Solomon's Mines,* which was inspired by Robert Louis Stevenson's *Treasure Island,* Haggard often equated archaeology with hunting for buried treasure. To many of its participants and observers, archaeological discovery was something like the Californian and Australian gold rushes (Ceram 118). In Egypt in particular, archaeological treasure hunting meant tomb robbing and the disturbance, removal, and often destruction of mummies. Haggard worried about the moral and cultural implications of tomb robbery and mummy desecration, which he himself practiced in a minor way. The tomb robbery and mummy unwrapping conducted by Hamarchis and Cleopatra in Haggard's novel named for her replays these concerns, and so does the protagonist's invasion and robbery of Queen Ma-Mee's tomb in "Smith and the Pharaohs." In that story, Smith discovers what Haggard must have learned from reading works on Egyptology: tomb robbery was itself an ancient practice. Smith carefully reburies the burned remains of the beautiful Ma-Mee and takes from her tomb items the original thief left behind, including Ma-Mee's mummified hand. His version of Egyptology, fueled by his fetishistic love for the image of Ma-Mee and for her hand, is, Smith learns from the ghost or *ka* of Ma-Mee herself, morally innocent and even noble compared to the original robber's motives. And Egyptology in general, Haggard believed, was both a scientific and a civilized way of honoring the ruins and relics of ancient Egypt, unlike the treatment they received from either the modern Egyptians or the Ottoman Turks. Yet Smith turns out to be (or dreams himself to be) the reincarnation of the antique sculptor Horus, who loved Ma-Mee ages ago. In his fantasies about antiquity, Haggard likes to have it both ways—to imagine himself as simultaneously ancient and modern, dead and alive.

Besides the ambivalent interplay between ancient and modern, the political implications of Haggard's romances involve his approval of certain kinds of authority, but—*pace* Queen Victoria—not necessarily the authority of women to rule over men. His views, even though he did not always express them explicitly, were thoroughly patriarchal, and patriarchy for Haggard as for many of his other male contemporaries was a corollary of imperialism. From various remarks about the intrusions of modern Europeans into Zulu country and elsewhere in Africa, including his fretting about tomb robbery and tourism in Egypt, it is possible though not convincing to claim that Haggard was actually opposed to imperialism. After all, when in *King Solomon's Mines* Allan Quatermain, Sir Henry Curtis, and Captain Good leave Kukuanaland in the hands of its rightful king, Umbopa or Ignosi, they do not disagree when he tells them: "No other white man shall cross the mountains, even if any may live to come so far. I will see no traders with their guns and rum.... I will have no praying-men to put fear of death into men's hearts, to stir them up against the king, and make a path for the white men who follow to run on. If a white man comes to my gates I will send him back." And so forth (234). Yet Haggard was a quite typical Tory imperialist not much different from his father (Etherington, *Rider Haggard* 92–98).

King Ignosi's rejection of what "the white men" have to offer agrees with Allan Quatermain's rejection of civilization and sedentary life in England. At the start of the romance that bears his name, Quatermain, like Alfred Tennyson's aging Ulysses, expresses his desire for a life of adventure, away from civilization: "The thirst for the wilderness was on me; I could tolerate [England] no more," and so forth. After all, Quatermain asks, what is civilization? It is "only savagery silver-gilt. A vainglory is it" (Haggard, *She, King Solomon* 419–20). In these passages from *King Solomon's Mines* and *Allan Quatermain,* Haggard expresses a conventional, romantic nostalgia for nature, adventure, and the primitive. When he explicitly states his own political views, as he does, for example, in *Cetawayo and His White Neighbours,* there can be no mistaking his belief in the rightness of British imperialism. He thoroughly approved of Theophilus Shepstone's takeover of the Transvaal, during which Haggard helped raise the Union Jack in Pretoria. He thought that act was necessary to protect the British and the Boers from the Zulus, the Zulus from the Boers, and the Zulus from one another. As to the British, he believed that "we alone of all the nations in the world appear to be able to control coloured races without the exercise of cruelty" (Haggard, "Transvaal" 78).

The political attitudes Haggard expresses in his romances are royalist and racist as well as imperialist. In *Days of My Life,* to his account of viewing the newly discovered mummies in the Boulak Museum, Haggard adds: "Poor kings! who dreamed not of the glass-cases of the Cairo Museum, and the gibes of tourists who find the awful majesty of their withered brows a matter for jests and smiles. Often I wonder how we dare to meddle with these hallowed relics, especially now in my age. Then I did not think so much of it; indeed I have taken a hand in the business myself" (1:257). Haggard's lament for the "poor kings" expresses sentiments that he also voiced in *She* and his other romances about lost civilizations. The governments of those civilizations are monarchies. Modernity involves a degeneration from past values, standards, authority, and religious belief, as embodied in a single dead or archaic ruler. The "glass-cases of the Cairo Museum," the casual sarcasm and ignorance of mere "tourists," and "meddling" with "hallowed relics"—whether under the sanction of archaeology or not—are all symptoms of the modern loss of reverence for "awful majesty."

Haggard's lost civilizations—the civilized predecessor of Kukuanaland in *King Solomon's Mines,* the kingdom of the Zu-Vendis in *Allan Quatermain,* and the original Kôr in *She* (though not Ayesha's terrifying reign)—are antique utopias through which Haggard expresses his rejection of modern civilization. Bradley Deane notes that there were many "tales of forgotten cities, rediscovered races, civilizations, and continents submerged beneath the sea or the ground, the hidden vestiges of ancient empires: over 200 such stories were published in Britain between 1871 and the First World War, many times the number that had appeared in all the years before" (206). Many of these stories were inspired by archaeological as much as by geographical discovery. At any rate, Deane contends that "lost worlds" stories express "a vision of imperial time in which encounters with the past serve less to illustrate theories of progress or decline than to imply a vast, cyclical chronology: empires come and empires go, but empire itself remains constant" (217).

This constancy of empire is at least implicit in *She* and Haggard's other "lost worlds" stories: imperial Kôr has fallen, but as Ayesha suggests, its survivors perhaps became the founders of imperial Egypt (*She* 183). "His description of Kôr's ruined capital strongly suggests Karnak and Luxor," Etherington writes, "even to such details as the resemblance of the stone columns to palm trees" (*Annotated* xxiv). Kôr is older than ancient Egypt; after the pestilence that caused its downfall, some of its inhabitants may have travelled north and established the Egypt of the pharaohs and pyramids. Meanwhile, Ayesha has established her matriarchal dictatorship in its place. One empire succeeds another, until the arrival of the British Empire, greatest of all. Of the Zu-Vendis, Allan Quatermain says, "They are exceedingly conservative, and look with disfavour on changes" (Haggard, *She, King Solomon* 537). They also enjoy "the blessings of comparative barbarism" (635). In other words, they are not too civilized; they combine the best elements of both civilization and savagery. Deane notes, "Lost world fiction dreams of a pre-historical mandate for empire articulated in the blood and sinews of the male body" (220)—a "mandate" clearer in both *King Solomon's Mines* and *Allan Quatermain* than in *She,* because Ayesha is a despotic "Diana in jack-boots," as Etherington calls her (*Haggard* 47).

Ayesha rules over a race, not her own, that sounds suspiciously like modern Egyptians. The Amahaggers speak an Arabic dialect (but not pure Arabic) and are "yellowish in colour," and "their appearance," writes Haggard, "had a good deal in common with that of the East African Somali, only their hair was not frizzed up, and hung in black locks upon their shoulders" (*She* 83). Ayesha later tells Horace Holly that possibly not all the denizens of Kôr were destroyed or migrated north, but "the barbarians from the south, or perchance my people, the Arabs, came down upon them, and took their women to wife, and [produced] the race of the Amahagger that is now is a bastard brood of the mighty sons of Kôr, and behold it dwelleth in the tombs with its fathers' bones," just as the modern Egyptians were doing (184).[4] In short, the cannibalistic Amahaggers are the spawn of racial degeneration.

For Haggard, as the fate of the beautiful but hapless Foulata in *King Solomon's Mines* suggests, nothing is worse than racial miscegenation. In *She,* Holly's marriage proposal to Ayesha, and Ayesha's own desire for Leo, who is Kallikrates's reincarnation, apparently do not signify crossing any racial divide. According to Etherington, however, "the deepest dyed villains" in Haggard's romances "are half-castes" (*Haggard* 102). In contrast to the "bastard brood" of the Amahaggers, Kukuanaland is a savage kingdom that, like the Zulu empire, Haggard hopes will remain savage and racially pure, but it is not and presumably never will become a civilization. Only a white race—or, perhaps, only *the* white race—can create a civilization.

Whether during his four years in southern Africa or later, Haggard became aware of the recent discovery of the ruins of ancient cities and citadels there. The Portuguese knew about them as early as the 1500s. The German explorer Karl Mauch rediscovered Great Zimbabwe in 1871, and there were many similar sites between the Limpopo and Zambesi rivers (Fontein; Kuklick). "Over all this huge expanse," writes Haggard in "The Real King Solomon's Mines" (1907), "are found spotted ancient ruins, whereof about five hundred are known to exist." He goes on to affirm the theory espoused by Mauch, Alexander Wilmot, "and other learned persons" that these southern African structures "were built by people of Semitic race, probably Phoenicians, or to be more accurate, South Arabian Himyarites," though he admits that this theory is "disputed by many experts" ("The Real" 21). In the same essay Haggard claims that, well before learning about these ruins or the theory of their Phoenician or Arabic origin, he had conceived and written *King Solomon's Mines*. "How I came to conclude that this people was Phoenician I have now no idea, for I do not believe that anyone suggested this to me. Nor, to the best of my memory, did I ever at any time hear of the great ruin of Zimbabwe, or that the ancients had carried on a vast gold-mining enterprise in the part of Africa where it stands" (19). This is one of several occasions when Haggard boasted about his originality in a disingenuous way; perhaps he was trying to counteract the charges of plagiarism that had been leveled against him.

In the novel named for him, Allan Quatermain says, "All my life I had heard rumours of a white race" who had colonized some portion of southeastern Africa and built "these ruined cities" (*She, King Solomon* 511, 432). Among the Zu-Vendis, Allan speculates that "their architecture and some of their sculptures suggest an Assyrian origin.... [T]hey may be one of the lost ten tribes." He also supposes that the original Zu-Vendis may have been Phoenicians (533–34). Haggard presented this notion again in *Elissa: The Doom of Zimbabwe* (1899). In his "Author's Note" he says that this "romantic sketch" is an attempt "to suggest incidents such as might have accompanied this first extinction of the Phoenician Zimbabwe" (viii). That ancient realm had long ago been toppled by waves of invading savages.

No more than Phoenician Zimbabwe, imperial Kôr, or the civilization that predates Kukuanaland is the Zu-Vendi realm in *Allan Quatermain* the work of a black African race. For Haggard as for many of his contemporaries, that was unthinkable. Given that Mauch's so-called discovery of the Zimbabwe ruins was publicized in 1872, and that the existence of these and many other ruins were familiar to Europeans in southern Africa well before Haggard wrote *King Solomon's Mines,* his claim to have invented out of whole cloth the ruined civilization—presumably Solomon's Ophir—in that novel is far-fetched. Haggard could even have come across this idea in reading John Milton. According to Basil Davidson, "the Portuguese, borrowing legend from the Arabs, had linked the gold of Sofala with the gold of Ophir; and the version had become so current in Europe as to give Milton one of the kingdoms that the fallen angel, in *Paradise Lost,* shows to Adam" (*Lost Cities* 251). This is "Sofala, thought Ophir" in book eleven (line 400) of Milton's epic. The myth was kept alive by Karl Peters in *King Solomon's Golden Ophir* (1899) and by many similar works well into the twentieth century. It reinforced the view that sub-Saharan Africans were incapable of civilizing themselves but needed the white race—and, more especially, needed the British—to tame them and put them to useful work in the fields and mines of southern Africa.

Haggard may also have been familiar with Hugh Walmsley's 1869 novel *The Ruined Cities of Zululand.* Walmsley locates "the gold fields of Solomon" and "the ruined cities of the mighty old Egyptians, the ancient gold diggers," in the same area as Haggard's Kukuanaland and the realm of the Zu-Vendis (Walmsley 134–35). A missionary in Walmsley's novel speculates that "the present race of Zulus, incontestably the finest in Southern Africa, sprang from the fusion of Pharaoh's seamen with the then cultivators of the soil" (48). The thought of miscegenation producing a superior race runs counter to orthodox opinion, including Haggard's, about racial mixings. The "bastard brood" of the Amahaggers in *She* may be the product of mixing Egyptians or Phoenicians with a sub-Saharan African race, but the result is obviously degeneration and not "incontestably the finest" race in southern Africa.

The preface that Haggard wrote for Wilmot's *Monomotapa* (1896) echoes Wilmot's theory, which was also Mauch's, that Phoenicians had colonized parts of Africa as far south as the Zambezi River. Wilmot in turn follows the lead of J. Theodore Bent, who, "under the auspices of the Royal Geographical Society, the British Chartered Company [which helped found Rhodesia], and the British Association for the Advancement of Science...as an archaeologist has performed excellent pioneer work" on the Zimbabwe ruins. "He has found sermons in the stones of colossal remains"—as did Mauch, Walmsley, Wilmot, and Haggard (3). According to Bent, the Shona or other Bantu societies could not have built Great

Zimbabwe because it was "a well accepted fact that the negroid brain could never be capable of taking the initiative in work of such an intricate nature" (quoted in Kuklick 140). Wilmot in turn, according to Henrika Kuklick, "made the story of the decline of the Great Zimbabwe civilization a cautionary tale for southern Africa's white settlers: the ancients had not withdrawn, but had weakened the quality of the kingdom's ruling stock by interbreeding with local Africans" (141). Haggard agreed with this assessment, and also with Wilmot's claim that Rhodesia was "eminently a white man's country" with Africans in ready supply as "cheap labour" (quoted in Kuklick 142).

The main "sermon" Haggard, Wilmot, and the others found in "the stones" of Zimbabwe was erroneous. The racist view that the ruins must have been erected by Phoenicians or some other white race was first authoritatively contested by archaeologist David Randall-MacIver in his 1906 book *Mediaeval Rhodesia,* although it continued to be expressed in works published in South Africa and Rhodesia well beyond that date. The myth continued to be repeated by many white Rhodesians and South Africans even after Rhodesia's unilateral declaration of independence, into the 1970s (Kuklick 158–62). Haggard never relinquished his belief that a white race, probably the Phoenicians, had long ago colonized southeastern Africa, as Cecil Rhodes and the British were doing in the modern era.

But what about Haggard's magnificent Zulus? Many of his novels feature that noble savage race. Even before the Zulu *impis* defeated the British forces at Isandhlwana in 1879, only to be defeated a year later at Ulundi, they were commonly portrayed as worthy opponents—untameably ferocious, however. They were a superior breed of savages—"incontestably the finest in Southern Africa," as the missionary in Walmsley's novel says. Beginning with Shaka, they had, after all, supposedly conquered most of the surrounding societies—"tribes" or "races" in Victorian parlance. It now seems clear that the Zulu *mfecane* or warfare and empire building among the "tribes" of southern Africa was not a case of Africans committing genocide against Africans but rather a defensive unification and resistance to European slave raiding and colonization (Wylie). To save Africans from destroying one another, good white imperialists like Sir Henry Bulwer and Theophilus Shepstone had to come to their rescue. Nevertheless, according to Haggard and many other white authors and filmmakers down to the present, the Zulus slaughtered every resistant African society (or "race") in their path. As the ultimate savage fighting machine, however, the Zulu army and the empire it constructed had its attractive features. The Zulu success in warfare was based on the ruthless, celibate discipline of young warriors—a supermasculine race for whom women, children, and domesticity were distinctly secondary. In the preface to one of his Zulu novels, *Maiwa's Revenge; or, The War of Little Hand* (1888), Haggard writes, in a tone as much admiring as condemnatory, that Shaka, "the Zulu Napoleon, never allowed a child of his to live. Indeed he went further, for on discovering his mother, Unandi, was bringing up one of his sons in secret, like Nero he killed her, and with his own hand" (vi). Haggard repeated this tale in his most important Zulu novel, *Nada the Lily* (1892).

Echoing the eyewitness but unreliable accounts of Nathaniel Isaacs and Henry Fynn (Wylie 83–95, 105–29), Haggard had no doubt that Shaka was a tyrant like King Twala in *King Solomon's Mines*. In his first book, *Cetawayo and His White Neighbours* (1882), Haggard wrote:

> The invincible armies of this African Attila had swept north and south, east and west, had slaughtered more than a million human beings, and added vast tracts of country to his dominions. Wherever his warriors went, the blood of men, women, and children was poured out without stay or stint; indeed he reigned like a visible Death, the presiding genius of a saturnalia of slaughter. (3)

The hyperbolic figure of "more than a million human beings" is typical of the earliest accounts by white observers of the Zulus. Most of Haggard's knowledge about the Zulus came from men like Fynn "who worked amongst the Zulu people" (Wylie 149), as Haggard himself did not. More explicitly admiring than this passage about the "African Attila" is Allan Quatermain's comment, in *King Solomon's Mines,* that one of the "things in the world...which cannot be prevented" is that "you cannot keep a Zulu from fighting" (*She, King Solomon's Mines* 198). If anyone is a match for the mighty, axe-wielding Zulu warrior Umbopa—"I am of the Zulu people, yet not of them," he says (69)—it is the gigantic Sir Henry Curtis, whose Danish ancestors were "a kind of white Zulus" (44).

Part of the respect Haggard and other white observers gave to the Zulus may have been because they were not cannibals. The Zulu war machine, it was reported, drove lesser African races sometimes to commit survival cannibalism (Wylie 26, 195). And Haggard and virtually every other Victorian writer agreed that the Zulus were, in a general way, like their first "king" Shaka, horrifically "bloodthirsty."[5] But Haggard, Walmsley, and most other writers do not accuse them of cannibalism. In Bertram Mitford's Haggardesque romance *The King's Assegai* (1894), it is other Africans, not the Zulus, who are "the eaters of men," as the title of chapter 11 has it. These other Africans are "held by [the] Zulus in the utmost contempt" (175). Not only did the Zulus, according to Haggard and Mitford, have the moral fiber to resist cannibalism and to scorn "the eaters of men," but also they were so utterly, resolutely, savagely masculine that the best of them, like Umbopa, could never fall victim to the wiles of women and the temptations of the flesh.

The Consolations of Necrophilia

As Joseph Conrad indicated in "Geography and Some Explorers," the "dark continent" was a "blank space" which, as a boy, he filled in with fantasies of romance and adventure. That is certainly what Haggard allowed his boyish imagination to do. Besides the imperialist, racist, and conservative politics of Haggard's romances, his interest in archaeology helped to stimulate his fantasies about women, death, and necrophilia. In *Days of My Life,* Haggard remembers how, on one occasion while visiting ancient ruins near Aswan, he was almost buried alive in a tomb in which there was "the mummy of a lady and the fragments of her painted mummy case" (1:260). The nightmare (or perhaps daydream) of being buried alive with a mummified "lady" is basic to Haggard's Gothic and necrophiliac treatment of archaeology in several of his romances, including both *She* and "Smith and the Pharaohs." Race, women, and death all come into play around Ayesha, the lost civilization of Kôr, and mummification. Ayesha's name is reminiscent of Isis; She might be an offspring or even a reincarnation of that Egyptian goddess.

Describing his fascination with the Egypt of mummies, tombs, and the Sphinx, Haggard half-jokingly declared, "I venerate Isis, and always feel inclined to bow to the moon!" (*Days* 1:255). Gerald Monsman reads *She* as "an allegory of Isis unveiled," and that phrase—"Isis unveiled"—served as the title of the founding work of Theosophy, published by Helena

Blavatsky in 1877. Monsman notes: "Isis, a moon-goddess like Astarte, was narrowly the divinity of agriculture but in her broader aspect she represented Nature, as testified to by an inscription on her veiled statue: 'I am all that has been, all that is, all that ever shall be, and no mortal has ever raised my garment. The fruit which I brought forth became the Sun'" (29). Haggard did not become a convert to Madame Blavatsky's new religion, but he was intrigued by Theosophy, as he was by other late Victorian manifestations of interest in the occult. Monsman points to a feature of the worship of Isis that seems to have attracted Haggard: "A vow of sexual abstinence was required for initiation into Isis's service, and punishment was meted out by the cult's deity if the priest broke his vow of celibacy" (29). Slain in a fit of jealousy by Ayesha, Kallikrates was a "forsworn" priest of Isis who had broken his vow to the goddess. Ayesha has been mourning and loving the dead priest's mummy for two thousand years.

Mummies were of central importance to Haggard's understanding of ancient Egypt. They had been familiar artifacts in Europe since the Middle Ages, when they were valued for medicinal purposes, and they received much attention throughout the nineteenth century, as they continue to do today. The Italian strongman and tomb robber Giovanni Belzoni "unearthed many mummies and was the first Westerner to enter the tomb of Seti I in the Great Pyramid" (Frost x), and as noted earlier, his 1820 *Narrative* was probably familiar to Haggard. According to Brian Frost, the "most prolific mummy unroller" in Britain was surgeon Thomas Pettigrew, whose "public demonstrations always drew huge audiences" (x). Pettigrew's *History of Egyptian Mummies* (1834) John Wortham calls "the most authoritative account of Egyptian embalming practices available to Egyptologists during the nineteenth century" (94). By the time Amelia Edwards wrote "Recent Discovery of Royal Mummies" for the *Illustrated London News* (February 4, 1882), she noted that new findings of mummies in Egyptian tombs were well publicized in the Victorian press. What is more, Haggard's brother Andrew, while stationed in Egypt, sent the family a mummy with which Haggard had some sort of extraordinary experience. According to Haggard's grandson Mark Cheyne: "The mummy was placed in Haggard's study and that night he sat up in this room till dawn. In the morning, he appeared quite distressed, and he found the house was covered in mummy dust. After breakfast he insisted on the mummy's removal and had it sent to the Norwich Museum" (quoted in Addy 2). Moreover, besides the rag doll "who must be obeyed" which apparently terrified Haggard in child-hood (according to Lilias Haggard; *The Cloak* 28), Ayesha may have been inspired by an "ushabti" or wooden funeral statuette in the Egyptian collection at Didlington Hall (Addy 36–38).

Well before *She,* mummies were familiar figures in fiction. Jane Webb published her Gothic-utopian romance *The Mummy! A Tale of the Twenty-second Century* in 1827. Théophile Gautier's *Roman de la momie* (1857–58) first appeared in translation as *The Romance of the Mummy* in 1863. In Gautier's tale, a young English nobleman, Lord Evandale, discovers a black sarcophagus in an Egyptian burial vault and removes the wrappings from the mummy he finds inside it. Frost writes that Evandale uncovers a beautiful female corpse "so well preserved she seems to be asleep rather than having been dead for thirty centuries." Evandale "immediately falls in love with the dead woman" and has her shipped back to his English residence. There, "so all-consuming is [his] obsession with the dead queen that he has remained a bachelor and spends much of his time gazing long-ingly at her coffin" (Frost 53–54). Similar necrophiliac motifs show up in other mummy stories such as Charles Mackay's *Twin Soul: The Strange Experiences of Dr. Rameses* (1887), Edgar Lee's *Pharaoh's Daughter* (1889), George Griffith's *Romance of Golden Star* (1897), and Guy Boothby's *Pharos the Egyptian* (1899) (Frost 64–66; Hurley, "Mummy-Fetish" 182). Toward the end of the 1800s there was a veritable explosion of mummy stories.

In her study of mummies in literature, Jasmine Day points out that the unwrapping of female mummies was often likened to rape, as in mummy stories by Jane Austin (not Austen) and Louisa May Alcott (47). William Prime's travelogue *Boat Life in Egypt and Nubia* (1857) describes an ac-tual episode of violating the corpse of a beautiful female mummy (Bar-rell, "Death" 110–11). In Bram Stoker's *Jewel of Seven Stars* (1903), when the mummy of Queen Tera is unwrapped, the male narrator says: "The figure…now lay completely nude before us.…As…the whole glori-ous beauty of the Queen was revealed, I felt a rush of shame sweep over me.…[I]t was…indecent; it was almost sacrilegious! And yet the white wonder of that beautiful form was something to dream of " (235). It turns out the beautiful mummy looks exactly like the narrator's daughter, who is Queen Tera's *ka* or reincarnation. Haggard's "Smith and the Pharaohs" (1920) offers yet another variation on the motif of falling in love with a beautiful mummy.

This is not to suggest that Haggard was unoriginal, or even that he read any or all mummy stories written by others, much less that he plagiarized from any of them. But archaeological findings, and mummies in particular, figure in a fairly lengthy tradition of romantic stories about necrophilia, specifically involving mummy love. When in "Smith and the Pharaohs" the protagonist falls in love at first sight with the image of a beautiful mummified queen named Ma-Mee, anyone who has also read Gautier's *Romance of the Mummy* might be excused for thinking that Smith is a reincarnation of Lord Evandale. And the obvious pun—Ma-Mee/mummy/mommy—leads one also to suppose that Haggard may have been parodying a tradition in which he participated, most notably in *She*.[6]

Though still alive after two thousand years, Ayesha is garbed in linen winding sheets like a mummy: "I could...clearly distinguish that the swathed mummy-like form before me was that of a tall and lovely woman," says Holly (*She* 146). As Ayesha does her first striptease before him, suddenly "the long, corpse-like wrappings fell from her to the ground" (158). Holly also spies on Ayesha grieving over the mummified corpse of Kallikrates. A member of the Gothic species of the living dead, Ayesha is a near-mummy who is in love with a mummy, reversing the gender roles in Gautier's tale and in Haggard's "Smith and the Pharaohs."

As if to ensure that the reader can't miss it, Haggard reinforces the theme of necrophilia—which on one level can be interpreted as the desire for *and* fear of a love that is everlasting—by embedding several other tales of mummy love in *She*. First, as they travel to Kôr, Holly and Leo sleep in a cave, where Billali recalls his boyhood enchantment by a beautiful mummy with white skin and yellow hair: "I remember when I was a boy I found the body of a fair woman lying where thou liest now, yes, on that very bench. She was so beautiful that I was wont to creep in hither with a lamp and gaze upon her.... Ay, day by day I came hither, and gazed on her till at last, laugh not at me, stranger, for I was but a silly lad, I learned to love that dead form" (114–15). When his mother discovers what he has been doing, she fears he is "bewitched," so "standing the dead woman up against the wall there," she "set fire to her hair, and she burnt fiercely, even down to the feet" (115). Like *She* as a whole, Billali's story is an example of "pornotropic" fantasy; more specifically, it is simultaneously about masturbation and fetishism, with the beautiful mummy as substitute phallus, itself going up in an orgasmic blaze when Billali's mother sets it aflame: trying to halt her son's erotic fixation on a corpse, mommy torches mummy. But Billali manages to cut off the mummy's feet before they burn up, and after telling Holly his story, he finds one "poor little foot" of the mummy under the bench where Holly has slept. Despite mommy's pyrotechnics, mummy love survives, albeit in even more fetishistic form. In psychoanalytic terms, male fear of the phallus is bound up with fear of female sexuality. The yellowish-skinned Amahaggers, Billali's craven people, are cannibals whose favorite way of killing their victims is "hot-potting," or placing a red-hot kettle over a person's head. This cannibal and castration scenario is overruled, however, by the magical and lethal powers of Ayesha.

When She gives Holly a tour of the tombs of Kôr, other stories involving necrophilia and fetishism emerge. Ayesha urges him to remove the wrappings from one of the mummies, and he discovers a woman in her thirties or younger, who "had certainly been...wonderfully beautiful," on whose arm, "its face pressed against her breast, there lay a little babe" (186). This "sweet" and yet "awful" Madonna and child scene is followed by other unveilings, including the discovery of two mummified lovers, "a young man and a blooming girl. Her head rested on his arm, and his lips were pressed against her brow." Holly recounts, "I opened the man's linen robe, and there over his heart was a dagger-wound, and beneath the girl's fair breast was a like cruel stab" (187). He proceeds to imagine an ancient Romeo and Juliet scenario, in which "this fair girl form—the yellow hair streaming down her, glittering against her garments snowy white, and the bosom that was whiter than the robes," was about to be married, but not to the man she desired. Just before the ceremony, the right man sprang from the crowd, grasped her, and kissed "her pale face in which the blood shot up like lights of the red dawn against the silent sky." Then swords were drawn and the right young man was stabbed to death, "but with a cry she snatched the dagger from his belt, and drove it into her snowy breast, home to the heart" (188).

In so fantasying about the deaths of the two lovers, Holly gives one more indication of Haggard's vivid porno-tropic imagination, in which ardent love or lust doesn't lead to fulfillment within the confines of the real world but is typically canceled by death. Richard Pearson is only stating the obvious when he writes, "The site of sexual exchange in Haggard is frequently the site of archaeology" (228). That site is also one of *Liebestod,* the romantic nexus in which longing exceeds life: the ardor of the lovers is so extreme that it is insupportable in the real world; it perishes, yet is perhaps somehow eternal.

As has often been noted, Haggard was evidently exploring his own baffled and unhappy sexual encounters when he wrote *She,* its sequels, and his other romances featuring femmes fatales, including *Cleopatra, The Yellow God,* and *Queen of the Dawn.* Indeed, Holly imagines the Juliet figure in terms that were especially meaningful to Haggard: "White stood the maid against the altar, fairer than the fairest there—purer than a lily" (188). Shortly before sailing to Capetown in 1875, Haggard had met Lilly Jackson, whom he intended to marry and always remembered as "the girl with the golden hair and violets in her hand" (according to Lilias Haggard; *The Cloak* 32). Squire Haggard disapproved; shipping his son off to Africa effectively ended the affair. During his colonial exile, and despite his love for Lilly, Haggard fathered an illegitimate child who died in infancy; its mother, Johanna Catherine Ford, died in 1885 (Coan 136–37). When Haggard returned to Britain in 1880, Lilly had married somebody else. He then met and quickly married, with the squire's blessing, Louisa Margitson, a placid, practical woman for whom Haggard seems to have felt little romantic attraction. Lilly's marriage meanwhile ended in separation. Louisa was "good and sensible"; she was real enough, but Lilly or "Lilith" signified for Haggard erotic longing and unattainable romance, purely decked out in white.

In "Smith and the Pharaohs," the ancient-modern split evident in all of Haggard's archaic romances is overcome by Smith's encounter—or dream of an encounter—with his beloved Ma-Mee. He learns—or dreams that he learns—he was once the sculptor Horus, the true love of the queen. In a sense, he still is; he possesses her hand, after all. It may be a dead hand, just like the bronze bust and also the image of Ma-Mee he first fell in love with in the British Museum. After that life-changing event, Smith becomes an Egyptologist, and in Egypt, seemingly by chance, he discovers the tomb of Ma-Mee, where he reburies her burnt remains and takes away her hand, the bust, and two rings, one of which he leaves with the French director of the Cairo Museum. Then he gets locked in that ghostly place overnight, where he has his encounter with the pharaohs, who accuse him of grave robbing, but is exonerated by none other than the ghost or *ka* of his beloved queen.

As a fetish, the embalmed hand of Ma-Mee is matched by the embalmed foot that Billali finds under the stone bench in *She.*[7] Holly says that the "poor little foot" was not "shrunk or shrivelled" but "plump and fair...a very triumph of embalming." He reflects: "Shapely little foot! Well might it have been set upon the proud neck of a conqueror bent at last to woman's beauty, and well might the lips of nobles and of kings have been pressed upon its jewelled whiteness" (116). Holly takes possession of the foot, putting it away in his "Gladstone bag, which," he says, "I had bought at the Army and Navy Stores—a strange combination, I thought" (116). And so it is—a "strange combination" of fetishism, of necrophilia ancient and modern, and of what it might feel like to be a "noble" or a "king" kissing that "jewelled whiteness." Holly does not tell us what later befalls this precious "triumph of embalming," but at the end of the tale he and Leo narrowly escape from the tombs of Kôr, minus the Gladstone bag and the precious foot. They take with them, however, two locks of Ayesha's hair: "And these locks we still have, the sole memento that is left to us of Ayesha as we knew her in the fullness of her grace and glory" (297). So one fetish replaces another, in a potentially endless chain of substitutions, while Holly and Leo swear their everlasting love for their antique and now (finally? temporarily?) deceased African queen. (Haggard revived her, like a series of fetish substitutions, in several of his later romances.)

One psychoanalytic study indicates that most necrophiliacs long for sexual relations uncomplicated by resistance or rejection; many are also motivated by the desire to be reunited with a lost lover or potential lover (Klaf and Brown). Although Ayesha hovers on the border between life and death, a sort of living mummy, her own necrophilia—that is, her seemingly everlasting love for the dead Kallikrates—combines both motivations, which were probably also among Haggard's motivations in writing *She.* The woman of Haggard's dreams would always be Lilly—or Ayesha, or Cleopatra, or Ma-Mee. In *She,* the portrayal of Ayesha as an unattainable and yet eternally faithful lover, at once ravishing, dangerous, magical, all-powerful in the world of the Amahaggers, and yet secretly vulnerable, reflects Haggard's fetishization of Lilly as well as his misogyny; the two were inseparable, like the dead Romeo and Juliet mummies that Holly uncovers and perhaps like Ayesha and Kallikrates (except that she has murdered him).

In "Smith and the Pharaohs" in particular, which begins and ends in museums, Haggard seems to recognize the connections between archaeology, fetishism, and necrophilia. After all, as Anne McClintock points out, "the museum—as the modern fetish-house of the archaic—became the exemplary institution for embodying the Victorian narrative of progress" (40). In Smith's case as in Haggard's, however, progress is not so important as regression: the search for lost origins, the search for the revival of the dead, and especially of dead love, and the search for a political constancy and conservatism that Haggard identified with Kôr, with the Zulus, with the kingdom of the Zu-Vendis, with the Phoenicians, with the Egypt of the pharaohs, and with an idealized and (he hoped) everlasting British Empire. The mummy-like beauty or the beautiful mummy—She or Ma-Mee—represented everything Haggard longed for but knew was not everlasting.

Haggard's adventure romances have always been popular; they continue to influence how their readers think about African "savages," especially about the Zulus. Another, very different Victorian novelist who wrote about southern Africa was Olive Schreiner. *The Story of an African Farm,* which Schreiner published in 1883 under the pseudonym "Ralph Iron," seems almost the antithesis to Haggard's adventure fantasies. As Cherry Clayton puts it in her study of Schreiner:

> Her novels can be read as the obverse of Rider Haggard's male romance quests, figured as a penetration of an exotic, sexualized landscape in search of treasure by a group of male adventurers. Schreiner's topics are difficult inner quests by women or feminized men in search of spiritual truth and wholeness of being within a culture that denies tenderness and imagination to men, and intellect and autonomy to women. (25)

The Story of an African Farm, writes Paula Krebs, "for all of its spirituality and experimentation, is at heart a Victorian realist novel, set in an Africa about which Britons were increasingly eager to learn." In contrast, in Haggard's stories "King Romance" reigned, filling "his southern Africa with adventure, passion, guns, and spears" (143). Schreiner's first and most important work of fiction has often been identified as the earliest "New Woman" novel: it foregrounds women's aspirations for better lives and livelihoods, including alternatives to marriage. *She,* in contrast, features an alluring, murderous female tyrant whose portrayal expresses Haggard's fear of granting women more power and rights than they already had. Horace Holly calls himself a misogynist; but the entire story is a misogynistic fantasy. It is also a profoundly racist fantasy. Did Schreiner, herself born and raised in southern Africa, manage to think beyond the limits of late Victorian and Edwardian racism, as she managed to think beyond patriarchy?

In her political writings, Schreiner defended the Boers and tried to prevent the war that broke out in 1899. In *Trooper Peter Halket of Mashonaland* (1897), she condemned Cecil Rhodes's bloody takeover of "Rhodesia," which included present-day Zimbabwe. That was precisely the region into which Haggard projected his fantasies of ancient white civilizations, falling prey to waves of savage invaders, including the Zulus. For Haggard, British rule was the only antidote to savagery. Rhodes was one of his heroes, and Rhodes became one of Rudyard Kipling's heroes. Schreiner imagined a future southern Africa in which Boers and British settlers had blended into a peaceful, unified white race. But she also imagined the black races providing the workforce for the dominant white race. While she decried white men's sexual exploitation of black women, she did not think of those women as the equals of white women (Krebs 136). "Even this most progressive of Victorians," writes Krebs, was "incapable of envisioning a truly multi-racial or non-racial future for South Africa" (111).

8

"Shadows of the Coming Race"

In Sir Arthur Conan Doyle's 1890 tale of mummy love "The Ring of
Thoth," the English Egyptologist Vansittart Smith chances upon an attendant in the Louvre secretly unwrapping a mummy. The attendant turns
out to be a nearly immortal Egyptian and lover of Atma, whose mummy he
is unwrapping. The ancient Egyptian tells Smith that he is "not one of the
down-trodden race of slaves who now inhabit the Delta of the Nile, but a
survivor of that fiercer and harder people who...built those mighty works
which have been the envy and the wonder of all after generations" (213), as
they were for Haggard. In Doyle's 1892 mummy story "Lot No. 249," however, an Englishman revivifies a male mummy in his Oxford rooms and
sends him forth to murder his enemies. Egypt in this second story is not
the locus of "mighty works" that "all after generations" have envied and
admired, but a source of evil. It is also a source of evil in Richard Marsh's
horror story *The Beetle* (1897).

For Helena Blavatsky, the unveiling of Isis meant the revelation of the
universal truths of religion. For Haggard, the unveiling of Ayesha was

a consummation of his porno-tropic, albeit mummified, daydreams. Isis
was the goddess She and Kallikrates worshipped. Ancient Egypt was the
home of the pharaohs and of Isis, and of Haggard's most alluring though
long-dead femmes fatales. Isis is also the goddess at the center of the ancient cult that provides the horror in *The Beetle*. An "Arab" or "diabolical
Asiatic" (293) magician and mesmerist has traveled to England to kidnap
a fresh victim to sacrifice to the goddess. The victim is the fiancée of an
eminent parliamentarian, Paul Lessingham. Traveling in Egypt when
he was a young man, Lessingham had himself been entrapped by members of the cult. Kept in a trance for "two unspeakable months," he was
forced to witness "orgies of nameless horrors" practiced by this "cult of the
obscene deity" (243). The horrors acquire more definition from the testimony of an Egyptian who had belonged to "this very idolatrous sect" (297).
He confessed that they offered "young women as sacrifices—preferably
white Christian women, with a special preference, if they could get them,
to young English women" (297). The victims were mutilated and burned
to death.

Mummy stories like *She,* "The Ring of Thoth," and Stoker's *Jewel
of Seven Stars* give credit to the ancient Egyptians (the modern race is a
degenerate version of the ancient one) for their engineering and artistic
feats and for their science of embalming—their attempts to achieve immortality, as their burial practices were interpreted. But *The Beetle* expresses no appreciation of Egypt's ancient civilization. It is only a source
of diabolical magic, terror, and what Kelly Hurley calls "the abhuman"
(*Gothic Body* 3–20). The title character—for "the diabolical Asiatic" can
shape-shift into a beetle or living scarab of variable size—represents
moral, religious, racial, and sexual degeneracy. He or she—the Beetle's
sexual identity is ambiguous—sometimes attacks its victims, both male
and female, in beetle form, suggesting a bizarre version of rape by insect.
And adding to the story's racist connotations, he or she is obsessed with
the whiteness of the victims' bodies.

The Beetle is one of many examples of imperial Gothic fiction that, in Stephen Arata's phrase, involve the motif of "reverse invasion." As in Thomas
De Quincey's "yellow peril" opium dreams, a nightmarish East threatens to
overwhelm the West with death and destruction (Barrell, Infection). "*The
Beetle* inverts the issue of colonization by presenting the East/West conflict
in terms of Oriental aggression," writes Hurley. Its plot involves

an Oriental incursion, with white slavery and genocide as its end, into the
very heart of London; and [it] distorts the issue further by presenting Egypt
as a site not of relatively stable English rule during Lord Cromer's occupation, but of Oriental misrule, under which innocent white tourists are kid-
napped, tortured, and murdered with impunity. (*Gothic Body* 127–28)

Besides the practice of human sacrifice, basic to the cult of Isis in Marsh's
tale is the scarab: the cult worships a bloodthirsty goddess but apparently
also worships beetles, and the story hints at the possibility of a world overrun by beetles. In other imperial Gothic stories the world, or at least a part
of it, is threatened with invasion by other monstrosities—underworld
creatures in Edward Bulwer-Lytton's *The Coming Race* (1872), Martians in
H. G. Wells's *The War of the Worlds* (1898), vampires in Bram Stoker's *Dracula* (1897). There is also, in Samuel Butler's *Erewhon* (1872), the threat—
one that would become a staple in twentieth-century science fiction—of a
world overrun by out-of-control machinery. Most of these stories share the
fantasy of evolution leading to catastrophe for the human species. And all
of their monsters—even machines—were racialized by their authors, most
obviously Count Dracula, who, like the Beetle, is a "diabolical Asiatic."

Monstrous Futures

In H. G. Wells's futuristic short story "The Empire of the Ants" (1905), a
portion of the Amazon basin is overwhelmed by extra-large, intelligent,
man-eating ants, who threaten to become "new competitors for the sovereignty of the globe" (*Stories* 107). Its rather buffoonish human characters
include a "Creole" ship's captain who cannot speak English properly and,
with the exception of the Englishman Holroyd, "the unappetising mixture
of races that constituted his crew" (105). A "Sambo" has alerted the Brazilian authorities—such as they are (inadequate, non-English officials)—
about the insect invasion: "In a few thousand years men had emerged from
barbarism to a stage of civilisation that made them feel lords of the future
and masters of the earth! But what was to prevent the ants from evolving
also?" Ordinary ants, says the narrator, "made no concerted efforts against
the greater world. But they had a language, they had an intelligence!"
Why should they stop evolving "any more than men had stopped at the

barbaric stage?" Indeed, "suppose presently the ants began to store knowledge, just as men had done by means of books and records, use weapons, form great empires, sustain a planned and organized war?" (98) Like the British invasion of Tasmania or the Martian invasion in *War of the Worlds,* the ant empire reflects badly on human imperialism. (Human, ant, and Martian imperialisms are all potentially genocidal.) The story also suggests that *Homo sapiens* does not know enough and cannot control either nature or natural selection in ways that would prevent the future colonization of the world by insects or by some even more alien species, or to prevent the extinction of civilization and humans altogether.

Just as antiquity supplied the nightmare of *The Beetle,* so Wells's futuristic fantasies—he called them "scientific romances"—paint nightmares based on the idea that evolution might produce the most antihuman of results. The differences between humans and Wells's various aliens and monsters, moreover, are exaggerated versions of the differences between human races. *The First Men in the Moon* (1901) is a more elaborate version of "The Empire of the Ants." The Selenites, who live in tunnels and caverns under the surface of the moon, at first appear to the two earthlings, Bedford and Cavor, "like ants in a disturbed ant-hill" (175). Although they walk upright, have hands, and appear to be more intelligent than humans, they nevertheless seem to be "insects." Like ants, they have tentacles and large eyes on the sides of their heads. Their skin is "hard and shiny, quite in the beetle-wing fashion" (145). Bedford says, "They're much more like ants on their hind legs than human beings, and who ever got to any understanding with ants?" (141). And a bit later he says that they are "insect men, that come out of a nightmare" (163). In venturing to the moon, Bedford and Cavor seem to have dived into a "broad sea of excited entomology" (248).

Unlike the Brazilian ants, the Selenites prove to be harmless. Once they can communicate with the earthlings, the Grand Lunar expresses his curiosity about life on Earth. When Cavor tells the Grand Lunar about human warfare, he immediately regrets doing so: the Selenites will surely want to avoid any further contact with Earth. They express no desire to behave like the invading Martians in *War of the Worlds* (1898), who attempt to colonize Earth and harvest humans as food. On the contrary, the colonizing impulse is expressed by Bedford. Under the influence of a hallucinogenic fungus, Bedford sounds like Cecil Rhodes, who declared that he "would annex the planets" if he could: "'We must annex this moon,' I said. 'There must be no shilly-shally. This is part of the White Man's Burthen. Cavor—we are—*hic*—Satap—mean Satraps! Nempire Caesar never dreamt. B'in all the newspapers. Cavorecia.—Bedfordecia. Bedfordecia—hic—Limited. Mean— unlimited!'" (125) As Leon Stover points out in the annotated edition, Bedford's idea of founding a colony as a company ("Limited") called "Cavorecia" or "Bedfordecia" is a satiric jab at the founding of Rhodesia in 1895 by Rhodes's British South African Company.

The Selenite state may not be an imperialist, warmongering one, but neither is it a democracy. It is instead an industrious "anthill," ruled undemocratically by the Grand Lunar. But this regime has features that Wells found attractive, or at least that he thought of as interesting alternatives to human arrangements. Like the future England that Wells depicts in *When the Sleeper Wakes* (1899), the realm of the Selenites has both dystopian and utopian features. According to Cavor, "in the moon...every citizen knows his place" (238). Stover notes that this remark "sums up the new ethic of the managerial revolution" (238 n. 209), indicating a society run by experts and technocrats—a society, in short, similar to the one Wells looks forward to in *Anticipations* (1901). Nevertheless, just what Wells thinks about the extreme specialization among the Selenites is unclear. Selenites "with big heads" are the intellectual class, and the Grand Lunar has the biggest: he is a "marvellous gigantic ganglion" (239). And he is surrounded by others with big heads who act as a living encyclopedia. In contrast, Selenites who work with machines are, almost literally, "machine hands" (242). All the different sorts of workers come in different shapes and sizes, depending on their roles. "Fine work is done by fined-down workers, amazingly dwarfed and neat. Some I could hold in the palm of my hand. There is even a sort of turnspit Selenite, very common, whose duty and only delight is to supply the motive power for various small appliances" (242).

Cavor begins to learn about Selenite "education" when he comes upon "a number of young Selenites in jars" whose limbs and organs are being shaped to match the tasks they will perform. He also learns that the various types of "operatives" are taught only to be obedient "machines," although he also discovers that there is "a sort of lunar police" in case anyone gets out of hand (242–43). He is afraid that this method of education is inhumane, and yet says, "Of course, it is really in the end a far more humane proceeding than our earthly method of leaving children to grow into human beings, and then making machines of them" (243). This is apparently also

Wells's opinion. At any rate, whatever one makes of the Selenite moon-scape, in one of his messages to Earth Cavor says, "I feel that I am casting back to the fable-hearing period of childhood again, when the ant and the grasshopper talked together and the bee judged between them" (237).

The War of the Worlds draws explicit analogies between the Martian invasion and British racism and imperialism. In the opening paragraph the narrator says that in the past, "terrestrial men fancied there might be other men upon Mars, perhaps inferior to themselves and ready to welcome a missionary enterprise" (41), like the supposedly "inferior races" in Asia and Africa. The comparison to British racism and imperialism continues when the narrator declares:

> Before we judge [the Martians] too harshly we must remember what ruth-less and utter destruction our own species has wrought, not only upon animals, such as the vanished bison and the dodo, but upon its own inferior races. The Tasmanians, in spite of their human likeness, were entirely swept out of existence in a war of extermination waged by European immigrants, in the space of fifty years. Are we such apostles of mercy as to complain if the Martians warred in the same spirit? (43)

This passage leaves unclear whether Wells is condemning the British for exterminating the "inferior race" of the Tasmanians or exonerating the Martians for behaving like the "European immigrants" according to Darwinian "survival of the fittest."

The Martians are not "men upon Mars," an inferior human race, but an alien species, with their "Gorgon groups of tentacles" (55), hideous to behold. Their lack of recognizable body parts corresponds to their reliance on machines. The narrator cites a satirist in *Punch* writing before the Martian invasion who said that

> the perfection of mechanical appliances must ultimately supersede limbs, the perfection of chemical devices, digestion—that such organs as hair, external nose, teeth, ears, and chin were no longer essential parts of the human being, and that the tendency of natural selection would lie in the direction of their steady diminution through the coming ages. (146)

Only brains and hands will remain and continue to evolve. The narrator applies this forecast to the Martians and speculates that they "may be descended from beings not unlike ourselves, by a gradual development of brain and hands (the latter giving rise to the two bunches of delicate tentacles at last) at the expense of the rest of the body" (146). According to this possibility, even if the Martian invasion fails, the species or "coming race" that humans will evolve into will be monstrosities similar to the Martians.

The "mechanical appliances" of the Martians—their Fighting and Handling Machines—are far in advance of human technology, yet also monstrous in appearance. The newspapers describe the Fighting Machines as "vast spider-like machines, nearly a hundred feet high, capable of the speed of an express-train, and able to shoot out a beam of intense heat" (103). The Handling Machine the narrator inspects resembles "a sort of metallic spider with five jointed, agile legs, and with an extraordinary number of jointed levers, bars, and reaching and clutching tentacles" (142). It is "a crab-like creature with a glittering integument, the controlling Martian, whose delicate tentacles actuated its movements, seeming to be simply the equivalent of the crab's cerebral portion" (143). Although the machines have "cerebral" Martians within them, the narrator at first wonders: "Were they intelligent mechanisms? ... Or did a Martian sit within each, ruling, directing, using, much as a man's brain sits and rules in his body?" (80). The narrator also occasionally refers to the machines and the controllers inside them as single units, as "the Martians," suggesting that they are cyborgs.

The narrator's question about whether the Martians and/or their machines are "intelligent mechanisms" suggests the further possibility that machines themselves may supersede organic creatures, a possibility that Samuel Butler and George Eliot also considered. The artilleryman the narrator reencounters late in the story has still another scenario to suggest about human evolution in the near term, assuming the Martians conquer the world. His suggestion sounds like a crackpot version of eugenics: the weak and the silly will be caught by the Martians, and if not killed immediately, raised in cages like tame animals, even pets, until they are slaughtered and eaten. And good riddance, he thinks. The smart and the strong, like himself and the narrator, will hide out in the sewers. Humans will have to behave like ants or rats—"vermin"—and go underground so the Martians will treat them as insignificant until they go away (171). He is digging a tunnel to connect to a sewer, and for awhile the narrator helps him. "The risk is that we who keep wild will go savage—degenerate into a sort of big, savage rat," says the artilleryman (171). This language echoes discourse earlier in the 1800s about going native and about "the residuum" as a degenerate race living like rats in the slums and sewers. The artilleryman, the narrator thinks, is insane. But Wells advocated a very similar version of eugenics in *Anticipations*.[1]

The evolutionary nightmare Wells depicts in *The Time Machine* (1895) is a fantasy of degeneration that has both racial and social class aspects. Some 802,000 years in the future, the Time Traveller encounters a world where humanity has split into two separate species: the effete, witless Elois who live in a false pastoral above ground, and the rat-like Morlocks who live underground and surface at night to feed on the Elois. Wells links evolutionary degeneration with the idea of entropy, based on the second law of thermodynamics. The universe itself is degenerating, dissipating its energy, cooling. Among the Elois and the Morlocks, the Time Traveller thinks that he "had happened upon humanity upon the wane...the sunset of mankind." He goes on:

> For the first time I began to realize an odd consequence of the social effort in which we are at present engaged. And yet, come to think, it is a logical consequence enough. Strength is the outcome of need; security sets a premium on feebleness. The work of ameliorating the conditions of life—the true civilizing process that makes life more and more secure—had gone steadily on to a climax. One triumph of a united humanity over Nature had followed another.... And the harvest was what I saw! (90)

This was the theme of the eugenics movement: civilization allows "feebleness" to subvert fitness; progress is its own undoing. The Time Traveller also concludes that the two symbiotic species he finds in this nightmarish future are the offshoots of the class divisions of the nineteenth century: the "social difference between the Capitalist and the Labourer was the key" (109). The aboveground Elois represent the aristocracy and bourgeoisie, no longer capable of exploiting the working class. Now the "human spiders," the Morlocks, the "ape-like" remnants of the working class, while continuing to clothe and feed the Elois, exploit them in the most basic way by treating them like sheep and eating them. The false pastoral proves to be a cannibalistic nightmare. The Time Traveller recovers his machine and escapes from the Morlocks into an even more monstrous future, where he comes close to witnessing the heat death of the universe and encounters monstrous, crab-like creatures on a terminal beach, which gives him a feeling of "abominable desolation" (146). Fortunately he is able to return to the present and tell his story. *The Time Machine,* writes Daniel Pick, is "an exemplary 'blue-print' of [late Victorian] degenerationist concerns" (157), which stressed the unfitness of "the lower orders" as evidence of the deterioration of the English or Anglo-Saxon "race."

All of Wells's major scientific romances can be interpreted as allegorical representations of the social class and racial conflicts of his time. *The Island of Dr. Moreau* (1896) depicts a Frankensteinian scientist attempting to humanize wild beasts by vivisection—a nightmare version of the imperialist and missionary so-called civilizing process both at home and abroad. The tortured Beast-Folk kill the mad doctor in revenge. And *When the Sleeper Wakes* (1899), which projects a future only two centuries after the 1890s, suggests that Wells did not expect warfare, imperialism, class conflict, and racial strife to disappear by then. Graham, the Sleeper, Wells's Rip Van Winkle, wakes up to technological and architectural marvels, just as does the protagonist of Edward Bellamy's *Looking Backward* (1888). In many respects, however, the human condition has worsened, while in many other respects not much has changed. Graham learns that highly mechanized megacities have sucked most of the population out of the countryside into the Labour Company or else into perennial unemployment and poverty: "The city had swallowed up humanity" (138). The few people who remained in the countryside had "neither means of being clothed nor fed....[T]o live outside the range of the electric cables was to live as an isolated savage" (138). The anemic, impoverished workers for the Labour Force are hardly better off.

Although in the Sleeper's brave new world the traditional aristocracy and monarchy no longer exist, social class inequality seems even more gaping. Capitalism is rampant, providing riches for the few and poverty for the masses. Print culture—"newspaper, book, schoolmaster, and letter"—has been replaced by "telephone, kinematograph and phonograph" with a loss of meaningful content. Both religion and democracy have disappeared. Through its "Babble Machine," the police state feeds the discontented workers disinformation or no information at all. Yet the police and armed forces are necessary to keep down revolutionary unrest. Graham is caught up in two revolutions. The first, led by Ostrog, overthrows the Council. The second overthrows Ostrog and would have installed the

Sleeper as master of half the world. (When he awakens, he learns that he already owns half the world.) In Paris, the rebelling workers threaten to establish "a Commune" (196), as if nothing has changed since the failed Commune of 1871.

Besides class conflict, another factor that has not disappeared from this dystopian future is racism, and along with racism, imperialism. To defeat the revolution that seeks to overthrow him, Ostrog calls in "negro" forces to Paris from Africa; their presumably unmitigated savagery throws fear into the population. These are "French speaking negroes. Senegal regiments, and Niger and Timbuctoo" (213). Ostrog tells Graham that the "negro police" are "useful.... They are fine loyal brutes," and despite speaking French, they have "no wash of ideas in their heads—such as our rabble has" (197). Graham is disturbed by the thought of the "negro police"; he tells Ostrog: "I have been thinking about these negroes. I don't believe the people intend any hostility to me, and, after all, I am the Master. I do not want any negroes brought to London. It is an archaic prejudice perhaps, but I have peculiar feelings about Europeans and the subject races" (202). Whether Wells shares Graham's "peculiar feelings" is unclear; but the British Empire remains intact, and Africa remains a region of ignorance and savagery. The narrator says, "The whole world was civilised; the whole world dwelt in cities; the whole world was property" (139). The last phrase is clearly ironic in relation to Wells's idea of what constitutes civilization; the notion of turning "the whole world" into "property," however, meshes with his conception of imperialism: "And everywhere now, through the city-set earth, save in the administered 'black belt' territories of the tropics, the same cosmopolitan social organisation prevailed" (139). Graham's "property" includes America and the British Empire, on which the sun still has not set. Nor have other empires—French, German, Russian—been decolonized. And Africa and the rest of the "black belt," it seems, remains as uncivilized as ever. Furthermore, Wells may have wanted his readers to ponder the idea of themselves as "sleepers" who need to wake up to the fact that they are the imperialist "owners" of half of the world.

According to the news coming out of France, "Paris is now pacified. All resistance is over.... The Black Police hold every position of importance in the city" (210). Apparently the Black Police have occasionally allowed their savagery to get the better of them, "and tortured and mutilated wounded and captured insurgents, men and women. Moral—don't go rebelling"

(211). But the Black Police are also "lively brave fellows," says the Babble Machine, who are educated enough to sing "songs written in praise of their ancestors by the poet Kipling" (211).[2] Graham and his Japanese servant Asano hear the listening crowd grumble, "Damned niggers," and then also hear more news from France: "Shocking outrage in Paris. Yahahah! The Parisians exasperated by the black police to the pitch of assassination. Dreadful reprisals. Savage times come again. Blood! Blood! Yaha!" (211). Although Ostrog tells Graham that he will not order the Black Police to come to England, he does so anyway. When Graham learns of this betrayal, he says to Ostrog: "These negroes must not come to London.... White men must be mastered by white men" (236). Ostrog brings on the black invasion anyway, and Graham at last realizes he must fight against Ostrog. He asks Helen Wooton, his sympathizer in revolution against the forces of Ostrog, if the coming battle is the product of "an older sin, a wider sin." The answer to this question could be racism, imperialism, or both, but seems to have nothing to do with the domestic class conflict that has led to the revolution in the first place. Helen wonders what he is referring to, and he replies: "These blacks are savages, ruled by force, used as force. And they have been under the rule of the whites two hundred years. Is it not a race quarrel? The race sinned—the race pays" (257). At the story's end, Graham takes to the air to battle against Ostrog and the black "aeronauts"—"savages" even though they speak French and can pilot airplanes—who are flying in from France.

In *When the Sleeper Wakes,* Wells does not do anything more to suggest how the "wider sin"—presumably that of racism and imperialism—connects to the class conflict that leads to the revolutions in both England and France. He is more overtly critical of imperialism if not of racism in some of his other stories and essays. But for Graham, one racist fear from Wells's age is laid to rest when he asks, "What of the yellow peril?" and learns that "the Chinese spectre had vanished" and that "Chinaman and European were at peace. The twentieth century had discovered with reluctant certainty that the average Chinaman was as civilised, more moral, and far more intelligent than the average European serf" (140). At the same time, Ostrog takes up a different strand of the theme of race when he tells Graham what he considers to be "the hope of mankind." This is the hope "that some day the Over-man may come, that some day the inferior, the weak and the bestial may be subdued or eliminated." Here Wells strikes a eugenicist note, with a nod to Friedrich Nietzsche's concept of the Über-mensch. Ostrog continues his eugenicist discourse about the improvement of the race: "The world is no place for the bad, the stupid, the enervated. Their duty—it's a fine duty too!—is to die. The death of the failure! That is the path by which the beast rose to manhood, by which man goes on to higher things" (200). If he fails to conquer "these swarming yelping fools," he tells Graham, "they will only fall to other masters. So long as there are sheep Nature will insist on beasts of prey. It would mean but a few hundred years' delay. The coming of the aristocrat is fatal and assured. The end will be the Over-man" (201). The novel makes clear that Ostrog is a tyrant; Wells just as clearly sympathizes with Graham's liberal views about domestic politics. Whether he also sympathizes with Graham's anti-black "archaic prejudice" is not so clear.

The eugenicist views Ostrog expresses are, however, similar to those Wells expresses in *Anticipations* (Childs 9–10; Greenslade 197). Wells's most hopeful anticipation concerns the emergence of what he calls "the New Republic," consisting of engineers, scientists, and other technocrats; this sounds very much like the regime Ostrog has established. Another, pessimistic anticipation concerns "the rapid multiplication of the unfit" (61–62)—that is, of all those millions of individuals at the bottom of "the social pyramid" whose potentially life-sustaining labor has been superseded by machinery (63). How will the society of the future rid itself of "these gall stones of vicious, helpless, and pauper masses"? (61–62). Wells's answer is the same as that of many other eugenicists such as Francis Galton, Karl Pearson, George Bernard Shaw, Virginia Woolf, and D. H. Lawrence: they must be prevented from multiplying, or if that fails, they must be exterminated (Childs). But the problem for the future involves much more than just how an industrialized society should deal with its "pauper masses." It involves how to deal with the outsized and presumably dangerous multiplication of all the world's races. Combining futurology with an Egyptian touch, Wells contends that while the New Republic is evolving, "that other great element, which I have called the People of the Abyss, will also have followed out its destiny." He continues:

> For many decades that development will be largely or entirely out of all human control. To the multiplying rejected of the white and yellow civilisations, there will have been added a vast proportion of the black and brown

races, and collectively those masses will propound the general question, "What will you do with us, we hundreds of millions, who cannot keep pace with you?" If the New Republic emerges at all it will emerge by grappling with this riddle; it must come into existence by the passes this Sphinx will guard. (199)

This Malthusian anticipation might be described as the black and brown plus the "rejected" white and yellow racial peril.

The Coming Machines

Most futuristic fantasies like Bellamy's *Looking Backward* and Wells's *When the Sleeper Wakes* depict greatly advanced science and technology. The central question is whether the machines of the future will liberate humans or make them so dependent that they become the slaves of the machines or themselves turn into robots. A corollary concerns technological determinism, or the degree to which machines displace humans with mechanical agency. These questions arose with the Industrial Revolution. "A Machine is not a Man nor a Work of Art," William Blake declared; "it is destructive of Humanity & of Art" (quoted in Eaves 903). In Thomas Carlyle's *Sartor Resartus* (1833), when Teufelsdröckh experiences despair and the "Everlasting No," he fears that the entire universe has turned into "one huge, dead, immeasurable Steam-engine, rolling on, in its dead indifference, to grind me limb from limb" (125–26). And in "Signs of the Times" (1829), Carlyle writes that "this age of ours" is "not an Heroical, Devotional, Philosophical, or Moral Age.... It is the Age of Machinery, in every outward and inward sense of that word" (226). Steam engines are all well and good, but there are also educational, political, literary, and even religious machines. "The true Church of England," Carlyle says, "lies in the Editors of its Newspapers" (241). In short, the success of industrialization has produced a cultural secularization and materialism that Carlyle deplores.

The early critics of industrialization, including those who championed trade unionism and other working-class movements, quickly recognized several threats posed by new machinery and "the factory system." The deleterious physical effects of factory labor, especially on child workers, soon became evident (Sussman 177). Engels cites the testimony of numerous medical authorities that factory labor produces physical deformities. According to one observer, "I can have no hesitation...in stating my belief...that a large mass of deformity has been produced at Bradford by the factory system" (quoted in Engels 176). Dr. Bisset Hawkins reported on "the lowness of stature, the leanness, and the paleness...among the factory classes" of Manchester, and added, "I have never been in any town in Great Britain, nor in Europe, in which degeneracy of form and colour from the national standard has been so obvious" (quoted in Engels 178). Engels also cites the admission by "one of the most important Manchester manufacturers, and the leader of the factory owners against the workers...that if this state of affairs were allowed to continue the Lancashire factory operatives would soon be a race of pigmies" (179). Such testimony was a major source of the later eugenicist discourse about the degeneration of the British working class and "the residuum." Eugenicists including Wells worried about improving the race more than improving conditions in workshops, factories, and mines.

A second major theme among early critics of the factory system concerned new machinery replacing handwork. Steam-powered looms were putting hand-loom weavers out of work. Beginning in 1811 the Luddites protested by sabotaging new machinery. They were defended in Parliament by Lord Byron; Luddism also serves as the backdrop of Charlotte Brontë's *Shirley* (1849). In the first two decades of the Victorian era, these issues were taken up by many other novelists, including Disraeli in *Coningsby* (1844) and *Sybil* (1845). In Dickens's *Hard Times* (1853), Coketown with its smoke and brick buildings is a city "of unnatural red and black like the painted face of a savage." This racially charged metaphor is echoed by one that likens a steam engine's piston to the head of "an elephant in a state of melancholy madness" plunging endlessly up and down (22). Instead of a civilized British community, Coketown is an "unnatural" jungle.

Many Romantic and Victorian writers agreed with Carlyle's claim that their age was growing increasing mechanical, which also meant materialistic. Matthew Arnold denounced "machinery" of all sorts in *Culture and Society*, while William Morris and the Arts and Crafts movement tried to renew art and culture on a non-machinic basis. "The great cry that rises from all our manufacturing cities, louder than their furnace blast," John Ruskin declared, "is all in very deed for this,—that we manufacture everything there except men" (180). For Ruskin, the seeming perfectness of machine-made goods was a sign of the enslavement of the machine "operatives" or factory workers. The roots of the modern and postmodern theme of machines enslaving or even exterminating humans lie in these Romantic and Victorian reactions to industrialization.

Within this anti-industrial discourse, the notion emerges that machines, which were increasingly making human labor superfluous, might become so powerful and even intelligent that they would render the entire human species superfluous. After Darwin's *Origin,* some writers even speculated that machines might be the new species that would eliminate humans in the struggle for survival. In *The Impressions of Theophrastus Such* (1876), George Eliot includes a chapter titled "Shadows of the Coming Race." Theophrastus contemplates the evolutionary future. "One sees that the process of natural selection must drive men altogether out of the field," he says, replaced by "the immensely more powerful . . . race" of machines (141). Eliot's chapter title echoes Edward Bulwer-Lytton's 1872 science fiction classic *The Coming Race,* in which the protagonist discovers the underground world of the Vril-ya, demonic creatures much advanced beyond humans, who fly about with mechanical wings and who have discovered a powerful source of energy called "vril." They threaten to surface and supplant or destroy humanity. Eliot is thinking as well about Samuel Butler's *Erewhon,* which also appeared in 1872. In Butler's novel, the author of "The Book of the Machines" has likewise concluded that machines are the coming race. "I shrink with as much horror from believing that my race can ever be superseded or surpassed," he writes, "as I should do from believing that even at the remotest period my ancestors were other than human beings" (222). Machines have evolved far more rapidly than natural organisms, however, and will soon gain intelligence and begin reproducing themselves. Machines might as well be organisms, because they belong to different "races and families" (214). Elsewhere Butler writes:

> Day by day . . . the machines are gaining ground upon us; day by day we are becoming more subservient to them; more men are daily bound down as slaves to tend them, more men are daily devoting the energies of their whole lives to the development of mechanical life. The upshot is simply a question of time, but that the time will come when the machines will hold the real supremacy over the world . . . is what no person of a truly philosophic mind can for a moment question. (Butler, *Notebooks* 46)

Butler later indicated that he intended "The Book of the Machines" to be a satire on anti-machine discourse: "It is a mistake to consider the machines as identities, to animalize them and to anticipate their final triumph over mankind" (quoted in Sussman 149). It seems clear, however, that he took the Erewhonians' anti-machine arguments quite seriously before deciding he was mistaken.

Fantasies of machines replacing, enslaving, and even devouring humans represent a major strain of science fiction that perhaps starts with Mary Shelley's *Frankenstein* (1818). No, the original Frankenstein's monster was not a robot or cyborg with a bolt through his neck, as he became in comic books and Hollywood films. But there is the business of the monster's bride that Frankenstein starts to make and then destroys. At first the mad scientist aspires to create a new "race" that will bless him as their creator; but as he works on the bride, he becomes horrified at the prospect of unleashing "a race of devils...upon the earth" (114). The ultimate nightmare is one of exterminating and replacing humans with this "race of devils."

The machinic aspects of Mary Shelley's monster story were elaborated by many authors in metaphors and stories about machines capable of devouring humans. This sort of mechanical cannibalism is evident, for example, in "The Steam King," an 1843 poem by Edward Mead which Engels quotes in his book on the condition of the working class: "Like the ancient Moloch grim...children are his food." Factory owners and capitalists are equally cannibals, along with the steam-powered machinery they own:

> His priesthood...a hungry band,
> Bloodthirsty, proud, and bold;
> 'Tis they direct his giant hand,
> In turning blood to gold.
> And his Satraps abhor'd, each proud Mill Lord,
> Now gorg'd with gold and blood,
> Must be put down by the nation's frown,
> As well as their monster God. (quoted in Engels 209)

In *The Time Machine,* Wells's working-class Morlocks practice a topsy-turvy cannibalism, devouring the evolutionary successors of Mead's industrial capitalists, the Elois. So do his Martian cyborgs, who in *War of the Worlds* "were heads, merely heads. Entrails they had none. They did not eat, much less digest. Instead, they took the fresh, living blood of other creatures, and *injected* it into their own veins.... Let it suffice to say, blood obtained from a still living animal, in most cases from a human being, was run directly by means of a little pipette into the recipient canal" (144). Wells's Martians, then, are technologically advanced vampires, hoping to batten on the blood of humans. This is, of course, what Count Dracula threatens to do presumably from here to eternity, or at any rate until he has turned everyone into a vampire.

Stoker's monster novel leaves unclear what the count will feed on after the human species has been superseded by his demonic version of a super-race. Like Haggard's *She,* Marsh's *The Beetle,* and Stoker's own *Jewel of Seven Stars, Dracula* focuses on a nightmare emanating from the distant past: the Middle Ages rather than Egyptian antiquity. But it also projects a future in which the human species has been replaced by a new "race of devils." Furthermore, both Stoker and his bloodthirsty count are heavily invested in current technological developments. Christopher Keep declares that Stoker's vampire novel "effectively dramatizes the relationship between the new communication and transportation technologies and the unmanageable problem of 'information.'" It may seem odd to think of *Dracula* as an industrial novel similar to *Coningsby* or *Hard Times,* but Keep points out that Stoker "shows a marked fascination" with the latest inventions: "Mina Harker uses a ... typewriter to transcribe and collate the various firsthand reports and documents that constitute the narrative; Jonathan Harker [uses] a Kodak camera [to take pictures of Dracula's new property in London]; and Dr. Seward records his diaries on a wax cylinder phonograph" (152). *Dracula* also features Winchester rifles, telegrams, and what another critic calls "one of the first cameo appearances of a telephone in a novel" (Winthrop-Young 111). Stoker expressed his fascination with new technologies in his other novels as well. In *The Lady of the Shroud* (1909), for example, the protagonist invents new weapons for a small Balkan nation, including noiseless airplanes and a "mysterious submarine built like 'a huge grey crab' which can immobilize a ship by shaking it from side to side" (Glover 52).

Dracula was published just two years after motion pictures were introduced in 1895, the year that also saw publication of *The Time Machine.* It is not evident that Stoker wrote his novel with an eye to its being turned into vampire movies, though there have been many of them. But Stoker was manager of the Lyceum Theatre in London, whose owner and star,

Henry Irving, often played Gothic, demonic roles like Dracula. Both Irving and Stoker were fascinated by special stage effects, including electrical ones, and they would have known about pre-cinematic illusions like Dr. Pepper's "Ghost" (Groth) and Thomas Armat's "electric Phantoscope" (Mannoni 429–32). Other new media also had phantasmatic effects. Richard Menke writes that "Victorian invocations of the electric telegraph often treat it as simultaneously objective and eerie, wholly truthful yet utterly mysterious." The earliest accounts of it "encouraged a particular sense of [its] ghostliness" (123); and it was no accident that Morse code and spiritualist table tapping began almost simultaneously. Ghostliness or spectrality was equally true of sound recording, the telephone, and radio.

Stoker understood that theater is, in a sense, itself a vampiric medium, in which an actor takes over a role—another human identity—or vice versa, the role takes over the actor, like demonic possession. And he may also have realized that cinema was going to be even more vampiric or phantasmatic than the stage.[3] Consider the ghostliness of the images in both early photographs and silent films.[4] The vampire can't be reflected in a mirror; his image is even more evanescent, or perhaps disembodied, than those fleeting, flickering images of actors on the silver screen. Nor does he cast a shadow.

Instead of cinema, Keep emphasizes the typewriter. He cites Jennifer Wicke's argument that for Stoker, vampirism "is not so much the antithesis of typewriting as another form of it, a means of transcription and multiplication that is both the central problem of the text and the ostensible solution to that problem" (152). Wicke indicates that the phrase she uses in the subtitle of her article, "vampiric typewriting," is an "oxymoron." By this she means that, superficially at least, the vampire and the various modern technologies, above all the typewriter, that are used to record Dracula's bloody deeds and defeat him seem completely at odds.[5] Once Jonathan Harker gets off the train in Transylvania, he leaves modernity behind: everything about Dracula's castle is medieval, and vampirism itself is a relic or a revenant of medieval superstitions. Yet Jonathan is surprised when he finds the count reading Bradford's railway timetables. Dracula's desire to move to London expresses his wish to be at the center of modernity, drinking up-to-date blood. Given the choice, no sane reader of Stoker's novel would opt to live in Transylvania rather than in 1890s London with

its newspapers and telegrams, its Kodak cameras and streetcars, its depart-
ment stores and typewriters, and the count is no exception.

By juxtaposing the new media of communications and the monster,
Stoker seems to put them in opposition. But the count is alive and well,
or at any rate undead and well, in the 1890s. Once he gets to London, he
is certainly in the swim of modern mass culture, definitely an au cou-
rant monster. And there are many ways, Stoker seems to have realized,
that the modern mass media and mechanical reproduction in general are
vampiric. Wicke contends that "the social force most analogous to Count
Dracula's...is none other than mass culture" and its means of reproduction, including "the developing technologies of the media in [their] many
forms, [such] as mass transport, photography...and mass-produced narrative" like Stoker's novel (476). Certainly both the novel and the many
films based on it have been commodities for mass consumption.

Wicke argues that "the same science, rationality and technologies
of social control relied on to defend against...Dracula are the source of
the vampiric powers of the mass culture with which Dracula...is allied"
(476–77). The typewriter in particular is central to the novel as the machine
that records it all, or the machine that copies it all, giving life to the count
and his bloodthirsty brood. Wicke notes that Mina's typewriter

> has a function called "Manifold" that allows it to make multiple copies in
> threes. This function is positively vampiric, even to the name it has been
> given, reverberating with the multiplicity of men Dracula is, the manifold
> guises of the vampire, and the copying procedure which itself produces
> vampires, each of which is...a replica of all the others. Here we step into
> the age of mechanical reproduction with a vengeance. (476)

The typewriter obliterates the sort of individual identity associated with
handwriting, and it can also be used to copy other writing and information at a rapid pace.[6] Consider, too, the blurring of identity through the
amalgamation of person and machine in the word "typewriter,"[7] suggesting a mechanical version of miscegenation. At the end, Jonathan Harker
says that the novel consists of "hardly one authentic document; [it is] nothing but a mass of typewriting," and therefore "we could hardly ask any
one...to accept these [typed pages] as proofs of so wild a story" (Gitelman
215). So the typewriter produces *in*authenticity instead of the reverse. In
"Dracula's Legacy," Friedrich Kittler argues that, with the emergence of

psychoanalysis at the same time as the new media that fascinated Stoker, the typewriting and stenography of Mina "undermines the very possibility of a discourse of the master" ("Dracula's Legacy" 63). Instead of a master discourse, modernity is the era of the discourse of the masses. By stressing that it is only "a mass of typewriting," Stoker acknowledges that his "wild," unbelievable Gothic romance is no exception to the modern rule of inauthenticity.

Wicke points out as well that "large sections of the ... typewritten manuscript derive from newspaper articles," such as the tabloid reports on Lucy as the "Bloofer Lady," preying on children on Hampstead Heath after dark (473). Like the count and the "weird sisters" who threaten Jonathan at Castle Dracula, Lucy as vampire evokes the *jouissance* of pornography, perhaps the basic element in all mass culture, or at least in all visual mass culture.[8] It is not that Lucy and the other vampires strip their victims naked and rape them, but they strip lust naked, revealing it as cannibalistic bloodlust or as the sadomasochistic roots of pornography. Moreover, vampirism strives to industrialize its version of porn by endlessly reproducing itself. That is one reason why Judith Halberstam calls Stoker's novel a "machinic text." Furthermore, by combining a wide range of transgressions against racial, class, gender, and sexual normalcy, the count is himself "a technology of monstrosity." Consider his degenerate, miscegenated racial composition, a "whirlpool" of threatening otherness. Dracula tells Jonathan that he is the last of a "conquering race":

> We Szekelys have a right to be proud, for in our veins flows the blood of many brave races who fought as the lion fights, for lordship. Here, in the whirlpool of European races, the Ugric tribe bore down from Iceland the fighting spirit which Thor and Wodin gave them, which their Berserkers displayed to such fell intent on the seaboards of Europe, aye, and of Asia and Africa, too, till the peoples thought that the were-wolves themselves had come. Here, too, when they came, they found the Huns, whose warlike fury had swept the earth like a living flame, till the dying peoples held that in their veins ran the blood of those old witches, who, expelled from Scythia, had mated with the devils in the desert. Fools, fools! What devil or what witch was ever so great as Attila, whose blood is in these veins? ... Is it a wonder that we were a conquering race? (41)

Blood and machinery, vampirism as an industrial and not just a medieval version of cannibalism, merge in Dracula as the final outcome of a demonic racial *and* machinic mixing and degeneration. Furthermore, the "gothic economy" of the novel, as with other Gothic romances, Halberstam notes, means that "attempts to consume Dracula and vampirism within one interpretive model inevitably produces vampirism," or a kind of vampiric reading at any rate (334).[9] The pleasures of the text ramify along with its supposedly forbidden sexual pleasures: the two are of course inseparable.

A world of vampires would be a world overrun by bloodless copies (and corpses), or by copies of copies without originals, a world of the living dead. We are today used to the idea that the postmodern condition is one of simulacra or endless images with nothing behind them. The intelligent machinery Butler worried about has emerged with the mass media and computers, while human identity has grown ever more machinic or even vampiric. Jean Baudrillard identifies the "precession of simulacra" with "hyperreality," a realm of the phantasmatic that has replaced the real. Reality itself, according to this postmodern logic, has been vampirized; it no longer casts any shadows. If this is correct, then perhaps *Dracula* is the first postmodern novel rather than the first great modernist one, which is what Wicke calls it.

Like Bulwer-Lytton's Vril-ya, Dracula and his multiplying family of vampires are post-humans, and they plan to turn all humans into versions of themselves—the past and future race of the living dead. In writing about post-humanity, many recent authors besides Baudrillard have claimed that computers and the Internet, for example, are "vampiring organic flesh, and draining its fluids into cold streams of telemetry" (Kroker and Weinstein 132). In *Data Trash* (1994), Arthur Kroker and Michael Weinstein add that history now "means the archiving of the human function and its recombination in the form of monstrous hybrids" (135). Like vampires, they claim, we post-humans in the age of the Internet have fallen prey to "the seduction of exterminism" (105) or cultural suicide. They acknowledge Marshall McLuhan's technological determinism when they offer the idea that "the data-net [is] an externalization of the human nervous system" (104), but they sound more like Bram Stoker when they write about the electronic harvesting of human flesh. Kittler, too, borrows from McLuhan the basic idea that machines and the media are externalizations of our bodies, which, in accelerating mode, are consuming and transforming those bodies into what, exactly?[10] Ever more "data trash," presumably the ultimate form of social waste (x). A body dump, according to Kroker and Weinstein, "is where flesh goes to be virtualized. Shopping malls, TV talk shows, computer consoles, fax machines, rock videos: all quick-time processing machines for harvesting the body of its organic juices, and draining bone and tissue into an indefinite spiral of telemetry" (104). Kroker and Weinstein are punning vampirically, but they may not be kidding when they write that the new "virtual class" of technocrats "for not understanding virtual hubris...is condemned to eternal repetition of the same data byte" (83).

Is Jennifer Wicke justified in interpreting all of the modern media in Stoker's novel as vampiric, or in claiming that Dracula himself "comprises the techniques of [mass] consumption" (475)? Certainly Dracula, forefather of Hannibal Lecter, is a figure of consumption gone awry, of consumption as cannibalistic lust and as a sort of medieval plague at the heart of modernity which causes it to cannibalize itself. The devil made him do it, or perhaps the devil made him. But London in the 1890s was a world capital of mass consumption, consisting of all of the ingredients of up-to-date mass culture. Stoker hoped, too, that his monster story would become a monster best-seller, and that it could easily be transferred to the stage for another version of mass consumption. (He himself wrote a stage version of it.) And *Dracula* incorporates a complex range of modern mass fetishes and phobias including occultism, anti-Semitism, anti-feminism, xenophobia, fears about sexual perversions, and anxieties about imperial and racial degeneration. The extent to which Stoker shared these fetishes and phobias with the mass readership of his day is unclear, but he was certainly willing to exploit them, vamping his readers in the process.

Stoker presents the relationship between vampirism and both science and the modern mass media as a sort of puzzle for the reader to figure out rather than a straightforward assertion that they are either aligned or antithetical. The late Victorian discourse of racial degeneration versus racial progress mediates between them. This combination—monstrosity, race, science—was fundamental to the emergence of science fiction from *Frankenstein* to H. G. Wells and Bram Stoker. It was also how many other writers between the 1890s and the 1930s problematized their relationship to both science and the mass media. It isn't simply that late Victorian and modernist writers were opposed to science, the new mass media, or mass culture. In regard to the media, many of them saw both the utopian and the dystopian potentials of the telephone, the phonograph, radio, and cinema (see, for example, Avery). The forms—the media—were wonderful, almost magical;

the content—mass culture, or what people did with the new media—was less than wonderful. Both the media and mass culture, however, were often conceived in Stoker's terms as vampiric, just as industrialism and machinery had earlier been conceived by many Romantic and Victorian writers as dystopian and as signs and causes of racial degeneration.

For many modernist as well as late Victorian writers (think of T. S. Eliot's "The Hollow Men" and "The Wasteland"), the danger came from what the masses would do with the new mass media, but also from what the media would do to the masses. Radio and the movies, like Wells's "Babble Machine," or like television and the Internet today, were often accused of having a hypnotic power that might overwhelm the masses with advertising, disinformation, and cultural trash. The upshot might be, as the historian G. M. Trevelyan opined in 1900, not invasion by the "yellow peril" from Asia but an internal collapse caused by the "white peril." In short, the new mass men and women, creatures of the mass media, would overwhelm the world as a self-replicating population of mental zombies, sucking the life's blood out of genuine culture and marching, like Stoker's vampires or Karl Čapek's robots, into totalitarianism and disaster.

Epilogue

Kipling's "The White Man's Burden" and Its Afterlives

> The prevailing force in my undergraduate days was not Socialism but
> Kiplingism. Our set was quite exceptional in its socialistic professions. And
> we were all...very distinctly Imperialists also, and professed a vivid sense of
> the "White Man's Burden."
>
> H. G. Wells, *The New Machiavelli*

At an 1898 meeting of the Anglo-African Writers' Club, its president,
H. Rider Haggard, introduced his friend Rudyard Kipling as a "true
watchman of our Empire." Haggard declared: "I do not believe in the divine right of kings, but I do believe...in a divine right of a great civilising
people—that is, in their divine mission. Yes, it is the voice of those true
watchmen of whom I speak that warns, that stirs the blood and braces
the minds of peoples, awakening them from the depth of sloth and self-
seeking." Haggard went on to say that Kipling, as a great patriot and
supporter of the British Empire, "has communed with the very Spirit
of our race" (Cohen, *Rudyard Kipling* 35–36). Haggard was referring to
the English "race," which he believed was the greatest imperial race the
world had ever known. He probably also meant the extended Anglo-
Saxon race—the white colonizers of India, North America, Australia,
New Zealand, and southern Africa. Both he and Kipling shared the faith
in the "divine mission" of the white race to conquer, rule, and attempt to
civilize all of the inferior, nonwhite races of the world.

This "divine mission" Kipling attempted to communicate to his friends in the United States by offering them his poem "The White Man's Burden." On November 22, 1898, he sent it to Theodore Roosevelt, who had just been elected governor of New York.[1] Kipling's specific aim was to encourage the United States to take over the Philippines, one of the territorial prizes of the Spanish-American War, and rule it with the same energy, honor, and beneficence that, he believed, characterized British rule over the nonwhite populations of India and Africa. A month earlier he had written to Roosevelt: "Now go in and put all the weight of your influence into hanging on permanently to the whole Philippines. America has gone and stuck a pickaxe into the foundations of a rotten house and she is morally bound to build the house over again from the foundations or have it fall about her ears" (*Letters* 2:350).

"The White Man's Burden" repeated this advice, adding a more abstract message about the white race's superiority and responsibility to the Filipinos and the other nonwhite peoples of the world. Forwarding Kipling's poem to Senator Henry Cabot Lodge, Roosevelt opined that it was "rather poor poetry" but that it made "good sense from the expansion standpoint." Agreeing about "the expansion standpoint," Lodge responded that it was "better poetry than you say" (Lodge and Redmond 384–85). Only later, in February 1899, was the poem published simultaneously in the *Times* of London and *McClure's Magazine* in the United States (Keating, *Kipling* 119).

Few poems have been more frequently cited, criticized, and satirized than "The White Man's Burden." It has served as a lightning rod for both the supporters and the opponents of imperialism, as well as of racism and white supremacy. This epilogue reviews the main context of Kipling's poem—America's colonization of the Philippines—and examines some of the uses to which "The White Man's Burden" has been put from 1898 to the present. Henry Labouchère's 1899 poem "The Brown Man's Burden" indicates that parodies and citations began to appear almost immediately. "The Black Man's Burden" was the title of many parodies and more serious poems in the African American press. While the Philippines was still an American colony, Edmund Morel's 1920 book *The Black Man's Burden* stood Kipling's message on its head by arguing against empire, and between the world wars other works with similar titles criticized racism in Britain and the United States.[2] Such criticism might be viewed as symptomatic of the decline and fall of the European empires and racism with them. But "The White Man's Burden" expresses a version of white supremacism that continues to influence the cultures and policies of Britain and its former colonies, including the United States, in the twenty-first century. Today's "neoracism" emphasizes cultural instead of biological differences between human populations, but it is still racism (Balibar and Wallerstein; McCarthy). The anti-Islamic phobia that was greatly exacerbated by 9/11 is an obvious example. So is the general anti-immigration sentiment in both the United States and Britain. And the invasions of Afghanistan and Iraq, stoked by anti-Islamic attitudes, have been rationalized by the imperialist belief that the United States, with Britain as its ally, can and should exercise what the Pentagon refers to as "full-spectrum dominance" throughout the world.

In the 1900s, most works that invoked Kipling's poem were parodic or critical in some fashion. It provoked criticism mainly because, as Peter Keating puts it, "there can be no doubt that the poem is profoundly racist in sentiment" (*Kipling* 120). But in response to America's "new imperialism" in Iraq, Afghanistan, and elsewhere, there have been various attempts to refurbish Kipling and "The White Man's Burden." Thus, for the title of his 2002 prizewinning book *The Savage Wars of Peace,* Max Boot chose a line from the poem, which he cites more fully and with explicit approval in the text itself. Although Boot and other current proponents of American imperialism deny or ignore this obvious fact, unless one wears a white blindfold, Kipling's poem makes the connection between imperialism and racism inescapable.

Is it despite or because of his racism and imperialism that Kipling will always be regarded, in the words of T. S. Eliot, as "very nearly a great writer" (quoted in Green 326)? The same question can be asked of other Victorian and modernist authors who took the empire as one of their themes. Kipling certainly did not recognize that the ideology of white supremacism he expressed throughout his career was any impediment to his faithful portrayal of India, South Africa, or any of the nonwhite or, for that matter, white peoples of the world. As his portrait of the lama in *Kim* suggests, Kipling like many other late Victorians was strongly attracted to Buddhism. He made a religion out of imperialism, however, and that ideology situated "the white man" with his "burden" at the top of history's great pyramid.

Kipling, the United States, and the Philippines

Whether or not Kipling's poem had any positive influence on public opinion, it is unlikely that it affected what the United States government decided to do about the Philippines. And if the many parodies of it are any indication, its influence may have been more negative than positive. Kipling flattered himself that Roosevelt in particular listened to his advice. But like many Americans by the 1890s, Roosevelt was already a believer in the duty or destiny of the white race to either civilize or exterminate the dark races of the world.[3] In *The Winning of the West* (1889), the future president of the United States had viewed the destruction of Native America by the advance of "the white man" as both inevitable and necessary for the sake of progress. Moreover, Roosevelt was pushing for war with Spain well before 1898. As leader of the "Rough Riders," he had helped win the battle of San Juan Hill in Cuba on July 1, 1898, and by then he was also advocating the annexation of the Philippines (*Letters and Speeches* 123). Although President McKinley was at first waffly about colonizing the archipelago—he confessed that, before the Spanish-American War, he didn't even know where the Philippines was (Morgan, *McKinley* 387–88)—Roosevelt, Lodge, and many other American politicians were already in favor of empire.

The doctrine of "Manifest Destiny" arose at the time of the war with Mexico in 1846–1848, which led to the addition of Texas, California, and most of the territory between them to the United States, and in the 1890s it seemed logical to many Americans to keep right on expanding into the Pacific and beyond. "Manifest Destiny" was often also expressed in terms of race: it was the destiny of the white, especially Anglo-Saxon race to conquer and civilize the American West and perhaps the entire uncivilized world (Horsman, *Race;* Healy 29–33). After the Civil War, along with social Darwinism, the idea that Anglo-Saxons around the world formed a unity in racial dominance suggested to many a reuniting, at least informally, of the British Empire with the United States, and this also is at least implicit in Kipling's poem. "Kipling hoped that the growing strength of the United States could be harnessed to the existing British Empire," writes Christopher Hitchens, and "race was the natural cement" (72).

In *The Poetry of Rudyard Kipling,* Ann Parry claims that "the response of the US public" to the aftermath of the Spanish-American War "was to reject imperialist adventures as alien to their political traditions" (87), but that notion is belied by the actions of the government and opinions in the mainstream press. Although an anti-imperialist minority, which included such prominent figures as Mark Twain, William James, Jane Addams, Samuel Gompers, and Andrew Carnegie, spoke out against the American seizure of the Philippines, it was never more than that—a minority.[4] The black press, too, was generally anti-imperialist, often siding with the dark "races" of the world, including the Filipinos, against white colonization (Marks; Gatewood). In the late 1890s African Americans were conflicted, however, because it was the Republican Party—the party of Lincoln—that was pro-empire, while the Democratic Party was still remembered for its proslavery stance. There was also an isolationist position whose advocates argued that precisely because Filipinos did not belong to the white race, the United States had no business taking over their territory and trying to civilize them: unlike Texas or California, the Philippines never could or should be turned into a state. That view was influenced by the fantasy of the "yellow peril," triggered in the United States by the migration of Chinese gold miners and railway workers into the West. But the war fever aroused by the conflict with Spain, the euphoria over easy victories, the argument that if the United States didn't take the islands then some other imperialist power would do so, and the general belief that anything Britain, France, or other nations could do America could do better overwhelmed both anti-imperialism and isolationism. Racism in this context was simply a given, treated as axiomatic.

The "splendid little war" against Spain, as Secretary of State John Hay called it, ended in 1899, but it was followed by the Philippine-American War. The Filipinos were already engaged in a revolution against Spanish rule, and once American forces took over Manila, the revolutionaries discovered that they had to fight on—this time against their new colonial overlords. After Admiral Dewey defeated the Spanish fleet in Manila harbor in 1898, the United States could have allowed the Filipino revolutionaries, led by Emilio Aguinaldo, to establish the republic that they had already proclaimed. Privately McKinley said, "If old Dewey had just sailed away when he smashed that Spanish fleet, what a lot of trouble he would have saved us" (quoted in Morgan, *McKinley* 388). Instead, for a variety of reasons—strategic, economic, racist—the U.S. Army arrived to take control of Manila, with the collaboration of the defeated Spaniards themselves. Aguinaldo and his forces were shut out from their capital city, and were inevitably thrust into the long conflict that ended in their defeat and the recolonization of the Philippines by the United States.

A prelude to both World War II and the Vietnam War, combat in the Philippines meant that American troops for the first time found themselves fighting in Asia. It proved to be a far longer, bloodier struggle than the one against Spain. Although Roosevelt claimed in 1902 that American forces had defeated the "Tagalog insurrection," as he insisted on calling it, the warfare didn't end then. He and other American officials labeled the post-1902 fighting "banditry" instead of either war or "insurrection" (Roosevelt, *Presidential Addresses* 2:571), which was similar to calling the Indian Rebellion of 1857–58 a "Mutiny." But on Luzon some conflict continued until at least 1911 (Pomeroy 97), and anti-imperialist resistance persisted in Mindanao and the other southern islands well beyond that date—indeed, down to the present. The Moro National Liberation Front is only the latest version of what has been called a "perpetual insurgency" (Bacevich 38). In recent years U.S. troops have been trying—this time with the good wishes of Philippines presidents Gloria Arroyo and Benigno Aquino III—to track down and capture or exterminate the supposedly Al-Qaeda-linked members of the Abu Sayyaf group, which on February 14, 2005, detonated bombs in the cities of Davao, General Santos, and Manila, killing at least twelve people and wounding many more.

During the Philippine-American War, on Luzon alone as many as a million Filipinos may have been killed either in combat or as "collateral damage" (Francisco). General J. Franklin Bell put the figure at 616,000, still enormous (Slotkin 119).[5] The official body count for American troops was 4,234 dead and buried in the Philippines; "scarcely any bodies were ever brought home," though "hundreds more later died in America of service-related diseases, 2,818 had been wounded, and the dollar cost came to six hundred million" (Wolff 360). What Kipling made of the bloody American conquest of the Philippines is unclear. He wrote "The White Man's Burden" before the fighting had turned into a major guerrilla war, and besides, he became much more concerned about the Anglo-Boer War.

As the fighting extended through the archipelago, however, plenty of evidence emerged that might have turned Kipling against what the American army was doing, as it did Mark Twain, for example, whose "To the Person Sitting in Darkness" is only the best-known of his critiques of U.S.

imperialism (Twain 22–39). "The devastation and hundreds of thousands of casualties wrought by American efforts to crush the so-called insurgency," writes Michael Adas, "made a mockery of...Kipling's celebration of the Americans as the latest of the Anglo-Saxon peoples to take up the 'white man's burden'" (155). Filipino POWs were frequently tortured or murdered; the "water cure"—or as it is now called by the Pentagon and CIA "water boarding"—was a standard practice. After the Balangiga massacre of U.S. soldiers by Filipino insurgents, the orders were to turn the entire island of Samar into a "howling wilderness" by killing everyone capable of bearing arms, including women and children aged ten years and up (Slotkin 117–19). Far more Filipinos were killed than wounded, reversing the normal pattern of warfare (Storey 126–29). What McKinley told Congress about the brutality of the Spanish troops trying to crush the anticolonial rebellion in Cuba applies just as well to the American troops in the Philippines: "It was not civilized warfare....It was extermination. The only peace it could beget was that of the wilderness and the grave" (quoted in Storey 139).

Torture and other brutal practices were rationalized by claims that the Filipinos were savages who fought like savages. Many of the American officers and troops had fought in the Indian wars in the West, and a lot of them behaved as if the only good Filipino was a dead one (Roth). White soldiers called their Filipino adversaries "googoos" and "niggers," but the Spaniards had called them "Indios," and comparisons between Filipinos and Native Americans cropped up everywhere in the press (Slotkin 109–10). The Filipinos were erroneously said to be divided into eighty-four separate "tribes," and "tribal" peoples were supposedly unfit for self-government. Newly elevated to the presidency after McKinley's assassination, Roosevelt told Congress on December 3, 1901, that "encouragement...to [the Filipino] insurrectos stands on the same footing as encouragement to hostile Indians in the days when we still had Indian wars" (*Presidential Addresses* 2:571). Elsewhere he compared Aguinaldo to Sitting Bull (*Letters and Speeches* 247). In his 1901 book *The Philippines: The War and the People*, Albert Robinson declared that the Filipino "presents a strong resemblance to the American red man" (229). Furthermore, "some tribes [of Filipinos] may be friendly, but it is quite probable that the hatchet will be buried in a very shallow place and very near at hand. Much will depend upon the vigor displayed by the nation and the missionary societies in efforts to civilize and Christianize them.

The process will not prove locally popular" (235). Robinson was right that "the process" did not prove "locally popular." But civilizing and Christianizing was difficult in part because, as the 1903 census indicated, the vast majority of Filipinos were already civilized and Christianized, albeit Roman Catholic rather than Protestant.

Kipling did not trouble himself any more than did McKinley, Roosevelt, or Robinson about what the Filipinos were actually like. As far as he was concerned, they were a "new-caught, sullen" people, "half devil and half child," and, like dark-skinned savages and barbarians elsewhere, in need of the strong hand and tutelage of the white man. Whether he was disturbed by or even aware of press reports regarding torture, concentration camps, and massacres of Filipino civilians by American troops is unknown. But his friendship with Roosevelt and later with William Cameron Forbes, who served as governor of the Philippines from 1909 to 1913, ensured that he viewed the results in a positive light.[6] He no doubt commiserated when the president wrote to him on November 1, 1904, about those who opposed American policy in the Philippines:

> Thus, in dealing with the Philippines I have first the jack fools who seriously think that any group of pirates and head-hunters needs nothing but independence in order that it may be turned forthwith into a dark-hued New England town meeting, and then the entirely practical creatures who join with these extremists because I do not intend that the islands shall be exploited for corrupt purposes. (Roosevelt, *Letters and Speeches* 357)

David Gilmour writes that Forbes convinced Kipling that American "imperialism was flourishing in the Pacific" (252; see also Stanley). In turn, Kipling assured Forbes that it was a "glorious experience" to see the progress British rule was making in Egypt and the Sudan, despite or because of the machine-gunning of eleven thousand Mahdist "dervishes" at the battle of Omdurman in 1898. Kipling added: "My fear (not that it's any of my business but we're all white men together) is that some fool Democratic spasm may land your people with a full-blooded modern constitution....May Allah preserve your land [the Philippines] from this fate and enable you to continue your works in peace" (quoted in Gilmour 240).

It was not exactly "some fool Democratic spasm" but Woodrow Wilson who in 1913 removed Forbes from the governorship of the Philippines— abruptly and unfairly, according to Kipling. In *Something of Myself*, Kipling says of Forbes:

There was an ex-Governor of the Philippines, who had slaved his soul out for years to pull his charge into some sort of shape and—on a turn of the political wheel in Washington—had been dismissed at literally less notice than he would have dared to give a native orderly. I remember not a few men whose work and hope had been snatched from under their noses, and my sympathy was very real. His account of Filipino political "leaders," writing and shouting all day for "independence" and running round to him after dark to be assured that there was no chance of the dread boon being granted—"because then we shall most probably all be killed"—was cheeringly familiar. (114)

Both Roosevelt and, more obviously, Forbes exemplified one of Kipling's primary fantasies throughout his fiction and poetry, that of the white colonial administrator whose labors receive little or no thanks from those he serves, both abroad and at home:

> Take up the White Man's burden—
> And reap his old reward:
> The blame of those ye better,
> The hate of those ye guard—
> The cry of hosts ye humour
> (Ah, slowly!) toward the light:—
> "Why brought ye us from bondage,
> Our loved Egyptian night?" (*Complete Verse* 322)

The work or "burden" of empire, Kipling believed, was typically thankless, frustrating, and often doomed to failure. "The White Man's Burden," writes John Kucich, "is perhaps the most famous expression of masochistic jingoism. With its rapturous celebration of sacrifice, toil, and ingratitude, it promotes an apocalyptic vision of history, bestowing on the imperialist the mantle of the Israelites—a chosen people tried by suffering" (8). Nevertheless, the lines about how "sloth and heathen folly" may "Bring all your hope to nought" have been read as a warning *against* imperialism (Love 198), but that is a stretch.

Perhaps the victory at Omdurman led Kipling to qualify "night" with the adjective "Egyptian" instead of Filipino, Asiatic, or Oriental. In any event, he clearly regarded 1898, in large measure also because of the Spanish-American War, as "a grand year for the White Man." Besides "The White Man's Burden," earlier in the year Kipling had penned "A

Song of the White Men," extolling the good that "the White Men" do
"When they go to clean a land":

> Oh, well for the world when the White Men tread
> Their highway side by side!...
> Oh, well for the world when the White Men join
> To prove their faith again!   (*Complete Verse* 280)

At last the (white) Americans were beginning to see the light and to do as
Britain had been doing for centuries. "Thank God" the Americans, Kipling wrote, were "on the threshold of the White Man's work, the business
of introducing a sane and orderly administration into the dark places of
the earth" (quoted in Gilmour 125–26).

By 1898 the popularity of his stories and poems helped Kipling believe
that he had the ability and the duty to serve as a spokesman for the British
Empire and, what amounted to the same thing as far as he was concerned,
for "the white man." The hubris evident in "The White Man's Burden"
also involves its author's assumption that his experience of India and the
United States and his friendship with great white men such as Haggard,
Cecil Rhodes, and Roosevelt equipped him to speak expertly about the
situation in the Philippines, a place containing multiple cultures about
which he knew nothing except what he had gleaned from the newspapers, and also to give advice not just to the United States but to the entire
"white race." Anxious about the Boer War, the rise of the Indian National
Congress, rivalries over imperialist expansion among the European nations and the United States, racial degeneration at home, and other signs
of the weakening of British control over its colonies, Kipling responded
in a mode of denial, by assuming "a basically uncontested empire," as
Edward Said puts it. "The division between white and non-white, in
India and elsewhere, was absolute, and is alluded to throughout...Kip-
ling's work; a Sahib is a Sahib, and no amount of friendship or camara-
derie can change the rudiments of racial difference" (Said, *Culture and
Imperialism* 134–35).

Kipling's racial absolutism allowed him to praise some aspects of Indian cultures and behaviors without relinquishing his belief in the racial
inferiority of all the nonwhite peoples of the world. That innate inferiority, however, meant the civilizing mission that justified the British Empire
could never be accomplished. The task of taming cannibals or savages was

endless; the white man with his burden might as well have been Sisyphus. Concerning British attempts to educate a class of Indians, the "Babus," in English language and literature, Kipling wrote to Haggard in 1913: "Well, whose fault is it that the Babu is what he is? *We* did it. We began in Macaulay's time: we have worked without intermission for three generations to make this Caliban. Every step and thought on the road is directly traceable to England and English influence" (Cohen, *Rudyard Kipling* 77). Painting Indians white was creating Babus, not white men. For Kipling, the idea of leaving the governance of India up to Indians was preposterous. He considered himself an expert on India, and yet he also asserted that the mind of the Indian was incomprehensible. He clearly believed himself expert enough to condemn Indian literature in terms at least as harsh as Macaulay's in his 1835 "Minute on Indian Education." In an 1886 letter Kipling says about the Ramayana, the Rig-Veda, and similar works: "I see every now and then at home some man who hasn't touched 'em lifting up his voice in praise of 'the golden mines of Oriental Literature' and I snort. There are one or two things worth the reading but to get at them one has to wade through a muck heap" (*Writings on Writing* 112).

In the aftermath of World War I, when it became evident that India was on the road to independence, Kipling despaired. In 1919 Haggard wrote about his friend: "Kipling believes ... that the worst thing that is happening to us as an Empire is what he calls 'the handing over of India'" (Cohen, *Rudyard Kipling* 111). This passage in Haggard's diary for August 25, 1919, begins with a comment about Kipling's anti-Semitism and the Russian Revolution: "Kipling ... is of opinion that we owe all our Russian troubles, and many others, to the machinations of the Jews. I do not know, I am sure, but personally I am inclined to think that one can insist too much on the Jew motive" (111–12). Haggard's hesitancy regarding "the Jew motive" indicates a relative modesty about using race to explain politics and history, or at least a modesty about jumping to conclusions, seldom evident in Kipling. For Kipling as for Benjamin Disraeli, Dr. Robert Knox, and many other Victorians, "all is race." No turn-of-the-century writer illustrates more clearly than the author of *Kim* the legacy of racism and its ties to imperialism that extends from the Enlightenment into the twenty-first century. If *Kim* expresses Kipling's appreciation and nostalgia for Indian culture at its literary best, "The White Man's Burden" expresses his racism and imperialist hubris at its worst.

The Burden of Rudyard Kipling

The idea that the majority of Filipinos were savages, "half devil and half child," in need of civilizing by the United States or some other branch of the white race (but not the Spaniards), is an obvious instance of the standard justification for imperial expansion used from the Renaissance to the twenty-first-century situation of "nation building" in Afghanistan and Iraq. Nevertheless, "The White Man's Burden" seemed offensive to many of its first readers, no doubt because of Kipling's preaching to Americans, but sometimes also because of the poem's white supremacist ideology. Besides Filipinos, it was especially offensive to African Americans. In *Black Americans and the White Man's Burden,* Willard Gatewood writes, "Dozens of poems entitled 'The Black Man's Burden' appeared in the months immediately following the publication of Kipling's work" (184).[7] Gatewood quotes as an example these verses by "a well-known black clergyman and editor of the influential *Christian Recorder,*" H. T. Johnson:

> Pile on the Black Man's Burden.
> 'Tis nearest at your door;
> Why heed long bleeding Cuba,
> Or dark Hawaii's shore?
> Hail ye your fearless armies,
> Which menace feeble folks
> Who fight with clubs and arrows
> And brook your rifle's smoke. (quoted in Gatewood 184)

Gatewood observes that there was even an organization, the Black Man's Burden Association, founded by J. H. Magee late in 1899 to advocate for rights for blacks at home and Filipinos and other "brown people" abroad (184).

J. Dallas Bowser's "Take Up the Black Man's Burden," which was published in the April 8, 1899, issue of *The Colored American,* recognizes that racism at home and imperialism abroad are inseparable, but is less a mocking of Kipling's poem than an expression of the theme of "black uplift" or self-improvement:

> Take up the Black Man's burden,
> "Send forth the best ye breed"

To serve as types of progress,
To teach, to pray, to plead.

As Booker T. Washington was advising them to do, African Americans, according to Bowser, should shoulder their own burden for the betterment of the world.[8] A month earlier, however, *The Colored American* had published a poem under the pseudonym "X-Ray," titled "Charity Begins at Home," which more directly confronts both white racism and Kipling's poem:

> To h——with the "White Man's Burden!"
> To h——with Kipling's verse!
> The Black Man demands our attention:
> His condition is growing worse.
> Why lose sleep over his burden?
> All mortals have their share,
> The black man's growing hardships
> Are more than he can bear.

This barb is closer than Bowser's verses to the editorial position of *The Colored American,* which on March 18, 1899, declared: "With all due respect for the alleged genius of one Rudyard Kipling, his latest conglomeration of rot about the 'white man's burden' makes us very, very tired. It has ever been the dark races who have borne the world's burdens" (Nichols 118).[9]

In 1907 the leading African American intellectual W. E. B. Du Bois entered the lists with "The Burden of Black Women." Therein, the "dark daughter of the lotus leaves that watch the Southern sea" grieves because "the Burden of white men bore her back, / and the white world stifled her sighs." The "White World's vermin and filth," writes Du Bois, include

> conquerors of unarmed men;
> Shameless breeders of bastards
> Drunk with the greed of gold.
> Baiting their blood-stained hooks
> With cant for the souls of the simple,
> Bearing the White Man's Burden
> Of Liquor and Lust and Lies!

Matters will not change until "the Black Christ be born!"

> Then shall the burden of manhood
> Be it yellow or black or white,

And Poverty, Justice and Sorrow—
The Humble and Simple and Strong
Shall sing with the Sons of Morning
And Daughters of Evensong. (Du Bois, "Burden" 291–93)

Besides Kipling's poem, Du Bois echoes the African American spiritual, in which the oppressed—indeed, all humanity—look forward to a time when we can lay our burdens down.

Kipling also had his British anti-imperialist critics and parodists. Wilfred Scawen Blunt declared that the true "white man's burden" was "the burden of his cash," and Richard Le Gallienne seemed to echo Robert Buchanan's earlier "Voice of the Hooligan," which attacked Kipling's schoolboy novel *Stalky & Co.* by declaring that "The White Man's Burden" expressed "the Englishman as brute" (quoted in Gilmour 131–32). In the journal *Truth,* radical M. P. Henry Labouchère published "The Brown Man's Burden"; it was republished in the February 25, 1899, issue of the *Literary Digest,* side by side with Kipling's poem and with still another parody by Ernest H. Crosby. The first stanza of Labouchère's parody reads:

Pile on the brown man's burden
To gratify your greed;
Go, clear away the "niggers"
Who progress would impede;
Be very stern, for truly
'Tis useless to be mild
With new-caught, sullen peoples
Half devil and half child.

In stanza five, Labouchère writes:

Pile on the brown man's burden,
Nor do not deem it hard
If you should earn the rancor
Of those ye yearn to guard.
The screaming of your Eagle
Will drown the victim's sob—
Go on through fire and slaughter.
There's dollars in the job. (Labouchère 219)

The gist of many of the early parodies is anti-imperialist, as in this bit of doggerel from a U.S. newspaper: "We've taken up the white man's burden of ebony and brown; / Now will you tell us, Rudyard, how we may put it down?" (quoted in Morgan, *McKinley* 434).

Nevertheless, Kipling and his poem had their admirers on both sides of the Atlantic. William Jennings Bryan, who took a "devious" stance toward McKinley's Philippines policy during the election campaign of 1899 (Lens 185), titled the Independence Day speech he gave in London on July 4, 1906, "The White Man's Burden." Although he was unhappy about the colonization of the Philippines by the United States, Bryan nonetheless agreed that "the white man" had a "burden" or responsibility to civilize the colonized.[10] If America was going to have an empire, then, Bryan argued, it had better be a humane one: "There is a white man's burden—a burden which the white man should not shirk even if he could" (quoted in Zwick).

In 1902 the American novelist Thomas Dixon published *The Leopard's Spots,* subtitled *A Romance of the White Man's Burden.* Dixon also penned *The Clansman* (1905), and it is on these two novels, together with the play based on the second one, that D. W. Griffith based his racist cinematic masterpiece *The Birth of a Nation* (1915), which was originally titled *The Clansman.* In Dixon's novels and Griffith's film, the Ku Klux Klan "is glorified for its work in bringing order from the chaos that followed" the Civil War (Cook, *Dixon* 68–69). Although some bad white men who claim to be KKK members terrorize and occasionally lynch blacks in Dixon's stories and Griffith's movie, the true Klansmen are heroic fighters for justice and a chivalric version of white supremacy. Dixon's and Griffith's KKK heroes, shouldering "the white man's burden" in South Carolina rather than India or the Philippines, aren't much different from Kipling's heroic but unappreciated colonial administrators.

After the Boer War, Kipling's literary reputation declined. He was too bumptious, too ideological, too racist to be considered a great writer. A number of his stories and poems, *The Jungle Books,* and *Kim* continued to be admired, though often in qualified terms. But since 9/11, writes Geoffrey Wheatcroft, "Kipling has resurfaced, and not just because of his lines about fighting on the Afghan plains" (84). "The White Man's Burden" in particular has been invoked by the defenders of America's "new imperialism" in Iraq and elsewhere. The editors of *Pox Americana: Exposing the American Empire* write:

> Today's imperialists see Kipling's poem mainly as an attempt to stiffen the
> spine of the U.S. ruling class of his day in preparation for what he called "the
> savage wars of peace." And it is precisely in this way that they now allude to
> the "white man's burden" in relation to the twenty-first century. Thus for
> the *Economist* magazine the question is simply whether the United States is
> prepared to shoulder the white man's burden across the Middle East. (Foster and McChesney 20).

The editors have Max Boot's *Savage Wars of Peace* in mind as one prominent instance of American neoimperialism. Boot claims that the U.S. military succeeded in the Philippines, in contrast to its later failure in Vietnam, and that the record of American colonial rule in the archipelago, though somewhat marred by racial arrogance, was generally constructive (126–28). "Benevolent assimilation" was, McKinley announced, the policy the United States would pursue in the Philippines, and according to Boot, it actually did so. But like (white) "colonialists everywhere," Boot claims, the U.S. administrators of the Philippines "received scant thanks," a phenomenon that leads to one of his several quotations from Kipling:

> Take up the White man's burden—
> And reap his old reward:
> The blame of those ye better,
> The hate of those ye guard.   (345)

For both Boot and Kipling, these lines express an interesting reversal on blaming the victim: there is nothing like conquest and empire, it seems, for making imperialists feel sorry for themselves.

What America did in the Philippines, Boot claims, is pretty much what it should be doing in Iraq. So too Michael Ignatieff predicted that the invasion and occupation of Iraq would follow the pattern of the Philippines from 1898 to 1946 (Foster and McChesney 18). Like Boot, Ignatieff deems the resemblance is a salutary one, because (he asserts) America's impact on the Philippines was largely positive. But the United States can do even better in Iraq:

> America's empire is not like empires of times past, built on colonies, conquest and the white man's burden. We are no longer in the era of the United

Fruit Company, when American corporations needed Marines to secure
their investments overseas. The 21st century imperium is a new invention
in the annals of political science, an empire lite, a global hegemony whose
grace notes are free markets, human rights and democracy. (Ignatieff 23)

The main difference between Boot and Ignatieff appears to be that the
former is happy with the idea of "the white man's burden," while the latter attributes it to an earlier, un-lite and perhaps unenlightened version of
empire.

Like Boot rather than Ignatieff, Robert Kaplan has no trouble em-
bracing Kipling. In his review of Kaplan's *Imperial Grunts: The American
Military on the Ground,* Andrew Bacevich points out that Kaplan has been
dubbed "America's Kipling" (34). Its author, writes Bacevich, is "bullish"
on America's new global empire: "The events of September 11, 2001, in-
augurated what Kaplan calls America's 'Second Expeditionary Era'—the
first had begun with the expansionist surge of 1898—in which US forces
once again sally forth to take up 'the white man's burden,' a phrase that he
employs without irony or apology" (Bacevich 35). Kaplan praises historian
Francis Parkman and western painter Frederic Remington as the "Kip-
lings" of "American imperialism" (Kaplan 9–10). And he believes that
Kipling got it right in regard to the Philippines, India, and Afghanistan
(Kaplan 175, 195).[11]

According to Boot, "the majority of Filipinos became reconciled to U.S.
rule or at least not violently opposed to it, and they were granted increasing
autonomy by Washington, far ahead of any comparable movement in European colonies" (125). This was just the way President George W. Bush
and his supporters wanted to interpret the record of America's colonization of the Philippines, with an eye to how they would like things to go in
Afghanistan and Iraq (and no doubt elsewhere). In *The Folly of Empire,*
John Judis notes that on October 18, 2003, while paying a brief visit to Manila, Bush praised the United States for transforming the Philippines into
"the first democratic nation in Asia." America, he proclaimed, "is proud
of its part in the great story of the Filipino people. Together our soldiers
liberated the Philippines from colonial rule. Together we rescued the islands from invasion and occupation" (quoted in Judis 1). And now, according to Bush, America was doing the same favor of bringing liberation
and democracy to Iraq. Bush was only repeating the standard chauvinistic
accounts of America's nation building in the Philippines, from Barrows

(1913) and Forbes (1928) to Ernest Lefever, who in *America's Imperial Burden* (1999) contends that not only was Britain's version of empire "civilizing and largely benign" (23) but so is America's. The Philippines is one of Lefever's examples (41). But he says nothing about the Philippine-American War or about Philippine nationalism and continued insurgency in the wake of that war. As far as he, Bush, Kaplan, and Max Boot are concerned, America successfully shouldered "the white man's burden" of imperial responsibility just as Kipling asked it to do (Lefever 22).

While it has often been held that America brought democracy, prosperity, and civilization to the Philippines, the actual record is rather different. Instead of freeing that nation from colonialism, "our soldiers" turned it into an American colony. I have already described the bloody quagmire that is nowadays called the Philippine-American War. In its aftermath, the new colonial masters of the islands worked hard to Americanize the Filipinos—short of giving the vast majority of Filipinos any genuine power or prosperity. Although the United States granted the Philippines independence in 1946, the American military presence meant that there would be no serious challenge to America's ultimate authority after the Japanese withdrew. The rulers of the Philippines have continued to come from the privileged elite who, so long as they support U.S. policies, are supported in return. In 1941 the Huk (or Hukbalahap) rebellion began as an uprising against Japanese rule; after the war it continued as an anticolonial communist insurgency, like the Vietminh in Indochina. The United States did everything it could to suppress the Huks, until the movement ran out of steam in the 1950s. But other forms of resistance have continued, in large measure because democracy in the Philippines has never been more than a "veneer." That is the term Judis employs; he writes that beneath the "veneer...a handful of families, allied to American investors and addicted to payoffs and kickbacks, [have] controlled Philippine land, economy, and society. The tenuous system broke down in 1973 when Ferdinand Marcos had himself declared president for life. Marcos was finally overthrown in 1986, but even today Philippine democracy is more dream than reality" (2).

Writing in the *New York Times,* in a piece titled "The White Man's Burden," economist Paul Krugman notes that Bush and other neoconservatives who regarded America's conquest and colonization of the Philippines as a model for what they hoped would transpire in Iraq might learn something if they paid closer attention to history. No evidence exists, Krugman says, to suggest that "control of the Philippines made us stronger" in strategic terms. And "the economic doctrines that were used to justify Western empire-building during the late 19th century... turned out to be nonsense. Almost without exception, the cost of acquiring and defending a colonial empire greatly exceeded even a generous accounting of its benefits" (Krugman 389). The moral that Bush and other neoconservatives drew from the example of the Philippines, Krugman contends—namely, that the invasion and occupation of Iraq would be good for the Iraqis and good for us—was a mirage. Calling "The White Man's Burden" the "perfect epitaph for the Bush administration," blogger Sharon Jumper adds, "Bush is such a nean-derthal, however, that were he to read the poem, he would likely think it laudatory of his current policies."[12]

Writing just before Kipling penned "The White Man's Burden," A. V. Dicey claimed: "The enforcement of the Pax Britannica throughout the British Empire, and the maintenance of civilized order throughout the length and breadth of the United States... is the main service which the Anglo-Saxon race renders to civilisation" (quoted in Rich 24). This was Kipling's faith. Citing Dicey in *Race and Empire in British Politics,* Paul Rich argues that "Anglo-Saxonist racial ideology had fallen into decline as the appeal to imperial race patriotism became increasingly unpopular in the wake of the Anglo-Boer War" (24). But the same "racial ideology" continued to be expressed, both in Britain and in the United States (not to mention France and other European countries), throughout the twentieth century. True, the ideologists of empire and "The White Man's Burden" toned down the explicit racism enmeshed in their support of Western imperialism, largely because of the emergence of fascism and Nazism and also because of the rise of decolonizing nationalisms throughout the world. Writing about the various "scandals"—war, genocide, slavery, loot-ing, the "drain" of wealth from India and other territories—that marked the origins of the British Empire, Nicholas Dirks remarks, "What is per-haps most disturbing in retrospect is the extent to which the scandals that were at the heart of imperial beginnings—not to mention the scandal of empire itself—have been either laundered or converted into narratives of imperial, nationalist, and capitalist triumph" (25). The scandals continue, and so does the laundering, as is evident in the patriotic fulminations of today's supporters of America's "empire lite" (maintained through war and the most powerful military in history) and their non-ironic echoes of Kipling's "The White Man's Burden."

Forever Kim

Despite his racism, his preachiness, and his dogmatic faith in the rectitude of the British Empire, Kipling was "very nearly a great writer." Perhaps in *Kim,* "The Man Who Would Be King," and several other stories and poems he achieved literary greatness. What constitutes that greatness? "I have never been able to read Kipling calmly," writes Salman Rushdie. "Anger and delight are incompatible emotions" (74). Yet he acknowledges that "no other Western writer has ever known India as Kipling knew it, and it is this knowledge of place, and procedure, and detail that gives his stories their undeniable authority" (75). Kipling's fictional successes, moreover, often stem from a contradiction basic to imperialist adventure tales. If the "burden" of "the white man" is to tame savages and barbarians, much of the non-burden of adventure lies in getting to know savages and barbarians—even getting familiar enough with them to go native, at least temporarily. Growing up in India until he was six, and then as a young reporter in Lahore, that is what Kipling did. His near-greatness as a writer is similar to Henry Mayhew's near-greatness as a social investigator. Both were journalists engaged in versions of ethnographic reporting. Mayhew's slumming and Kipling's real and imaginary versions of going native resulted in vivid portrayals of exotic characters and customs that still make for entertaining reading.

The writers of boys' adventure fiction depict plucky British lads behaving savagely in order either to defeat the savages or to escape from their clutches. Once that occurs, the story is over; the plucky lads ordinarily return safely to civilization. Sometimes, like Haggard's Allan Quatermain, the lads go adventuring among the savages in later stories. Ralph, Jack, and Peterkin in Robert Ballantyne's *Coral Island* (1857), for example, go home at the end of that best-seller, then head for "darkest Africa" in *The Gorilla Hunters* (1861). But where is home for Kim? He is a shapeshifter whose only home is on the road in India, forever playing "the Great Game" of espionage for the British secret service and forever serving as the lama's faithful *chela* or disciple. Kim plays both roles with delight, and his obvious enjoyment is shared by the reader. Kipling's Irish Indian scamp seems never to experience a dull moment.

Kipling asserted that *Kim* is "nakedly picaresque and plotless" (*Something of Myself* 132). It isn't plotless, but Kipling understood "the picaresque connection with Cervantes," writes Angus Wilson, who adds that the lama and Kim "recall…Quixote and Sancho Panza, a deeper, more original recall than Pickwick and Sam Weller" (129). As a novel of the road, *Kim* depicts its hero's adventures as always leading to something new and exciting, into a wide-open future of more adventures and more enjoyment. *Kim* is "concerned with movement rather than with the goal," writes Phillip Mallett (118); the Irish scamp and the other spies foil the Russian and French agents, but that seems anticlimactic: Kim's adventures are not over. The story is an innovative combination of the picaresque and the idyllic, which is similar to how Kipling viewed the British Empire—its youthful energies ever expanding through conflict and war, yet ever expanding the Pax Britannica. Michael Gorra, who calls *Kim* an idyll, contends that it omits history. The Ilbert Bill and the Indian National Congress play no role in it; the Indian Rebellion is viewed as an inexplicable "madness" that afflicted a few troops of sepoys. John McClure also claims that *Kim* omits history, which would involve "change and development" for both India and the protagonist. It emphasizes instead "either side of the historical process…the plenitude of the moment and the finality of the eternal" (80). Kim is focused on "the moment," the lama on "the eternal." The kaleidoscope of races, creeds, and cultures that Kim experiences seems in constant flux, and yet nothing fundamental changes. "Dotting *Kim*'s fabric is a scattering of editorial asides on the immutable nature of the Oriental world" (Said, *Culture and Imperialism* 149). Kipling wished to believe that the British Empire was also immutable.

Does Kim need to grow up, to choose between the roles of spy or disciple, or to become an English-educated imperial functionary like Colonel Creighton? Zoreh Sullivan writes that Kim's "journey towards 'education' [is also] a journey towards loss" (166). The brief description of St. Xavier's, where Kim is sent to be educated like an English boy, makes it sound penitential: " 'The Gates of Learning' shut with a clang" (174). Prominent in the St. Xavier episodes is the bullying the English drummer boy inflicts on Kim. Apart from that, the narrator says, "you would scarcely be interested in Kim's experiences as a St. Xavier's boy" (175). Kim manages to do well as a student, but while he is at St. Xavier's, only his adventures when he is on vacation or playing hooky are rendered in much detail. Sullivan continues: "The life of a Sahib in school, or out of it, is inevitably a life of cold competition whose final reward will be Kim's function as a cog in the imperial machine. His life on the road with the lama, on the contrary, is a carnival that inverts and democratizes the imperial hierarchy of class, creed, color and race" (172). But is Kim destined to become a Sahib? Or will he continue to be the lama's *chela*? At the novel's end, Kipling leaves the future of his Irish Indian Peter Pan in suspense, though with the impression that Kim will always do what is best for himself, for the lama, and for India, as though these aims were identical. His value as a "state nomad" (Richards 28) may be so great that Colonel Creighton would never want to turn him into a full-fledged "white man" or imperial functionary like himself.

Kim's brief time at St. Xavier's, where he is studying to be a civilized English boy, seems equivalent in the novel to the improbable ideal of taming India. As far as Kipling was concerned, ruling India was one thing; taming it was another and was altogether out of the question. In his otherwise perceptive analysis of *Kim*, Ian Baucom says the novel contains "a cultural reformatory disguising itself as a wonder house" (86). Apart from Kim's unappealing schooling at St. Xavier's, however, the only deliberate cultural reform going on is the dual, contradictory training he receives to become an effective spy and to comprehend the lama's Buddhism. Kim's most important education, which has prepared him for both roles, comes from the streets of Lahore. The novel depicts a few missionaries but no systematic attempt to reform Indian cultures or religions. India comes across as a wonderful spectacle, the externalized version of "the Wonder House"—a spectacle that is always changing but never progressing in any meaningful direction. And so, Kipling seems to say, India always has been and always will remain, in a perpetual childhood something like Kim's own apparently unending adolescence.[13]

Kim "lived in a life wild as that of the Arabian Nights, but missionaries and secretaries of charitable societies could not see the beauty of it" (3–4). That comment expresses a contradiction central to *Kim* and to many other literary works that deal with the imperialist theme of taming cannibals or civilizing savages. The "wild" side of the frontier provides the stories; the tame side represents the end of the thousand and one nights. When all of the savages still left alive have been subdued if not civilized, and when all of the heroes like Kim, Allan Quatermain, and Ralph Rover have settled down into sedentary, civilized routines, the great adventure will be over. The vanishing of adventure and romance is a standard theme in late Victorian fiction. "Soon the ancient mystery of Africa will have vanished," Haggard wrote in 1894. "Where will the romance writers of future generations find a safe and secret place, unknown to the pestilent accuracy of the geographer, in which to lay their plots?" (quoted in Etherington, *Rider Haggard* 66).

Various critics over the years have observed that Kipling had an inadequate idea of civilization. Robert Buchanan famously accused him of expressing a "hooligan imperialism"; Oscar Wilde said that Kipling "is a genius who drops his aspirates"; and Henry James asserted that his writings contained "almost nothing civilized save steam and patriotism" (quoted in Orel, *Critical Essays* 6–7). Kim is charming precisely because he is not civilized or tame. He is a wild boy who, the reader hopes, will never grow up to become a proper "white man" shouldering the "burden" of imperial rule. He is also an Irish orphan, and the Irish, Kipling believed, were "the Orientals of the West" (quoted in Gilmour 242). For that racist reason, or perhaps in spite of it, Kim is able to slip through all social and cultural doors and barricades and to be "the Little Friend of all the World."[14]

Underlying much of Kipling's writing, and that of many other British writers who dealt with the empire, is the contradiction between their own lived experience, involving the excitement of adventure and encounters with exotic peoples and cultures, and the twinned ideologies of imperialism and racism that caused them consciously, in the name of civilization, to belittle the lures of adventure and the exotic as always standing in need of "the white man's" rule. Presented with the false dichotomy between savagery and civilization, Kipling, Haggard, and many others asserted the rectitude of "The White Man's Burden" while also discovering countless ways of evading that burden. Wells put it succinctly in his *Outline of History* when he declared, "It was quite characteristic of [the 1890s and early 1900s] that Mr. Kipling should lead the children of the middle and upper-class British public back to the Jungle" (quoted in Green 306). That was not where Kipling and many other imperialist writers intended to lead their readers, but that was the locale of adventure and often also of great stories.

NOTES

Introduction

1. In his "Reformation of Manners, A Satyr" (1702), Defoe calls slave traders crueler than the Spanish conquistadors, who "drank the Blood of Gold and *Mexico*" (Defoe 389). But usually he defended that trade and "Negro" slavery as making good economic sense and as a potentially civilizing influence on the slaves and on Africa.

2. "I am as free as nature first made man, / Ere the base laws of servitude began, / When wild in woods the noble savage ran." John Dryden, *The Conquest of Granada* (1672), part 1, act 1, scene 1.

3. The reason for the difference between white and black people, Hume suspects, is not cultural; rather, "nature...made an original distinction between these breeds of men" (86). According to Roxann Wheeler, "the ideology of human variety broadly changed" in the 1700s in Britain from cultural factors such as religion and governance to "characteristics of the human body—color, facial features, and hair texture. At the end of the century, the contours of racial ideology were more established than a century before.... The transference from a cultural emphasis to a bodily emphasis was imperfect, of course, and occurred at various places in different realms that used racial ideology as a reference point" (291; see also Kitson 4).

4. Despite postcolonialism and the new imperial history, the topics of race and racism are downplayed or completely overlooked in several mainstream accounts of nineteenth-century British history. To paraphrase the title of Paul Gilroy's 1987 book, for the authors and editors of these accounts, there still "ain't no black in the Union Jack." The index to Kenneth Hoppen's seven-hundred-page *Mid-Victorian Generation* (1998) in the new *Oxford History of England* lists three

entries for "racialism" but none on race or racism. There is no entry on race or racism in the index to the 1999 revised edition of Kenneth Morgan's *Oxford History of Britain*, and John Cannon's 2001 *Oxford Dictionary of British History* is equally silent on that topic. Race and racism are missing as well in the second, 2007 edition of Norman McCord and Bill Purdue's *British History, 1815–1914*, also published by Oxford. John Plowright's *Routledge Dictionary of Modern British History* (2006) mentions "racism" once, in its article about Enoch Powell (211), but otherwise doesn't mention it. For Plowright, moreover, "modern British history" has very little to do with the British Empire. He includes articles on Ireland, on slavery and its abolition, and on the first and second Anglo-Boer Wars, but nothing about Australia, New Zealand, Canada, India, Egypt, or Kenya. None of these texts even hints at the fact that racism has been a constituent ideological aspect not just of modern European imperialisms but of modern history in general. When racism is abundantly apparent in modern cultures and histories, isn't it racist to ignore that fact?

5. Despite decolonization starting in the 1940s, the European and American imperial nations still exercise much power through what Kwame Nkrumah in 1961 called "neocolonialism," which means mainly economic domination coupled with the exercise of supposedly informal political influence.

6. An example of identifying all savagery with cannibalism is the Reverend Frederic Farrar's 1867 essay "Aptitudes of Races." A friend of Darwin's, Farrar was also an abolitionist. Nevertheless, regarding the African "negro," wrote Farrar, no Europeans "have weaned him, on his native continent from his cannibalism, his rain-doctors, his medicine-men, his mumbo-jumbo." (122). And Africans were not alone among "savages," who, according to Farrar, all made man eating a self-destructive custom.

7. According to Lippmann's liberal approach, if stereotyping is the basic process of public opinion, then it is basic to democracy. As versions of the "hermeneutics of suspicion," the other theoretical approaches—psychoanalysis, Marxism, poststructuralism—call liberalism and public opinion into question even while also critiquing authoritarian rhetoric and oppression. Yet according to all four approaches, all forms of representation are misrepresentation.

8. In *Difference and Pathology* (1985), Sander Gilman writes that "the closed world of language...carries and is carried by the need to stereotype." Furthermore, "stereotypical structures...dominate...daily mental life" (27). Nevertheless, Gilman claims it is imperative to "make the distinction between pathological stereotyping and the stereotyping all of us need to do to preserve our illusion of control over the self and the world" (18). Lippmann also insists on the importance of "detecting" stereotypes, because they can have nefarious consequences (85–102). So stereotyping is synonymous with the normal but defective mental operations of everyone, although some stereotypes are harmful or pathological. Detecting the pathological variety would seem to be the first step toward eliminating them, but Gilman instead writes: "The goal of studying stereotypes is not to stop the production of images of the Other, images that demean and, by demeaning, control. This would be the task of Sisyphus. We need these stereotypes to structure the world. We need crude representations of difference to localize our anxiety, to prove to ourselves that what we fear does not lie within" (240). But do "we need" anti-Semitism or homophobia? It is not possible to read Gilman without concluding that he wishes to eradicate those thought monstrosities. Because Gilman, however, starts from the assumption that stereotyping is representation in general, he seems unable to say just what diagnosing the "pathological" variety would accomplish. Many other experts on stereotyping disable themselves in the same manner.

9. According to Theodor Adorno and the other members of the Frankfurt School, ideology and modern mass culture are virtually synonymous, and their basic units are stereotypes. Thus, writing about film and television, Adorno declares that "the vocabulary of [their] image-writing is composed of stereotypes" (55). In *Dialectic of Enlightenment*, Adorno and Max Horkheimer argue that "the culture industry" produces "enlightenment as mass deception" (120–67). The "deception" involves "the stereotyped appropriation of everything...for the purposes of mechanical

reproduction" (127) and for the mass market. Hence the "false consciousness" of Herbert Marcuse's "one-dimensional man" consists of stereotypes, including the affirmation of the status quo as good or even "much better than before" (*One-Dimensional* 12).

10. For an account of the various forms of slavery through history, see David Brion Davis.

11. The more one looks for exceptions to the colonizer/colonized binary, the more one can find them. The relations between missionaries and non-missionary colonizers were often conflictual. Another distinction emerges between the colonizers in most imperial contexts and metropolitan authorities. White settlers in pre-1776 North America, for example, were in the position of the colonizer vis-à-vis Native Americans. But they were in the position of the colonized vis-à-vis the British government in London. Even more complex were those situations in which Native Americans became plantation and slave owners, as did some Cherokees, only to find themselves sent into exile on the Trail of Tears by President Andrew Jackson's Indian removal policy in the 1830s. Escaped slaves often joined Indian communities, while there were also numerous cases of whites captured by Indians during raids and warfare who, when they had a chance to return to white "civilization," chose to remain with their captors (see chapter 3). Were the white captives still in the position of colonizer, or had they in turn been colonized by the Indians? And what about slaves who escaped to freedom in Canada? Were they still in the position of the colonized? Or had they gone over to the side of the colonizers? These and many other complex, hybrid situations emerge in any detailed history of colonial relations.

12. Bhabha does not note that the term and concept of "the fetish" developed through early Portuguese slave trading and colonization in West Africa, predating Marxism (commodity fetishism) and Freudianism (sexual fetishism) by several centuries. The twin modern concepts of fetishism stem from the Portuguese stereotype of African religious beliefs as fetish worship. Does this mean that Bhabha's argument also follows, at least in part, a stereotypic logic?

13. Surveying psychoanalytic approaches to racism, Phil Cohen writes: "The foundations for a social psychology of prejudice were laid by Gordon Allport's *The Nature of Prejudice* (1954)....[His] theory was heavily cognitivist, drawing on and further elaborating the notion of stereotypification advanced by gestalt psychologists and phenomenologists in the 1920s and 1930s" (182). Neither the gestalt psychologists nor the phenomenologists nor Allport and his followers complicated their social-psychological versions of the stereotype via history. Stereotyping hence emerges from social psychology as always and invariably some version of "cognitive dissonance," like Bhabha's comparison of "the stereotype" (singular) to "the fetish" (singular), as if they were timeless products of the human psyche. According to this ahistorical line of argument, West Africans in the 1400s were no different from modern Westerners: they also believed in fetishes.

14. Fanon's other major writings, including *Wretched of the Earth,* are less concerned with psychology than with history and economics, but are nevertheless insistent on the colonizer/colonized binary.

15. Because Bhabha has authored separate essays on "the stereotype" and "hybridity," it is unclear how he would answer this question, although it seems likely his answer would be both.

1. Missionaries and Cannibals in Nineteenth-Century Fiji

1. To claim that Western mediation means non-Western subalterns cannot "speak" at all negates the entire projects of anthropology and "subaltern studies," as Spivak is well aware. For a critique of the more extreme position she seems to take at the end of her famous essay, see Lazarus (10).

2. A. B. Brewster includes a detailed account of Baker's death in *The Hill Tribes of Fiji* (26–34), first published in 1922. He updates that account with the help of a native informant and eyewitness in *King of the Cannibal Isles,* his history of Fiji and Thakombau's government from 1871 forward (120–26). According to Brewster, who "became intimately acquainted with" Baker's

murderers, "they were heartily sorry for what they had done," but they "hotly resented the accusation of having eaten the boots. They said they were not such fools" (*Hill Tribes* 27). They did, however, Brewster adds, try to eat a cake of soap they found in Baker's gear, thinking it a piece of bread made from bananas. But they found it bitter and threw it away (*King* 122).

3. I put "cannibals" in quotation marks in this paragraph because no community anywhere at any time has consisted of full-time eaters of human flesh. Anthropophagy has never been the main attribute of any culture or society. Rather than using quotation marks throughout the chapter, I will assume the reader understands "cannibal" and variants of it as provisional and of questionable utility. I do not see any clear reason to distinguish between "cannibalism" and "anthropophagy," as Obeyesekere recommends. Although she does not focus on Fiji, Shirley Lindenbaum offers a good recent overview of the issues. Most reports of cannibalism may have been false, but, like other racial categories and stereotypes, cannibals have been important figures in Western philosophy (Avramescu).

4. Hooper appears to be referring to Obeyesekere's *Cannibal Talk,* which was forthcoming when Hooper wrote. Brewster notes, "It might be considered that cannibalism is a delicate topic, and one to be avoided, but as a rule my native friends would discuss it quite openly and freely, attributing it to the darkness and ignorance of the olden times" (*Hill Tribes* 29).

5. About the only items on which both sides agree are that the main bone of contention concerns empirical evidence and that many accounts of cannibalism are untrustworthy. The skeptics aren't arguing that there is no reliable evidence about non-Western cultures, only that there is little or no reliable evidence about cannibalism. Thus, none of the skeptics takes a thoroughgoing poststructuralist position like that of Michel de Certeau, who in his essay on Montaigne's "Of Cannibals" writes that "the cannibals slip away from the words and discourses that fix their place.... They are never *there*. Nomadism is not an attribute of ... the Cannibal[s]: it is their very definition. What is foreign is that which escapes from a place" (70).

6. It is perhaps symptomatic that most of the cannibals whose names I know are white monsters: Sweeney Todd, Dracula, Hannibal Lecter, Jeffrey Dahmer, Armin Meiwes. Three of these are fictional—a trivial point, though it suggests that the fictional variety are historically at least as significant as the real ones.

7. No anthropologist today accepts Freud's ogre story in its details. For a sympathetic albeit critical summary of *Totem and Taboo* by an anthropologist, see Robert Paul (271–76). Similarly, in *Divine Hunger,* anthropologist Peggy Sanday makes use of Freud's account, but without assuming that it is anything more than a speculative story of origins.

8. For Patterson, see Lamb, Smith, and Thomas, *Exploration and Exchange* (180–86); for Dillon, J. W. Davidson; for Lockerby, Im Thurn and Wharton. Wilkes's five-volume *Narrative* is polyvocal, incorporating the various reports of his officers. Captain John Erskine includes Jackson's "Narrative" as an appendix in his *Journal of a Cruise* (411–77). In *Life in Feejee,* Mary Wallis summarizes the observations of various firsthand observers. Berthold Seeman's *Viti* contains a chapter on Fijian cannibalism, summarizing various authorities and witnesses, including Fijians.

9. Ta'unga does not provide an account of his pre-Christian life. But that the Rarotongans were (supposedly) cannibals before their conversions to Christianity is evident from, for instance, Buzacott (54). Alan R. Tippett, himself both a missionary and an anthropologist, read approximately one hundred letters and reports by Fijian native missionaries in parts of Melanesia; in these documents, written in Fijian, "cannibalism is a recurrent theme" (130). For Ta'unga, Maretu, and Bulu, see also Peggy Brock, "New Christians as Evangelists."

10. According to Obeyesekere, Endicott "could not possibly have witnessed" the "cannibal feast" he describes (160); "Cannibal" Jack was no better than a "novelist" (181–84); and Dillon was a thoroughly unreliable "trickster" (222). He also lumps missionaries together with other Westerners as apt to indulge in "cannibal talk," a discourse that gave "the settler, the missionary, and the traveler the license to lie" (154). But this is to make liars out of a great many people, both missionaries and non-missionaries, and both Westerners and non-Westerners. Except for one brief

citation of the Reverends Thomas Williams and Walter Lawry (154), Obeyesekere does not investigate missionary texts from Fiji. Besides Sahlins, anthropologists who treat missionary accounts of cannibalism in Fiji as credible include Ralph Linton (129–31), Tippett (39–80), and Nicholas Thomas (70–79), who points out that, contrary to the usual rejection of missionary discourse by professional anthropologists, "missionaries such as Maurice Leenhardt and Carl Strehlow produced celebrated examples of cultural ethnography, which have never had a secondary or merely semi-professional status" (14–15).

11. Though Haweis also warned that "amidst these enchanting scenes, savage nature still feasts on the flesh of its prisoners" (quoted in Samson, "Ethnology" 102). Haweis's sentiment is repeated in the Reverend John Davies's *History of the Tahitian Mission, 1799–1830*. Davies quotes James Wilson, captain of the *Duff*, which transported the first group of missionaries to Polynesia, writing to the LMS directors: "[Tahiti's] inhabitants are more mild generous and hospitable, and have fewer horrid customs" perhaps than other Polynesians, but certainly fewer such customs than "the New Hollanders," sunk in "deplorable wretchedness," and also than the ferocious "New Zealanders," with their "furious temper, and horrid customs" (quoted in Davies 31).

12. Johnston, *Missionary Writing*, 117–19. George Vason is an interesting case of a missionary turned native. See Lamb, Smith, and Thomas, *Exploration and Exchange* (156–69). For a detailed but hagiographic history of the Wesleyans in Fiji, see Findlay and Holdsworth, *The History of the Wesleyan Methodist Missionary Society* (3:363–469).

13. For a fictional contrast, see Herman Melville's *Typee* (1845). Although he himself engages in "cannibal talk," Melville trusts nothing missionaries say or do.

14. There are numerous "unspeakable" moments in the writings of all the Wesleyan missionaries in Fiji, as when Thomas Williams declares, "Atrocities of the most fearful kind have come to my knowledge, which I *dare* not record here" (*Fiji,* 133). Nevertheless, given his graphic accounts of warfare, cannibalism, torture, infanticide, widow strangling, and treacherous murder, what exactly was "unspeakable"? One answer lies in the realm of sexual behavior (or, from the missionary standpoint, hellish misbehavior). From Ballantyne's *Coral Island* to Conrad's *Heart of Darkness* and beyond, the trope is also a frequent one in imperialist adventure fiction.

15. "Tui" means chief or "king"; Tanoa was at that time "king" of Bau.

16. Superior races produce vigorous, honorable characters, modeled by the Victorian gentleman. Inferior races produce weak characters, including cannibals.

17. The Fijians in the 1800s were descendants of migrants from both Polynesia and Micronesia. In his study of the origins and spread of the theory of Aryanism, Tony Ballantyne does not mention Fiji, and I have not encountered any speculations that the Fijians were Aryans, as the Maoris and even the Australian Aborigines were sometimes held to be.

18. In 1853 Captain John Erskine met Thakombau and told him he should give up cannibalism and should lotu if he expected any support, moral or otherwise, from Queen Victoria (Erskine 186–88). Thakombau often got similar messages from visiting captains and white traders (Samson, "Ethnology"). If Fijian chiefs sought political gains through conversion, ordinary Fijians may have done so as well—not least to free themselves from their chiefs and priests, and also from warfare and cannibalism. For the political significance of religious conversion in general, see Gauri Viswanathan, *Outside the Fold*.

2. King Billy's Bones

1. On Windschuttle's attempt at genocide denial, see the essays in Robert Manne, ed., *Whitewash,* and my review essay "'Black Armband' versus 'White Blindfold' History in Australia." For the question of genocide in the entire Australian context, see Henry Reynolds, *An Indelible Stain?*

2. In her examination of Robinson as a "self-made man," Cassandra Pybus notes his "inexhaustible capacity for self-enhancement and self-delusion" (108).

3. See my *Dark Vanishings*. Russell McGregor's *Imagined Destinies: Aboriginal Australians and the Doomed Race Theory* takes the 1880s as its main starting point, but versions of that theory were in circulation much earlier.

4. In *Victorian Anthropology,* George Stocking points out that the Aborigines Protection Society, founded in 1837 by antislavery advocates, "may be regarded as the oldest lineal ancestor of modern British anthropological institutions" (240–41). On missionary ethnography, see Stocking (87–92) and Christopher Herbert (150–203).

5. Bernard Cohn develops an interesting typology of the forms of colonial knowledge, though his focus is India. Cohn identifies a number of "investigative modalities" that the British practiced in India throughout the history of the Raj. He notes that the "first step was... to learn the local languages" (4). This linguistic basis enabled the development of the other modalities. The "historiographic modality" led to the production of historical accounts of India's huge variety of states, empires, cultures, and societies and also of the British presence in the subcontinent. The "observational/travel modality" entailed narratives of trips to and through India in various patterns and utilizing a variety of "set pieces, such as the description of Indian holy men and their austerities, encounters with traveling entertainers, and a sati seen or heard about" (7). The "survey modality" encompassed "a wide range of practices, from the mapping of India to collecting botanical specimens" (7). The "enumerative modality" involved weighing and measuring everything and everyone, as for example in censuses. The "museological modality" entailed creating collections of Indian art, texts, archaeological specimens, and so forth. And the "surveillance modality" differed from the survey form mainly in emphasizing policing and control, including the origin in India of the technique of fingerprinting (11). Some but not all of these "investigative modalities" of colonial knowledge can be found in Robinson's *Journals*.

6. See H. Ling Roth, *The Aborigines of Tasmania* (1890), and E. B. Tylor's preface to that volume.

3. Going Native in Nineteenth-Century History and Literature

1. Here is an example of the racist idea of the "mimicry" of "the natives," from G. A. Henty's 1884 boys' adventure novel *By Sheer Pluck:* "The intelligence of the average negro is about equal to that of a European child of ten years old.... They are fluent talkers, but their ideas are borrowed. They are absolutely without originality.... Living among white men, their imitative faculties enable them to attain a considerable amount of civilisation. Left to their own devices, they retrograde into a state little above their native savagery" (118). In short, a black African can "ape" the white man, but it is easy for him to backslide into his "native savagery," close to the apes. From this obviously racist perspective, "mimicry" is the opposite of "originality," and it marks the limit to an African's ability to become fully civilized.

2. I have summarized the story of Pearce partly from Marcus Clarke's great prison novel *For the Term of His Natural Life.* Clarke renames Pearce "Gabbett." Pearce escaped twice from Macquarie Harbor in Tasmania, the first time with seven comrades, four of whom were killed and eaten. In his second escape attempt, Pearce was accompanied by only one other convict, whom he killed and ate. He was recaptured and executed in 1824. For the historical details, see Robert Hughes, *The Fatal Shore,* 219–26.

3. Frontiersmen such as Daniel Boone were the pioneers of civilization, but in many ways they behaved like Indians. Natty Bumppo's allegiance is split between past and future, wilderness and civilization, redskin and paleface. The early Canadian novelist John Richardson depicts in *Wacousta* a white man turned Indian warrior during the 1760s. And in Robert Montgomery Bird's Indian-hating novel *Nick of the Woods,* a white renegade says, "I'm a white Injun, and there's nothing more despicable" (quoted in Drinnon 163).

4. According to the editor of Rutherford's memoir, "generally... the Europeans that have adopted the life of the savage have been men driven out from civilization, or disinclined to systematic

industry...but...savage life has a strong charm for many minds," including "independence, the exemption from regular labour, and...the variety of adventure, which it promises to ardent and reckless spirits" (quoted in Bentley 141).

5. As to Europeans participating, along with the indigenous societies they joined, in cannibal feasts, there were also stories from colonial frontiers of behavior that seems, if possible, even worse. In his *Journals,* George Augustus Robinson relayed a story about white sealers on Kangaroo Island who tortured an Aboriginal woman by slicing off some of her thigh and making her eat it. And there was a similar story from southern Africa about a white man forcing an African to eat some of his own flesh (Elbourne 85).

6. See *Sketch of a Residence among the Aboriginals of Northern Queensland for Seventeen Years* by James Morrill, included in John Morgan, *The Life and Adventures of William* Buckley, 194–238.

7. Gordon had in fact helped draft the order to evacuate the Sudan, so in disobeying it he was, in a sense, disobeying himself (Nutting 3). In his biography of Gladstone, Philip Magnus writes: "Fearless, erratic, brilliant, perverse, always notoriously undisciplined, Gordon's power of self-deception matched that of Gladstone and his religious fanaticism matched that of the Mahdi" (310).

8. In 1862 Dr. Robert Edmund Scoresby-Jackson published his authoritative *Medical Climatology,* which gave the green light to the climates of many British colonies, even (with qualifications) Jamaica. He theorized, however, that all "who leave their native soil to reside in foreign climates would ultimately *die out* were this not prevented by the return of their offspring to spend a portion of their lives in the mother country, or through the transfusion of new blood into the veins of their descendants by intermarriage with immigrants fresh from the parent stock" (quoted in Anderson, *Cultivation* 13). Scoresby-Jackson relied in part on James Clark's *Sanative Influence of Climate,* which also claimed that the climates of most of the colonies were "salubrious."

9. Conrad is more definite about what happens to the pair of white men that leads them to destroy themselves in his other African story, "An Outpost of Progress," written shortly before *Heart of Darkness.* Kayerts and Carlier are men of the "crowd"—mass men, in other words—for whom "the contact with pure unmitigated savagery, with primitive nature and primitive man, brings sudden and profound trouble into the heart." They are no better than "pigs" or "dogs" or the savages they encounter. In contrast, Kurtz, according to Marlow, is an exemplary human being, a model of European civilization. Both stories express Conrad's total disbelief in the hyperbolic rhetoric of imperialism and its civilizing mission.

10. Historian Howard Malchow speculates that Heathcliff may have been the mixed-race offspring of a British sailor and an enslaved African woman (39–40). Literary critic Terry Eagleton claims that "Heathcliff starts out as the image of the famished Irish immigrant" (*Heathcliff* 19).

11. See Eliza Lynn Linton, "The Wild Women," and Mona Caird, "A Defense of the So-Called 'Wild Women.'"

12. My comments on Annie Besant are based on Gauri Viswanathan's insightful analysis of her ideas in *Outside the Fold* (177–207). For Aryanism, see Tony Ballantyne, *Orientalism.*

4. "God Works by Races"

1. The British secret service which employs Kim calls itself an "ethnographic survey." Burton's activities in Sindh and elsewhere were often tantamount to espionage; he was also one of the founders of the Anthropological Society, the more racist of the two competing London-based societies in the 1860s (Stocking).

2. For Edward Lane, see Said, *Orientalism,* 158–64. For Burton's celebrations of Arabic "chivalry" in relation to Disraeli, see my *Rule of Darkness,* 158–71. On the general British fascination with Arabia, see Tidrick, *Heart-Beguiling Araby.*

3. Besides Isabel Burton, the roster of British women who traveled to Islamic countries and remained there for extended periods, living to a greater or lesser extent like the natives, includes Lady Hester Stanhope ("Queen of the Arabs" and one of Isabel's heroines); Lady Jane Digby, who

had married Sheik Mijwal el Mezrab and who befriended the Burtons in Damascus; and Byron's cousin Lady Ann Blunt (Melman).

4. See Disraeli's letter of January 1, 1834, to Benjamin Austen, in *Letters: 1815–1834,* 385. Nothing came of this proposal; Edward Lane's translation of the *Arabian Nights* began to appear in 1838. Richard Burton was a later translator.

5. There were frequent discussions about restoring the Jews to Palestine even before Disraeli's time. According to Mayir Vereté, there were discussions about restoring the Jews to Palestine in the 1790s. Disraeli has been credited with penning the anonymous manuscripts published in *Unknown Documents on the Jewish Question: Disraeli's Plan for a Jewish State* (1947), though there is no evidence for his authorship. See Ann Pottinger Saab, "Disraeli, Judaism, and the Eastern Question."

6. This is a theme in Eric Hobsbawm and Terence Ranger's *Invention of Tradition.* See especially Bernard Cohn, "Representing Authority in Victorian India," in *Colonialism and Its Forms of Knowledge,* 165–209.

7. Disraeli was traveling after the 1829 Treaty of Adrianople, and the London Protocol of 1830, under which Greece was supposedly an independent kingdom. The crown was offered first to Prince John of Saxony (who refused it), then to Prince Leopold of Saxe-Coburg (who withdrew after first accepting it). In early 1833 the son of King Ludwig of Bavaria became Otto I of Greece.

8. Isaiah Berlin writes: "When Disraeli presided over the elevation of Queen Victoria to the throne of the Empress of India, and all that went with it, the gorgeous trappings of empire, the elephants and the durbars, and all those eastern splendours which had succeeded the realistic, hardheaded rule of the East India Company and inspired the vast and occasionally hollow periods of later imperialist rhetoric, it is difficult to resist the impression that something of this stemmed from Disraeli's genuine orientalism" (271).

9. In his August 16, 1845, letter to the *Morning Post* on "Young England Philosophy," Disraeli cites not only Blumenbach, "the Newton of physiology," but also James Cowles Prichard's *Researches into the Physical History of Mankind* (which appeared in various expanded editions from 1813 to 1851) as providing the scientific basis for his own racial classification. Prichard, however, was critical of Blumenbach's "Caucasian" category (Baum). Disraeli, *Letters: 1842–1847,* 180–84. I owe this point to Paul Smith.

10. "Among these [Syrian] mountains we find...everywhere liberty—a proud, feudal aristocracy, a conventual establishment, which in its ramifications recalls the middle ages, a free and armed peasantry whatever their creed; Emirs on Arabian steeds, bishops worthy of the apostles, the Maronite monk, the horned head-gear of the Druses" (*Tancred* 400). This sounds like Carlyle's medievalizing in *Past and Present,* only set in the Middle East.

11. It is ironic that George Eliot, author of the philo-Semitic *Daniel Deronda* (1876), should have viewed Disraeli through anti-Semitic lenses. In *Deronda,* Eliot was trying to counteract not just anti-Semitism but also what she saw as Disraeli's erroneous racial ideas. In an early letter Eliot declared that Disraeli's "theory of 'races'...has not a leg to stand on.... The fellowship of race, to which D'Israeli exultingly refers the munificence of Sidonia, is so evidently an inferior impulse which must ultimately be superseded that I wonder even he, Jew as he is, dares to boast of it" (*Letters* 45). "Boasting" is, perhaps, not inappropriate, because Disraeli's "theory of 'races'" was a compensatory attempt to fight racism with racism. "No one can fail to notice that he boasted of his Jewish origins almost too insistently, and mentioned them in and out of season at some risk to his political career, and this despite his eccentric but genuine Christianity" (Berlin 268). For excellent accounts of Jews and Judaism in Victorian and early modern British culture, see Michael Ragussis and Bryan Cheyette.

12. John Vincent declares that "Disraeli's racial doctrine went the whole hog. Not only was race the key to history, but some races were far superior to others. There were master races, and

then there were the rest" (27). It might be more accurate to say that for Disraeli there was *one* master race—the Hebrew, or at any rate the Semitic or Arabic—the only race, as Disraeli liked to emphasize, to whom God had revealed His grand truths. It would make little sense, however, to interpret Disraeli's racism as proto-fascist, as some scholars have done, both because racial explanations for history were the common currency of nineteenth-century intellectuals and because Disraeli was so obviously seeking, through his philo-Semitism, to trump versions of Anglo-Saxonism, Aryanism, and anti-Semitism that were themselves intellectual forebears of fascist and Nazi racism.

5. Race and Class in the 1860s

1. Robert Young contends that, starting in the 1850s, there was an "increased emphasis on racial difference, on the permanence of the intellectual capacities, or incapacities, of the different races, and the similar differentiations that could be made between the classes" (96). Gareth Stedman Jones writes, "The idea of settlement [creating social work 'colonies' in the slums] was not a product of the situation in the 1880s, but, like Poor Law Reform, the Charity Organisation Society, and Octavia Hill's housing schemes, grew out of the crisis of the 1860s" (259). Neil MacMaster, commenting on Europe in general, declares, "The elaboration of a modern and aggressive racism from the 1860s was thus one expression of a profoundly insecure bourgeois society that constantly played upon and interwove the rhetoric of race and class" (65).

2. Foucault gives the historical priority to "race war," but argues that as modern nation-states established themselves, such warfare moved to the "periphery"—in other words, to war against foreign enemies and to empire building. In Britain's domestic affairs, class conflict among people mainly of the same "race"—English—took precedence from the Industrial Revolution forward, although it can be traced back much further, to the revolution of the 1640s or even to the Norman invasion. In the last instance, the myth of the Norman yoke referred simultaneously to races (Normans versus Anglo-Saxons) and to classes (aristocracy versus working classes). In the 1800s, the doubling of race and class is evident in historical novels such as Sir Walter Scott's *Ivanhoe* and Charles Kingsley's *Hereward the Wake*.

3. On Anglo-Saxonism, see MacDougall, *Racial Myth in English History;* and Horsman, "Origins of Racial Anglo-Saxonism in Great Britain before 1850." In official discourse and also journalism about the working classes, much attention was paid to issues of health, diet, and sanitation as well as education in the 1830s and 1840s. Except for anti-Irish attitudes and the metaphor of "white slavery" (or "wage slavery"), however, writers in those decades did not otherwise tend to racialize the poor.

4. "Race accounted for social inequalities by attributing them to nature," writes Kenan Malik (6). In *Colonial Desire,* Young argues that "historically social ideas of race and culture developed simultaneously" and that throughout the 1800s there was a general "racialization of knowledge" (64). Here I am attempting to explain why that racialization of knowledge was especially intense in the 1860s and after.

5. Robert Latham's *Natural History of the Varieties of Man* also appeared in 1850. Gobineau's multivolume *Essai sur l'inégalité des Race humaines* was published in 1853–1855, followed by an English translation two years later. The 1850s could be considered the decade when racism, under supposedly scientific auspices, became a dominant ideology, but the influence of these works became fully evident in the next decade.

6. In her study of science and race, Nancy Stepan rejects the term "pseudoscience." Scientific racism, she contends, may have been "bad science," but it adhered to many of the standards and methods that still qualify as science. Few nineteenth-century scientists "knowingly broke the accepted canons of scientific procedure of their day" (xvi), even though they expressed racial, social class, and historical biases and stereotypes in their arguments. Her key point is that science is never

isolated from the social contexts in which it develops. In *The Mismeasure of Man,* however, Stephen Jay Gould argues that the race scientists ought to have known better. It is not the case that the race scientists, anthropologists, and evolutionists were discovering anything new about race and racial differences in the 1850s and 1860s. Instead, as Neil MacMaster puts it, they "picked up the pre-existing prejudices and stereotypical attitudes of European and white colonial societies, repackaged them as scientific theory, and then mirrored them back to a literate public." This was just as true of Darwin and his followers as of earlier "race ideologues" (MacMaster 18).

7. The concept of "prehistory" was in large measure due to Huxley's and Darwin's friend and ally Sir John Lubbock. His *Pre-Historic Times as Illustrated by Ancient Remains and the Manners and Customs of Modern Savages* appeared in 1865.

8. These are the Australians, the "Negritos" (Tasmanians, Melanesians), "Amphinesians" (Polynesians, the Maori), American Indians, "Esquimaux," Mongolians, Negroes, Bushmen, "Mincopies" (Andaman Islanders), and the two major "stocks" that inhabit Europe, North Africa, and most of western Asia, which are the civilization-founding "Xanthochroi" (white people) and the "Melanochroi," who are darker-skinned and "long-headed."

9. Well before John Beddoe theorized about the "nigrescence" of the Irish in *The Races of Britain* (1885), Huxley in 1870 wrote about the "so-called black Celts" (quoted in Bonnett 324).

10. Watts's *Wild Tribes* is mainly descriptive, after the manner of Dickens's *Sketches by Boz.* Unlike Mayhew, Watts does not offer a race-based theory about the "savage denizens" of the slums of London (7), but presents only a series of racial, and racially demeaning, metaphors. By the mid-1850s "wild tribes" had become a standard metaphor for the poor, along with metaphors of disease and "vermin" (8). Watts, however, stresses the racial otherness of the poor as much as or more than earlier writers: many of them are "wild Milesians" (12), "filthy" Jews (33), Lascars, Malays, and even English or Irishmen in disguise, like "Hafiz Khan," the fake Turkish rhubarb seller, who tells Watts about other "dodges" or disguises, such as "the Hindoo-and-trac' [tract] dodge—the Uncle Tom—the persekuted Nigger go," and so on, because, he claims, these are highly appealing to Christian charity (83).

11. "Gamboge," derived from the same root word as Cambodia, refers to a Southeast Asian tree from which is derived a vivid yellow pigment. Compare J. C. Parkinson, writing in 1869: "There is a little colony of Orientals in the centre of Bluegate-fields, and in the centre of this colony is the opium den. . . . The livid, cadaverous, corpse-like visage of Yahee, the wild excited glare of the young Lascar who opens the door, the stolid sheep-like ruminations of Lazarus and the other Chinamen coiled together on the floor, the incoherent anecdotes of the Bengalee squatted on the bed, the fiery gesticulations of the mulatoo and the Manilla-man who are in conversation by the fire, the semi-idiotic jabber of the negroes huddled up behind Yahee, are all due to the same fumes" (quoted in Marriott 169). This could be the opium den that provides the opening scene for Dickens's unfinished *Mystery of Edwin Drood,* also published in 1869.

12. Marriott quotes Baptist Noel in 1835: "England sends out her missionaries to the coasts of Guiana, to the tribes of Southern Africa, to the islands of the South Pacific, to North and South India, to Malacca and Canton: but 518,000 souls in the metropolis, within easy reach of hundreds of Christian ministers, and of thousands of intelligent Christian laymen with wealth and leisure, are almost entirely overlooked" (108).

13. In 1868 historian J. R. Green declared that clergymen who had been thoughtlessly charitable now "stand aghast at the Pauper Frankenstein they have created" (quoted in Stedman Jones 246). See also John Hollingshead on "mistaken charity" (223–31).

14. The *Times* of London maintained that "the Emancipation Proclamation meant servile war," and that "the black blood of the African" was a danger to "innocent women and children." It also compared American slaves or ex-slaves with British workers in declaring, "There is no society which cannot be destroyed by the process of setting loose those 'dangerous classes' which are always to be found in every community whether urban or rural" (quoted in Lorimer 168).

15. Besides Koven, see also Christopher Herbert's chapter on Mayhew's "cockney Polynesia" in *Culture and Anomie,* 204–52; and Brantlinger and Ulin, "Policing Nomads."

6. The Unbearable Lightness of Being Irish

1. W. R. Greg, for instance, treats "the frugal, foreseeing, self-respecting Scot" as though he were a "Saxon" instead of a "Celt." In his essay, the latter term means Irish (Greg 361).

2. Robert Kee's account of events at Wexford includes torture and massacres on both sides, but without the note of cannibalism the *Times* introduces as an aspect of United Irishmen's behavior (1:108–21). Half a century after their rebellion and the Act of Union, the liberal *Spectator* in 1848 condemned the Irishman as a "wild man," asserting, "The aboriginal inhabitant of Ireland ... [is] an animal in human form that avowedly exults in ferocity, malevolence, and the love of blood" (quoted in de Nie 120).

3. See, for example, Donal Kerr, *A Nation of Beggars?*

4. As both L. P. Curtis and Michael de Nie demonstrate, cartoons in the English press sometimes depicted the Irish threat as an oversized ogre, a Frankenstein's monster, but more often as a diminutive, monkey-like or goblin-like figure, as in the 1846 *Punch* cartoon "Young Ireland in Business for Himself," in which a sinister, ape-like dwarf is selling "pretty little pistols for pretty little children" to an Irish ragamuffin, who is already armed with two swords, a pistol, and a blunderbuss (de Nie 110).

5. For AE (George Russell) as for Yeats, "Celticism was a way of coming into contact with the supernatural. [AE] found in the tales told him by peasants and the stories of ancient Irish literature the same figures who inhabited his own dreams. Celticism became for him a means for dealing with ancestral memory, with an imagined past full of mystical power" (Fallis 61).

7. Mummy Love

1. In regard to archaeology in Egypt, Napoleon's expedition in 1798 led to the multivolume *Description de l'Égypte* (1809–1813). Sir John Gardner Wilkinson published his multivolume *Manners and Customs of the Ancient Egyptians* starting in 1837, followed by John Kenrick's *Ancient Egypt under the Pharaohs* in 1850. And the German archaeologist Richard Lepsius produced his *Egyptian Chronology* in 1849 and his *Book of Egyptian Kings* the year after. Many other works on ancient Egypt appeared throughout the nineteenth century.

2. Haggard's romances that deal with ancient Egypt include *Cleopatra, The World's Desire* (coauthored by Andrew Lang), *The Way of the Spirit, Morning Star, Moon of Israel, The Ancient Allan, Wisdom's Daughter, Queen of the Dawn,* and the novelette or long short story "Smith and the Pharaohs."

3. Tomb robbing commenced as soon as there were tombs to rob, or at any rate tombs worth robbing. In his history of archaeology, C. W. Ceram writes, "It seems almost uncanny to us today to find, among the papyrus collections from the period of Ramses IX (1142–1123 B.C.), a document relating to a tomb-robbery trial that took place three thousand years ago" (157). See also Peter France, *The Rape of Egypt.*

4. John Barrell notes the widespread idea that the modern Egyptians were neither Caucasian nor black but "an entirely hybrid or mongrel race" ("Death" 117). He points out that for British tourists, "admiration of the ancient Egyptians seems to grow at the expense of any respect for the civilization of modern Egyptians" (98). In Florence Nightingale's *Letters from Egypt* (1854), for example, ancient Egyptians may have formed the first civilization, but modern Egyptians are "beasts" or even "reptiles" (quoted in Barrell, "Death" 107–8).

5. Dan Wylie notes that "the portrayal of Shaka in Esther Roberts's *The Black Spear* (1950) is adequately summed up by the original dust-jacket design, in which the very clouds ooze blood. This romance is heavily influenced by Haggard, from the quest-plot down to the fair-skinned heroine, Sewele the Rain Goddess, being termed 'She-who-must-be-obeyed'" (186–87).

6. The French director of the Cairo Museum adds another meaning to this series of puns: "Ma-Mie," or "my darling." See Haggard, "Smith and the Pharoahs" 165.

7. In part because it was easier to take pieces like feet or hands rather than entire mummies out of Egypt, stories in which mummified body parts figured were common, such as in Gautier's "La pie de la momie." The seven-fingered hand in Stoker's *Jewel of Seven Stars* is another example. Flaubert kept a mummy's foot on his writing desk. There is also an evident connection between sexual and commodity fetishism, which both Nicholas Daly and Kelly Hurley have examined.

8. "Shadows of the Coming Race"

1. Wells later repudiated what he considered to be facile versions of eugenics. See McLean, *Early Fiction* 154–57.

2. The reference to Kipling is ironic; it suggests Wells's ambivalence toward imperialism, whether British or otherwise. The single poem Kipling wrote in highly qualified praise of Africans is "Fuzzy-Wuzzy," in which a cockney soldier says: "So 'ere's to you, Fuzzy-Wuzzy, at your 'ome in the Soudan; / You're a pore benighted 'eathen but a first-class fightin' man" (*Complete Verse* 399).

3. Whether or not Stoker saw any motion pictures before publishing *Dracula,* he probably read about them, and it's likely that he understood their phantasmatic possibilities from both stage illusion and photography. "Thus, Stoker's *Dracula* was both conceived at exactly the same time as the new medium of film, and in some sense also imagined its advent" (Marsh and Elliott 469).

4. New media of communications typically seem uncanny. The telegraph was often seen as "magical" and "a spirit like Ariel," for example. See Morus, Thurschwell, and Sconce. The connection between electricity and Gothic romances begins with *Frankenstein:* the Shelleys expressed their interest in galvanic experiments to resurrect life. Furthermore, an early version of the "magic lantern" was christened "the lantern of fear," and the earliest attempt at producing animation with that instrument shows a skeleton juggling a skull (Mannoni 48, 39). Antoine Furetière's 1690 *Dictionnaire universel* defined the *lanterne magique* as "a small optical machine which makes visible in the darkness on a white wall several ghosts and monsters so hideous, that those who do not know the secret believe that this is done by magic" (quoted in Mannoni 67).

5. Stoker's novel would be incoherent, Wicke argues, a mishmash of "journal entries, letters, professional records and newspaper clippings," but these are "collated and typed by the industrious Mina" (469), who makes sense out of the mishmash. Besides typing, Mina enjoys exchanging letters and notes in shorthand with Jonathan. Wicke comments: "Vampirism springs up, or takes command, at the behest of shorthand. Although the pages we open to start our reading of the book look like any printed pages, there is a crucial sense in which we are inducted into Count Dracula lore by…stenography" (471). And as to the photographs Jonathan brings to Transylvania, Wicke notes these are "really also…celluloid analog[s] of vampirism in action" (472). Perhaps so, although she adds, "If a vampire's image cannot be captured in a mirror, photographs of a vampire might prove equally disappointing" (473).

6. See also Pamela Thurschwell: "During the 1880s and 1890s supernatural fiction, as well as aesthetic writings, suggest that reproduction may be seductive in new and 'unnatural' forms— the vampirism of *Dracula* and its carbon paper; the mesmeric birth of the opera star in *Trilby;* the aesthetic seductions and mimetic reproductions of *Dorian Gray.* Reproduction comes to seem both queer and occult in these texts" (46).

7. See Friedrich Kittler, *Gramophone, Film, Typewriter* 183. Kittler goes even further by comparing early typewriters directly to vampires. With the early typewriters, "all the agency of writing passes on in its violence to an inhuman media engineer who will soon be called up by Stoker's *Dracula.* A type of writing that blindly dismembers body parts and perforates human skin necessarily stems from typewriters built before 1897, when Underwood finally introduced visibility.

Peter Mitterhofer's Model 2, the wooden typewriter prototype of 1866...did not even have types and a ribbon. Instead, the writing paper was perforated by needle pins" (210–11).

8. Fredric Jameson writes that "the visual is essentially pornographic," and that "pornographic films are thus only the potentiation of films in general, which ask us to stare at the world as though it were a naked body" (*Signatures* 1). In *Dracula* it isn't movies, of course, but all of the other new media that Stoker brings into play which bring vampirism into play. That is to say, they are all put to quasi-pornographic use. Adding up the typewriter, the camera, the phonograph, telegrams, and tabloids, one arrives at the nearly allegorical alignment between vampirism and mass culture, or, better, the media of cultural reproduction, that Keep, Wicke, Kittler, and Halberstam all see in Stoker's novel.

9. In *Telegraphic Realism,* Richard Menke writes: "By the end of the century, *Dracula* ... stanches the gothic predations of the count with a bureaucratic romance of information management" (10).

10. In fact Kittler, like McLuhan, takes the step beyond technological momentum: "Media *determine* our situation" (*Gramophone* xxxix; emphasis added).

Epilogue

1. On a trip to Washington, D.C., in 1895, his friend Henry Adams had introduced Kipling to various up-and-coming conservative politicians, including John Hay, Henry Cabot Lodge, and Theodore Roosevelt. Kipling may have found the ideas of Henry's brother Brooks Adams especially congenial. He owned a copy of Brooks's *Law of Civilisation and Decay* (1895), and in 1900 Brooks published *America's Economic Supremacy,* which argues that "the United States must shortly bear the burden England has borne, must assume the responsibilities and perform the tasks which have within human memory fallen to the share of England, and must be equipped accordingly" (quoted in Hagiioannu 69). Kipling may or may not have felt that the United States was already assuming the role of imperial leadership that had theretofore belonged to Britain, but the message of "The White Man's Burden" is unmistakable: America should do so, at least in the Philippines.

2. "The bard of a modern Imperialism has sung of the White Man's burden" (3), Morel begins. He gives an ironic, musical interpretation to "burden": "The notes strike the granite surface of racial pride and fling back echoes which reverberate through the corridors of history, exultant" (3). But "what of that other burden," he goes on to ask, that of the black man? His book is an exposé "of the atrocious wrongs which the white peoples have inflicted upon the black," particularly in Africa (vi). Morel had been a leader in the campaign to expose and end atrocities in the Congo, and had published such earlier works as *King Leopold's Rule in Africa* and *Red Rubber.* In *The Black Man's Burden,* Morel offers a highly critical history of European imperialism in various parts of Africa, from the earliest days of the slave trade to the devastating effects of industrial, capitalist exploitation.

3. In *U.S. Expansionism,* David Healy writes that for many turn-of-the-century white Americans, "the conclusion was inescapable: it was not only possible for the civilized to lead the backward toward the light, it was actually their moral duty to do so. If the task was hard, and its duration long—as long as the foreseeable future—then this opportunity and duty could fittingly be called...'the White Man's Burden'" (15).

4. The "platform" of the American Anti-Imperialist League, October 1899, reads in part: "We condemn the policy of the present national administration in the Philippines. It seeks to extinguish the spirit of 1776 in those islands. We deplore the sacrifice of our soldiers and sailors....We denounce the slaughter of the Filipinos as a needless horror. We protest against the extension of American sovereignty by Spanish methods" (Nichols 117).

5. Arguing that Bell and other Americans may have had reason to exaggerate the number of Filipino deaths as a sign of military effectiveness, Richard Slotkin offers "estimates based on army

records…[of] between 16,000 and 20,000 rebels killed in action and…an additional 200,000 civilian deaths" (119).

6. On Forbes, see Stanley, *A Nation in the Making* 99–107.

7. Besides Gatewood's 1975 book, other works critical of racism in America that have made use of Kipling and his famous or infamous title include B. F. Riley, *The White Man's Burden: A Discussion of the Interracial Question with Special Reference to the Responsibility of the White Race to the Negro Problem* (1910); Louis R. Harlan, "Booker T. Washington and the 'White Man's Burden'" (1966); Matthew Holden, *The White Man's Burden* (1973); and Winthrop Jordan, *White Man's Burden: Historical Origins of Racism in the United States* (1974), a condensed version of Jordan's magisterial 1968 study *White over Black: American Attitudes toward the Negro, 1550–1812.* More recently, a film titled *White Man's Burden* (1995), directed by Desmond Nakano and starring John Travolta and Harry Belafonte, critiques both racism and class prejudice in the United States by reversing the standard roles of race and class domination. Travolta plays a downtrodden white worker and Belafonte his wealthy, overbearing boss. Reviewing the film for *Rolling Stone,* Peter Travers calls it a "noble experiment" that, however, "only fitfully hits home" (Travers 92).

8. Louis R. Harlan writes that Booker T. Washington "so thoroughly subscribed to the 'White Man's Burden' of leadership and authority that, in seeming forgetfulness that he was Negro, he actually took up the burden himself" (442).

9. It is not always clear that the parodists of "The White Man's Burden" were critiquing either its politics or its racism. They were sometimes just mocking the effrontery of an Englishman presuming to advise the United States about how to conduct its business. There were also parodies with such titles as "The Poor Man's Burden" and even "The Old Maid's Burden." Labor leader George E. McNeill, champion of the eight-hour day, published "The Poor Man's Burden" in 1903; the poor were of all races. And E. A. Brininstool's feminist barb "The White Woman's Burden" appeared in the *Los Angeles Times* on March 6, 1899; it reads in part:

> Ring off on the "White Man's Burden,"
> And talk of a woman's right;
> Tell of the jawing she has to stand
> From early morn till night.
> If the "white man's" burden is heavy,
> What do you think 'twould be,
> If he had to cook and dig and scrub,
> And never from work be free?

See also "The White Woman's Burden" by suffragette Hester Gray, in *Common Cause,* November 27, 1914, 565–66.

10. That was, indeed, the view of the first American officials to govern the Philippines, including Forbes, William Howard Taft, and such "humanitarian imperialists" as David Prescott Barrows. Thus, although Barrows considered the Filipinos to be "civilized," they were at such a low level of civilization that they could not be trusted with self-government. Before going to the Philippines, Barrows had taken an interest in the ethnography of American Indians in California, and he held that the Filipinos were inferior to those Native Americans "who had developed extensive tribal organization and even confederacies" (Clymer 502–3). As Kenton Clymer notes, humanitarian imperialism and the idea of "the white man's burden" ran counter to the social Darwinism that Barrows and many others accepted (507). For Taft, see Oscar M. Alfonso, "Taft's Early Views on the Filipinos."

11. Among neoimperialist admirers of Kipling, Niall Ferguson is more circumspect than either Kaplan or Boot when it comes to citing Kipling and "The White Man's Burden." In *Empire: The Rise and Demise of the British World Order and the Lessons for Global Power,* his highly favorable

survey of the mighty British Empire, Ferguson notes some of its destructive aspects but insists that it grew increasingly humane, that it promoted democracy, and that ultimately more good than evil came from it (304). The "lessons" it holds for the new American empire are also, he thinks, good ones, although he believes Americans may not have sufficient pluck or Britishness or something or other to be very good imperialists. He doesn't quite say that America should now "take up the white man's burden," as Kipling advised the United States to do during the Spanish-American War: "No one would dare," he writes, "use such politically incorrect language today" (316). Obviously he is tempted to use that language but doesn't for fear of being accused of the racism that Kipling and other British imperialists expressed.

Like Kipling's, Ferguson's notion that the British Empire grew increasingly humane is belied on many fronts—for example, by the brutal repression of the Mau-Maus in Kenya in the 1950s (Elkins; Anderson, *Histories*). In the introduction, Ferguson fondly remembers his childhood in Kenya. He mentions without explaining "the days of White Mischief," but "we had our bungalow, our maid, our smattering of Swahili—and our sense of unshakeable security. It was a magical time" (xv). Clearly, he was never thrown into prison like Jomo Kenyatta, much less lynched on a "White Mischief" gallows. In his main text, Ferguson mentions Kenya only once more, as a former British colony which has not "managed to sustain free institutions" (308), even though it is today a democracy, albeit a shaky one. In any event, Ferguson argues that "just like the British Empire before it, the American Empire unfailingly acts in the name of liberty, even when its own self-interest is manifestly uppermost" (316). Given America's record of subverting democratically elected governments such as Allende's in Chile while supporting dictators such as Pinochet—or Ferdinand Marcos or Saddam Hussein in the 1980s—the notion that it "unfailingly acts in the name of liberty" is either naïve or disingenuous. I agree with Harry Harootunian, who in *The Empire's New Clothes* writes that Ferguson's pontificating—his "lessons" for America—are "sophomoric" (107), as was Kipling's earlier advice to the United States about the Philippines.

12. Citing Cornel West's *Democracy Matters: Winning the Fight against Imperialism* (2004), Thomas McCarthy writes that "the arrested development of democracy in America…must be examined [in terms of] the pervasiveness of white supremacy in our history. The failure to come fully to terms with the deeply racist and imperialist strains in our national past remains a fundamental weakness of our political culture" (69).

13. Donald Randall comments that Kim, "still in the care of two partial and incompatible fathers, Mahbub [Ali] and Teshoo Lama, is left suspended on the brink of an impossible manhood. The predicament implied by Kim's truncated Bildung, his insuperable adolescence, mirrors the problem of imperial consolidation," or of "an empire that has not discovered…its appropriate coming of age" (158). As a number of critics have noted, the idea of "the Great Game" itself suggests childhood or adolescent pleasures that the players hope will never end (Bivona 70).

14. In *Empire of Analogies,* Kaori Nagai writes, "Kipling, by representing his imperial hero as Irish, at once contains Irish rebellion and reclaims the Irish as loyal subjects" (10). At several points Nagai refers to Kipling's portrayals of potential or actual Irish "mutinies," including "The Mutiny of the Mavericks"—Kim's father's regiment.

Works Cited

Adas, Michael. "Improving on the Civilizing Mission? Assumptions of United States Exceptionalism in the Colonization of the Philippines." In *The New American Empire: A 21st-Century Teach-In on U.S. Foreign Policy,* edited by Lloyd C. Gardner and Marilyn Young, 153–81. New York: New Press, 2005.

Addy, Shirley M. *Rider Haggard and Egypt.* Accrington, Lancashire: AL Publications, 1998.

Adorno, Theodor W. *Critical Models: Interventions and Catchwords.* Translated by Henry Pickford. New York: Columbia University Press, 1998.

Adorno, Theodor W., and Max Horkheimer. *Dialectic of Enlightenment.* Translated by John Cumming. New York: Continuum, 1997.

Akşin, Sina. *Turkey: From Empire to Revolutionary Republic.* London: Hurst, 2007.

Alfonso, Oscar M. "Taft's Early Views on the Filipinos." *Solidarity* 4 (June 1969): 52–58.

Althusser, Louis. "Ideology and Ideological State Apparatuses." In *Lenin and Philosophy, and Other Essays,* 127–86. Translated by Ben Brewster. New York: Monthly Review Press, 1971.

Anderson, Benedict. *Imagined Communities: Reflections on the Origin and Spread of Nationalism.* London: Verso, 1992.

Anderson, David. *Histories of the Hanged: Britain's Dirty War in Kenya and the End of Empire.* London: Weidenfeld and Nicolson, 2005.

Anderson, I. P. S. "A People Who Have No History?" In *Reading Robinson: Companion Essays to "Friendly Mission,"* edited by Anna Johnston and Mitchell Rolls, 59–76. Hobart, Tasmania: Quintus Publishing, 2008.

Anderson, Warwick. *The Cultivation of Whiteness: Science, Health, and Racial Destiny in Australia.* Melbourne: Melbourne University Press, 2002.

Archer, Thomas. *The Pauper, the Thief, and the Convict; Sketches of Some of Their Homes, Haunts, and Habits.* London: Groombridge and Sons, 1865.

Arendt, Hannah. *Imperialism.* Part 2 of *The Origins of Totalitarianism.* 1951. New York: Harcourt, Brace and World, 1968.

Arens, William. *The Man-Eating Myth: Anthropology and Anthropophagy.* Oxford: Oxford University Press, 1979.

Arnold, Matthew. *Culture and Anarchy.* Edited by J. Dover Wilson. Cambridge: Cambridge University Press, 1963.

——. "The Incompatibles." In *English Literature and Irish Politics,* edited by R. H. Super, 238–85. Ann Arbor: University of Michigan Press, 1973.

——. "On the Study of Celtic Literature." In *Lectures and Essays in Criticism,* edited by R. H. Super, 291–395. Ann Arbor: University of Michigan Press, 1962.

Asoian, Boris R. *Apartheid, "The White Man's Burden."* Moscow: Progress Publishers, 1988.

Augstein, Hannah, ed. *Race: The Origins of an Idea, 1760–1850.* London: Thoemmes, 1996.

Avery, Todd. *Radio Modernism: Literature, Ethics, and the BBC, 1922–1938.* Burlington: Ashgate, 2006.

Avramescu, Catalin. *An Intellectual History of Cannibalism.* Princeton: Princeton University Press, 2009.

Axtell, James. "The White Indians of Colonial America." In *The European and the Indian: Essays in the Ethnohistory of Colonial North America,* 168–206. New York: Oxford University Press, 1981.

Bacevich, Andrew. "Robert Kaplan: Empire without Apologies." *The Nation,* September 26, 2005, 34–38.

Bagehot, Walter. *Physics and Politics.* Chicago: Ivan R. Dee, 1999.

Bailey, Frank Edgar. *British Policy and the Turkish Reform Movement: A Study in Anglo-Turkish Relations, 1826–1853.* Cambridge: Harvard University Press, 1942.

Balibar, Étienne, and Immanuel Wallerstein. *Race, Nation, Class: Ambiguous Identities.* London: Verso, 1991.

Ballantyne, Robert M. *The Coral Island.* Oxford: Oxford World's Classics, 1990.

Ballantyne, Tony. *Orientalism and Race: Aryanism in the British Empire.* Houndmills: Palgrave, 2002.

Banton, Michael. *The Idea of Race.* London: Tavistock, 1977.

——. *Racial Theories.* Cambridge: Cambridge University Press, 1987.

Barker, Francis, Peter Hulme, and Margaret Iversen, eds. *Cannibalism and the Colonial World.* Cambridge: Cambridge University Press, 1998.

Barkham, P. "136 Years on, Fiji Says Sorry for Its Cannibal Past." *Times* (London), October 15, 2003, 3.

Barrell, John. "Death on the Nile: Fantasy and the Literature of Tourism, 1840–1860." *Essays in Criticism* 41 (April 1991): 97–127.

———. *The Infection of Thomas De Quincey: A Psychopathology of Imperialism.* New Haven: Yale University Press, 1991.

Barrow, David Prescott. *A Decade of American Government in the Philippines, 1903–1913.* Yonkers, N.Y.: World Book Company, 1914.

Barthes, Roland. *Mythologies.* New York: Hill and Wang, 1972.

Baucom, Ian. *Out of Place: Englishness, Empire, and the Locations of Identity.* Princeton: Princeton University Press, 1999.

Baudrillard, Jean. *Simulations.* Translated by Paul Foss, Paul Patton, and Philip Beitchman. New York: Semiotext(e), 1983.

Bauman, Zygmunt. *Modernity and the Holocaust.* Ithaca: Cornell University Press, 1989.

Bayly, Christopher A. *Atlas of the British Empire: The Rise and Fall of the Greatest Empire the World Has Ever Known.* New York: Facts on File, 1989.

Bentley, Trevor. *Pakeha Maori: The Extraordinary Story of the Europeans Who Lived as Maori in Early New Zealand.* London: Penguin, 1999.

Berlin, Isaiah. *Against the Current: Essays in the History of Ideas.* London: Hogarth Press, 1979.

Bernasconi, Robert. "The Ghetto and Race." In *A Companion to Racial and Ethnic Studies,* edited by David Theo Goldberg and John Solomos, 340–47. Oxford: Blackwell, 2002.

Bernasconi, Robert, and Anika Maaza Mann. "Locke, Slavery, and *The Two Treatises.*" In *Race and Racism in Modern Philosophy,* edited by Andrew Valls, 89–107. Ithaca: Cornell University Press, 2005.

Bhabha, Homi K. "The Other Question: Stereotype, Discrimination and the Discourse of Colonialism." In *The Location of Culture,* 66–84. London: Routledge, 1994.

Biddiss, Michael. *Father of Racial Ideology: The Social and Political Thought of Count Gobineau.* New York: Weybright and Talley, 1970.

Bivona, Daniel. *British Imperial Literature, 1870–1940: Writing and the Administration of Empire.* Cambridge: Cambridge University Press, 1998.

Blake, Robert. *Disraeli's Grand Tour: Benjamin Disraeli and the Holy Land, 1830–31.* London: Weidenfeld and Nicholson, 1982.

Bonnett, Alastair. "How the British Working Class Became White: The Symbolic (Re)formation of Racialized Capitalism." *Journal of Historical Sociology* 11, no. 3 (September 1998): 316–40.

Bonwick, James. *Daily Life and Origin of the Tasmanians.* 1870. New York: Johnson Reprint Company, 1967.

———. *The Last of the Tasmanians.* 1870. New York: Johnson Reprint Company, 1970.

Boot, Max. *The Savage Wars of Peace: Small Wars and the Rise of American Power.* New York: Basic Books, 2002.

Booth, Michael R. *English Melodrama.* London: Herbert Jenkins, 1965.

Booth, William. *In Darkest England and the Way Out.* London: Salvation Army, 1890.

Bowser, J. Dallas. "Take Up the Black Man's Burden." *The Colored American.* April 8, 1899. http://boondocksnet.com.

Braddon, Mary Elizabeth. *The Octoroon; or, The Lily of Louisiana.* 1861–62. Hastings, U.K.: Sensation Press, 1999.

Bradshaw, David. "Eugenics: 'They Should Certainly Be Killed.'" In *A Concise Companion to Modernism,* edited by David Bradshaw, 34–55. Oxford: Blackwell, 2003.

Brady, Ivan. "Cannibalism." In *Encyclopedia of Cultural Anthropology,* vol. 1, edited by David Levinson and Melvin Ember, 163–66. New York: Henry Holt, 1996.

———. "The Myth-Eating Man." *American Anthropologist* 84 (1982): 595–611.

Brantlinger, Patrick. "'Black Armband' versus 'White Blindfold' History in Australia: A Review Essay." *Victorian Studies* 46, no. 4 (Summer 2004): 655–74.

———. *Dark Vanishings: Nineteenth-Century Discourse about the Extinction of Primitive Races.* Ithaca: Cornell University Press, 2003.

———. "The Famine." *Victorian Literature and Culture* 32, no. 1 (2004): 193–207.

———. "Mass Media and Culture in *Fin-de-Siècle* European Culture." In *Fin-de-Siècle and Its Legacy,* edited by Mikuláš Teich and Roy Porter, 98–114. Cambridge: Cambridge University Press, 1990.

———. "Missionaries and Cannibals in Nineteenth-Century Fiji." *History and Anthropology* 17, no. 1 (March 2006): 21–38.

———. *Rule of Darkness: British Literature and Imperialism, 1830–1914.* Ithaca: Cornell University Press, 1988.

Brantlinger, Patrick, and Don Ulin. "Policing Nomads: Discourse and Social Control in Early Victorian England." *Cultural Critique* (Fall 1993): 33–63.

Brendon, Vyvyen. *Children of the Raj.* London: Weidenfeld and Nicolson, 2005.

Brewster, A. J. *The Hill Tribes of Fiji: A Record of Forty Years' Intimate Connection with the Tribes of the Mountainous Interior of Fiji....* New York: Johnson Reprint Company, 1967.

———. *King of the Cannibal Isles: A Tale of Early Life and Adventure in the Fiji Islands.* London: Robert Hale, 1937.

Briggs, Asa. *Saxons, Normans and Victorians.* Hastings, U.K.: The Historical Association, 1966.

Brock, Peggy. "New Christians as Evangelists." In *Missions and Empire,* edited by Norman Etherington, 132–52. Oxford: Oxford University Press, 2005.

Brodie, Fawn. *The Devil Drives: A Life of Sir Richard Burton.* New York: Norton, 1967.

Brontë, Charlotte. *Jane Eyre.* London: Penguin, 1996.

Brontë, Emily. *Wuthering Heights.* Oxford: Oxford University Press, 1976.

Brown, Paula, and Donald Tuzin, eds. *The Ethnography of Cannibalism.* Washington, D.C.: Society for Psychological Anthropology, 1983.

Buchanan, Robert. "The Voice of the Hooligan." *Contemporary Review* 76 (December 1899): 774–89.

Bulu, Joel. *Joel Bulu: The Autobiography of a Native Minister in the South Seas.* London: T. Woolmer, 1884.

Burrow, J. W. "Evolution and Anthropology in the 1860s: The Anthropological Society of London, 1863–71." *Victorian Studies* 7, no. 2 (December 1963): 137–54.

Burton, Antoinette. Review of *Oxford History of the British Empire,* vols. 3 and 5. *Victorian Studies* 44, no. 1 (2001): 167–69.

Burton, Isabel. *The Life of Captain Sir Richard F. Burton.* Boston: Milford House, 1973.

Burton, Richard F. *The Book of a Thousand Nights and a Night.* 10 vols. London: Burton Club, 1886.

———. *The Jew, the Gypsy and El Islam*. Chicago: Herbert S. Stone, 1897.

———. *The Lake Regions of Central Africa*. 2 vols. New York: Horizon, 1961.

———. *Personal Narrative of a Pilgrimage to Al-Madinah and Meccah*. 2 vols. New York: Dover, 1964.

Butler, Samuel. *Erewhon*. Harmondsworth: Penguin, 1976.

———. *The Notebooks of Samuel Butler*. London: Hogarth Press, 1985.

Buzacott, Rev. A. *Mission Life in the Islands of the Pacific*. London: John Snow, 1866.

Caird, Mona. "A Defense of the So-Called 'Wild Women.'" *The Nineteenth Century* 31 (1892): 811–29.

Calder, J. E. *Some Account of the Wars, Extirpation, Habits, etc. of the Native Tribes of Tasmania*. Hobart: Henn, 1875.

Calvert, Rev. James. *Fiji and the Fijians*. Part 2. *Mission History*. New York: D. Appleton, 1859.

Cannon, John, ed. *Oxford Dictionary of British History*. Oxford: Oxford University Press, 2001.

Cargill, Rev. David. *The Diaries and Correspondence of David Cargill, 1832–1843*. Edited by A. J. Schütz. Canberra: Australian National University Press, 1977.

Carlyle, Thomas. *Chartism*. In *English and Other Critical Essays*, 165–238. London: Dent, 1964.

———. *Sartor Resartus*. London: Dent, 1964.

———. "Signs of the Times." In *Scottish and Other Miscellanies*, 223–45. London: Dent, 1923.

Ceram, C. W. *Gods, Graves, and Scholars: The Story of Archaeology*. 2d ed. New York: Alfred A. Knopf, 1967.

Chakrabarty, Dipesh. *Provincializing Europe: Postcolonial Thought and Historical Difference*. Princeton: Princeton University Press, 2000.

Chakravarty, Gautam. *The Indian Mutiny and the British Imagination*. Cambridge: Cambridge University Press, 2005.

Chatterjee, Partha. *The Nation and Its Fragments: Colonial and Postcolonial Histories*. Princeton: Princeton University Press, 1993.

Cheyette, Bryan. *Constructions of the "Jew" in English Literature and Society: Racial Representations, 1875–1945*. Cambridge: Cambridge University Press, 1993.

Childs, Donald. *Modernism and Eugenics: Woolf, Eliot, Yeats, and the Culture of Degeneration*. Cambridge: Cambridge University Press, 2001.

Clarke, Marcus. *His Natural Life*. Harmondsworth: Penguin, 1970.

Clayton, Cherry. *Olive Schreiner*. New York: Twayne, 1997.

Clifford, James. Introduction to *Writing Culture: The Poetics and Politics of Ethnography*, edited by James Clifford and George Marcus, 1–26. Berkeley: University of California Press, 1986.

———. "On Ethnographic Allegory." In *Writing Culture: The Poetics and Politics of Ethnography*, edited by James Clifford and George Marcus, 99–121. Berkeley: University of California Press, 1986.

Clymer, Kenton. "Humanitarian Imperialism: David Prescott Barrows and the White Man's Burden in the Philippines." *Pacific Historical Review* 45 (1976): 495–515.

Coan, Stephen. "'The Most Extraordinary Romance': H. Rider Haggard and the Writing of *She*." In *She: Explorations into a Romance,* edited by Tania Zulli, 115–38. Rome: Aracne, 2009.

Cohen, Morton, ed. *Rudyard Kipling to Rider Haggard: The Record of a Friendship.* London: Hutchinson, 1965.

Cohen, Phil. "Psychoanalysis and Racism: Reading the Other Scene." In *A Companion to Racial and Ethnic Studies,* edited by David Theo Goldberg and John Solomos, 170–201. Oxford: Blackwell, 2002.

Cohn, Bernard. *Colonialism and Its Forms of Knowledge: The British in India.* Princeton: Princeton University Press, 1991.

———. "Representing Authority in Victorian India." In *The Invention of Tradition,* edited by Eric Hobsbaum and Terence Ranger, 165–209. Cambridge: Cambridge University Press, 1983.

Colley, Linda. *Captives.* New York: Pantheon, 2002.

Conklin, Beth A. *Consuming Grief: Compassionate Cannibalism in an Amazonian Society.* Austin: University of Texas Press, 2001.

Conrad, Joseph. *Heart of Darkness.* New York: W. W. Norton, 2006.

———. *Lord Jim.* London: Penguin, 1989.

———. "An Outpost of Progress." In *Tales of Unrest,* 143–98. New York: Charles Scribner's, 1898.

Cook, Captain James. *Journals.* Edited by J. C. Beaglehole. 4 vols. Rochester: Boydell Press, 1999.

Cook, Raymond A. *Thomas Dixon.* New York: Twayne, 1974.

Cooper, Frederick. *Colonialism in Question: Theory, Knowledge, History.* Berkeley: University of California Press, 2005.

Cove, John J. *What the Bones Say: Tasmanian Aborigines, Science and Domination.* Ottawa: Carleton University Press, 1995.

Crèvecoeur, Hector St. John. *Letters from an American Farmer and Sketches of Eighteenth-Century America.* New York: Penguin, 1986.

Cromer, Earl of. "The Government of Subject Races." In *Political and Literary Essays, 1908–1913,* 3–53. London: Macmillan, 1913.

Cumming, Constance G. *At Home in Fiji.* New York: A. C. Armstrong, 1889.

Curtis, L. Perry. *Anglo-Saxons and Celts: A Study of Anti-Irish Prejudice in Victorian England.* Bridgeport, Conn.: University of Bridgeport, Conference on British Studies, 1968.

Dalrymple, William. *White Mughals: Love and Betrayal in Eighteenth-Century India.* New York: Viking, 2003.

Daly, Nicholas. "That Obscure Object of Desire: Victorian Commodity Culture and Fictions of the Mummy." *NOVEL: A Forum on Fiction* 28, no. 1 (Autumn 1994): 24–51.

Daniel, Glyn. *A Hundred and Fifty Years of Archaeology.* Cambridge: Harvard University Press, 1976.

Darwin, Charles. *The Voyage of the Beagle.* Garden City, N.Y.: Doubleday, 1962.

———. *The Descent of Man.* New York: Prometheus Books, 1998.

David, Deirdre. *Rule Britannia: Women, Empire, and Victorian Writing.* Ithaca: Cornell University Press, 1995.

Davidson, Basil. *The Black Man's Burden: Africa and the Curse of the Nation-State.* New York: Three Rivers Press, 1992.

———. *The Lost Cities of Africa.* Rev. ed. Boston: Little, Brown, 1970.

Davidson, J. W. *Peter Dillon of Vanikoro, Chevalier of the South Seas.* Melbourne: Oxford University Press, 1975.

Davies, Rev. John. *The History of the Tahitian Mission, 1799–1830.* Cambridge: Cambridge University Press, 1961.

Davis, David Brion. *Slavery and Human Progress.* Oxford: Oxford University Press, 1984.

Davis, Thomas. *Literary and Historical Essays, 1846.* Washington, D.C.: Woodstock Books, 1998.

Day, Jasmine. *The Mummy's Curse: Mummymania in the English-Speaking World.* London: Routledge, 2006.

Deane, Bradley. "Imperial Barbarians: Primitive Masculinity in Lost World Fiction." *Victorian Literature and Culture* 36, no. 1 (2008): 206–25.

Deane, Seamus. *Celtic Revivals: Essays in Modern Irish Literature, 1880–1980.* London: Faber and Faber, 1985.

De Certeau, Michel. *Heterologies: Discourse on the Other.* Minneapolis: University of Minnesota Press, 1986.

Defoe, Daniel. *Robinson Crusoe.* Edited by Evan Davis. Peterborough, Ont.: Broadview Editions, 2010.

De Gusta, D. "Fijian Cannibalism: Osteological Evidence from Navatu." *American Journal of Physical Anthropology* 110, no. 2 (1999): 215–41.

De Nie, Michael. *The Eternal Paddy: Irish Identity and the British Press, 1798–1882.* Madison: University of Wisconsin Press, 2004.

Derrida, Jacques. "Différance." In *Margins of Philosophy.* Translated by Alan Bass, 3–27. Chicago: University of Chicago Press, 1982.

Dickens, Charles. *Great Expectations.* Oxford: Oxford University Press, 1989.

———. *Hard Times.* Oxford: Oxford University Press, 1989.

———. *The Mystery of Edwin Drood.* Oxford: Oxford University Press, 1989.

Dippie, Brian. *The Vanishing American: White Attitudes and U.S. Indian Policy.* Lawrence: University Press of Kansas, 1982.

Dirks, Nicholas. *The Scandal of Empire: India and the Creation of Imperial Britain.* Cambridge: Harvard University Press, 2006.

Disraeli, Benjamin. *Alroy.* Bradenham ed., vol. 5. New York: Alfred A. Knopf, 1927.

———. *Coningsby, or The New Generation.* New York: Penguin, 1983.

———. *Contarini Fleming, a Psychological Romance.* Bradenham ed., vol. 4. New York: Alfred A. Knopf, 1934.

———. *Letters of Benjamin Disraeli: 1815–1834.* Edited by J. A. W. Gunn et al. Toronto: University of Toronto Press, 1982.

———. *Letters of Benjamin Disraeli: 1842–1847.* Edited by M. G. Wiebe et al. Toronto: University of Toronto Press, 1989.———. *Lord George Bentinck: A Political Biography.* London: Routledge, Warne, and Routledge, 1861.

———. *Lothair.* Bradenham ed., vol. 11. New York: Alfred A. Knopf, 1934.

———. *Tancred; or, the New Crusade.* Bradenham ed., vol. 10. New York: Alfred A. Knopf, 1934.

Disraeli, Isaac. *The Genius of Judaism.* London: Edward Moxon, 1833.

Dolin, Tim. "Race and the Social Plot in *The Mystery of Edwin Drood.*" In *The Victorians and Race,* edited by Shearer West, 84–100. Aldershot: Ashgate, 1996.

Doyle, Sir Arthur Conan. *The Best Supernatural Tales of Arthur Conan Doyle.* New York: Dover, 1979.

Drinnon, Richard. *Facing West: The Metaphysics of Indian-Hating and Empire Building.* Minneapolis: University of Minnesota Press, 1980.

Du Bois, W. E. B. "The Burden of Black Women." In *W. E. B. Du Bois: A Reader,* edited by David Lewis, 291–93. New York: Henry Holt, 1995.

———. "The Conservation of Races." 1897. In *Nations and Identities,* edited by Vincent P. Pecora, 190–99. Oxford: Blackwell, 2001.

Dyer, Richard. *White.* New York: Routledge, 1997.

Eagleton, Terry. *Crazy John and the Bishop, and Other Essays on Irish Culture.* Cork: Cork University Press, 1998.

———. *Heathcliff and the Great Hunger: Studies in Irish Culture.* London: Verso, 1995.

Easterly, William Russell. *The White Man's Burden: Why the West's Efforts to Aid the Rest Have Done So Much Ill and So Little Good.* New York: Penguin, 2006.

Eaves, Morris. "Blake and the Artistic Machine: An Essay in Artistic Decorum." *PMLA* 92, no. 5 (October 1977): 903–27.

Edwards, Amelia. "Recent Discovery of Royal Mummies and Other Egyptian Antiquities." *Illustrated London News,* February 4, 1882, 113.

Elbourne, Elizabeth. "Between Van Diemen's Land and the Cape Colony." In *Reading Robinson,* edited by Anna Johnston and Mitchell Rolls, 77–94. Hobart: Quintus Publishing, University of Tasmania, 2008.

Eliot, George. *The Impressions of Theophrastus Such.* Iowa City: University of Iowa Press, 1994.

———. *The Mill on the Floss.* Boston: Houghton Mifflin, 1970.

———. *Selections from George Eliot's Letters.* Edited by Gordon S. Haight. New Haven: Yale University Press, 1985.

Elkins, Caroline. *Imperial Reckoning: The Untold Story of Britain's Gulag in Kenya.* New York: Henry Holt, 2005.

Endelmann, Todd. "'A Hebrew to the End': The Emergence of Disraeli's Jewishness." In *The Self-fashioning of Disraeli, 1818–1851,* edited by Charles Richmond and Paul Smith, 106–30. Cambridge: Cambridge University Press, 1998.

Engels, Friedrich. *The Condition of the Working Class in England.* Stanford: Stanford University Press, 1958.

Erskine, Captain John E. *Journal of a Cruise among the Islands of the Western Pacific....* London: John Murray, 1853.

Etherington, Norman. *The Annotated She: A Critical Edition of H. Rider Haggard's Victorian Romance.* Bloomington: Indiana University Press, 1991.

———. *Rider Haggard.* Boston: Twayne, 1984.

Evans, Julie. *Edward Eyre, Race and Colonial Governance.* Dunedin, New Zealand: University of Otago Press, 2005.

Ewen, Elizabeth, and Stuart Ewen. *Typecasting: On the Arts and Sciences of Human In-equality.* Rev. ed. New York: Seven Stories Press, 2008.

Eze, Chukwudi Emmanuel, ed. *Race and the Enlightenment: A Reader.* London: Blackwell, 1997.

Fabian, Johannes. *Time and the Other: How Anthropology Makes Its Object.* New York: Columbia University Press, 1983.

Fallis, Richard. *The Irish Renaissance.* Syracuse: Syracuse University Press, 1977.

Fanon, Frantz. *Black Skin, White Masks.* New York: Grove Press, 1967.

——. *The Wretched of the Earth.* Translated by Constance Farrington. New York: Grove Press, 1991.

Farrar, Frederic William. "Aptitudes of Races." Transactions of the Ethnological Society, n.s. 5 (1867): 115–26.

Farwell, Byron. *Queen Victoria's Little Wars.* New York: Harper and Row, 1972.

Faverty, Frederic. *Matthew Arnold the Ethnologist.* Evanston: Northwestern University Press, 1951.

Ferguson, Adam. *An Essay on the History of Civil Society.* 1767. Philadelphia: A. Finley, 1819.

Ferguson, Niall. *Empire: The Rise and Demise of the British World Order and the Lessons for Global Power.* New York: Basic Books, 2004.

Findlay, G. G., and W. W. Holdsworth. *The History of the Wesleyan Methodist Missionary Society.* 5 vols. London: Epworth Press, 1921.

Fontein, Joost. *The Silence of Great Zimbabwe: Contested Landscapes and the Power of Heritage.* London: University College London Press, 2006.

Forbes, William Cameron. *The Philippine Islands.* 2 vols. Boston: Houghton Mifflin, 1928.

Foster, John Bellamy, and Robert McChesney, eds. *Pox Americana: Exposing the American Empire.* New York: Monthly Review Press, 2004.

Foucault, Michel. *"Society Must Be Defended": Lectures at the Collège de France, 1975–76.* New York: Picador, 2003.

France, Peter. *The Rape of Egypt: How the Europeans Stripped Egypt of Its Heritage.* London: Barrie and Jenkins, 1991.

Francisco, Luzviminda. "The First Vietnam: The Philippine-American War, 1899–1902." In *The Philippines Reader: A History of Colonialism, Neocolonialism, Dictatorship, and Resistance,* edited by Daniel P. Schirmer and Stephen R. Shalom, 8–19. Boston: South End Press, 1987.

Franklin, Benjamin. *Works.* Edited by John Bigelow. Vol. 2. New York: Putnam's, 1904. Franklin, J. Jeffrey. *The Lotus and the Lion: Buddhism and the British Empire.* Ithaca: Cornell University Press, 2008.

Freud, Sigmund. *Totem and Taboo.* New York: W. W. Norton, 1913.

Frost, Brian J. *The Essential Guide to Mummy Literature.* Lanham, Md.: Scarecrow Press, 2008.

Froude, James Anthony. *The English in Ireland in the Eighteenth Century.* 3 vols. New York: Charles Scribner's Sons, 1897.

——. *The Two Chiefs of Dunboy; or, An Irish Romance of the Last Century.* New York: Charles Scribner's Sons, 1889.

Gardner, Donald. "Anthropophagy, Myth, and the Subtle Ways of Ethnocentrism." In *The Anthropology of Cannibalism,* edited by Laurence R. Goldman, 27–50. Westport, Conn.: Bergin and Garvey, 1999.

Garrett, John. *To Live among the Stars: Christian Origins in Oceania.* Suva: World Council of Churches, 1982.

Gatewood, Willard. *Black Americans and the White Man's Burden, 1898–1903.* Urbana: University of Illinois Press, 1975.

Gibbons, Luke. *Gaelic Gothic: Race, Colonization, and Irish Culture.* Galway: Arlen House, 2004.

Gilbert, W. S. *Bab Ballads and Savoy Songs.* Teddington, Middlesex: The Echo Library, 2007.

Gill, Rev. W. W. *Jottings from the Pacific.* London: Religious Tract Society, 1885.

Gilman, Sander L. *Difference and Pathology: Stereotypes of Sexuality, Race, and Madness.* Ithaca: Cornell University Press, 1985.

Gilmour, David. *The Long Recessional: The Imperial Life of Rudyard Kipling.* New York: Farrar, Straus and Giroux, 2002.

Gitelman, Lisa. *Scripts, Grooves, and Writing Machines: Representing Technology in the Edison Era.* Stanford: Stanford University Press, 1999.

Gladstone, William Ewart. *Bulgarian Horrors and the Question of the East.* London: John Murray, 1876.

Glover, David. *Vampires, Mummies, and Liberals: Bram Stoker and the Politics of Popular Fiction.* Durham: Duke University Press, 1996.

Gobineau, Count Arthur de. *The Inequality of Races.* Translated by Adrian Collins. Los Angeles: Noontide Press, 1966.

Godsall, Jon R. *The Tangled Web: A Life of Sir Richard Burton.* Leicester: Matador, 2008.

Goldberg, David Theo. *The Racial State.* Oxford: Blackwell, 2002.

Goldie, Terrie. *Fear and Temptation: The Image of the Indigene in Canadian, Australian, and New Zealand Literatures.* Kingston, Ont.: McGill–Queen's University Press, 1989.

Goldman, Laurence R., ed. *The Anthropology of Cannibalism.* Westport, Conn.: Bergin and Garvey, 1999.

Gorra, Michael. "Rudyard Kipling to Salman Rushdie: Imperialism to Postcolonialism." In *The Columbia History of the British Novel,* edited by John Richetti, 631–57. New York: Columbia University Press, 1994.

Gould, Stephen Jay. *The Mismeasure of Man.* New York: W. W. Norton, 1981.

Gray, Peter. *The Irish Famine.* New York: Harry N. Abrams, 1995.

Green, Roger Lancelyn, ed. *Kipling: The Critical Heritage.* London: Routledge and Kegan Paul, 1971.

Greenslade, William. *Degeneration, Culture and the Novel, 1880–1940.* Cambridge: Cambridge University Press, 1994.

Greg, W. R. "On the Failure of 'Natural Selection' in the Case of Man." *Fraser's* (September 1868): 353–62.

Groth, Helen. "Reading Victorian Illusions: Dickens's *Haunted Man* and Dr. Pepper's 'Ghost.'" *Victorian Studies* 50, no. 1 (Autumn 2007): 43–65.

Gunson, Neil. *Messengers of Grace: Evangelical Missionaries in the South Seas, 1797–1860.* Melbourne: Oxford University Press, 1978.

Guttman, W. L., ed. *A Plea for Democracy: An Edited Selection from the 1867 Essays on Reform and Questions for a Revised Parliament.* London: MacGibbon and Kee, 1967.

Haggard, H. Rider. *Cetawayo and His White Neighbours.* London: Trübner, 1882.

——. *The Days of My Life.* 2 vols. London: Longmans, Green, 1926.

——. *Elissa: The Doom of Zimbabwe; Black Heart and White Heart: A Zulu Idyll.* London: Longmans, Green, 1900.

——. *King Solomon's Mines.* Peterborough, Ont.: Broadview, 2002.

——. *Maiwa's Revenge; or, The War of Little Hand.* London: Longmans, Green, 1888.

——. "The Real King Solomon's Mines." In *The Best Short Stories of Rider Haggard,* edited by Peter Haining, 18–25. London: Michael Joseph, 1981.

——. *She.* London: Penguin Books, 2001.

——. *She, King Solomon's Mines, Allan Quatermain.* New York: Dover, 1951.

——. "Smith and the Pharaohs." In *The Best Short Stories of Rider Haggard,* edited by Peter Haining, 148–91. London: Michael Joseph, 1981.

——. "The Transvaal." *Macmillan's Magazine* 36 (May 1877): 71–79.

Haggard, Lilias. *The Cloak That I Left: A Biography of the Author Henry Rider Haggard KBE.* London: Hodder and Stoughton, 1951.

Hagiioannu, Andrew. *The Man Who Would Be Kipling: The Colonial Fiction and the Frontiers of Exile.* New York: Palgrave Macmillan, 2003.

Haight, Gordon S., ed. *Selections from George Eliot's Letters.* New Haven: Yale University Press, 1985.

Halberstam, Judith. "Technologies of Monstrosity." *Victorian Studies* 3, no. 3 (Spring 1993): 333–52.

Hall, Catherine. *Civilising Subjects: Metropole and Colony in the English Imagination, 1830–1867.* Chicago: University of Chicago Press, 2002.

Hall, Catherine, Keith McClelland, and Jane Rendall. *Defining the Victorian Nation: Class, Race, Gender and the Reform Act of 1867.* Cambridge: Cambridge University Press, 2000.

Hannaford, Ivan. *Race: The History of an Idea in the West.* Baltimore: Johns Hopkins University Press, 1996.

Harlan, Louis R. "Booker T. Washington and the 'White Man's Burden.'" *American Historical Review* 71, no. 2 (January 1966): 441–67.

Harootunian, Harry. *The Empire's New Clothes: Paradigm Lost, and Regained.* Chicago: Prickly Paradigm Press, 2004.

Headrick, Daniel. *The Invisible Weapon: Telecommunications and International Politics.* Oxford: Oxford University Press, 1991.

——. *The Tools of Empire: Technology and European Imperialism in the Nineteenth Century.* Oxford: Oxford University Press, 1981.

Healy, David. *U.S. Expansionism: The Imperialist Urge in the 1890s.* Madison: University of Wisconsin Press, 1970.

Henty, G. A. *By Sheer Pluck.* London: Blackie, 1884.

Herbert, Christopher. *Culture and Anomie: Ethnographic Imagination in the Nineteenth Century.* Chicago: University of Chicago Press, 1991.

Heuman, Gad. *The Killing Time: The Morant Bay Rebellion in Jamaica.* Knoxville: University of Tennessee Press, 1994.

Himmelfarb, Gertrude. *The Idea of Poverty in England in the Early Industrial Age.* London: Faber, 1984.

Hiraiwa-Hasegawa, M. "Cannibalism among Non-human Primates." In *Cannibalism: Ecology and Evolution among Diverse Taxa,* edited by Mark Elgar and Bernard Crespi, 323–38. Oxford: Oxford University Press, 1992.

Hitchens, Christopher. *Blood, Class, and Empire: The Enduring Anglo-American Relationship.* New York: Nation Books, 2004.

Hobsbawm, Eric. *Labouring Men.* London: Weidenfeld and Nicolson, 1964.

Hobsbawm, Eric, and Terence Ranger, eds. *The Invention of Tradition.* Cambridge: Cambridge University Press, 1983.

Hochschild, Adam. *King Leopold's Ghost.* Boston: Houghton Mifflin, 1998.

Holden, Matthew. *White Man's Burden.* New York: Chandler, 1973.

Hollingshead, John. *Ragged London in 1861.* London: Smith, Elder, 1861.

Hooper, Steven. "Cannibals Talk." *Anthropology Today* 19, no. 6 (2003): 20.

Hoppen, Kenneth. *The Mid-Victorian Generation, 1846–1886.* New Oxford History of England. New York: Oxford University Press, 1998.

Horkheimer, Max, and Theodor W. Adorno. *Dialectic of Enlightenment.* Translated by John Cumming. New York: Continuum, 1997.

Horkheimer, Max, Theodor Adorno, et al. *Aspects of Sociology.* Translated by John Viertel. Boston: Beacon Press, 1972.

Horsman, Reginald. "Origins of Racial Anglo-Saxonism in Great Britain before 1850." *Journal of the History of Ideas* 37 (1976): 387–410.

——. *Race and Manifest Destiny: The Origins of American Racial Anglo-Saxonism.* Cambridge: Harvard University Press, 1981.

Hughes, Robert. *The Fatal Shore: The Epic of Australia's Founding.* New York: Vintage, 1986.

Huhndorf, Shari M. *Going Native: Indians in the American Cultural Imagination.* Ithaca: Cornell University Press, 2001.

Hulme, Peter. "Introduction: The Cannibal Scene." In *Cannibalism and the Colonial World,* edited by Francis Barker, Peter Hulme, and Margaret Iverson, 1–38. Cambridge: Cambridge University Press, 1998.

Hume, David. *Political Essays.* Cambridge: Cambridge University Press, 1994.

Hurley, Kelly. *The Gothic Body: Sexuality, Materialism, and Degeneration at the Fin de Siècle.* Cambridge: Cambridge University Press, 1996.

——. "The Victorian Mummy-Fetish: H. Rider Haggard, Frank Aubrey, and the White Mummy." In *Victorian Freaks: The Social Contexts of Freakery in Britain,* edited by Marlene Tromp, 180–99. Columbus: Ohio State University Press, 2008.

Huxley, Thomas Henry. *Man's Place in Nature, and Other Anthropological Essays.* Vol. 7 of *Collected Essays.* 9 vols. New York: Greenwood, 1968.

——. "*Emancipation—Black and White.*" Vol. 3 of *Collected Essays.* 9 vols., 66–75. New York: Greenwood, 1968.

——. "On the Methods and Results of Ethnology." Vol. 7 of *Collected Essays.* 9 vols., 253–70. New York: Greenwood.

Hyam, Ronald. *Empire and Sexuality: The British Experience.* Manchester: Manchester University Press, 1990.

Ignatieff, Michael. "The American Empire: The Burden." *New York Times Magazine,* January 5, 2003, 22–27.

Im Thurn, Everard, and Leonard Wharton, eds. *The Journal of William Lockerby, Sandalwood Trader in the Fijian Islands during the Years 1808–1809....* London: Hakluyt Society, 1925.

Jahoda, Gustav. *Images of Savages: Ancient Roots of Modern Prejudice in Western Culture.* London: Routledge, 1999.

James, Lawrence. *Raj: The Making and Unmaking of British India.* New York: St. Martin's Griffin, 2000.

Jameson, Fredric. *The Political Unconscious: Narrative as a Socially Symbolic Act.* Ithaca: Cornell University Press, 1981.

———. *Signatures of the Visible.* New York: Routledge, 1992.

Johnston, Anna. *Missionary Writing and Empire.* Cambridge: Cambridge University Press, 2003.

Johnston, Anna, and Mitchell Rolls, eds. *Reading Robinson: Companion Essays to Friendly Mission.* Hobart: Quintus Publishing, University of Tasmania, 2008.

Johnston, Sir Harry H. *British Central Africa: An Attempt to Give Some Account of a Portion of the Territories under British Influence North of the Zambesi.* 3d ed. London: Methuen, 1906.

Jones, Gareth Stedman. *Outcast London: A Study in the Relationship between Social Classes in Victorian Society.* Oxford: Clarendon Press, 1971.

Jordan, Winthrop. *The White Man's Burden: Historical Origins of Racism in the United States.* New York: Oxford University Press, 1974.

Joy, Bill. "Why the Future Doesn't Need Us." *Wired* (April 2000): 238–46.

Joyce, James. *Collected Poems.* New York: Viking, 1957.

———. *The Critical Writings.* New York: Viking, 1959.

———. *Dubliners.* New York: Penguin Books, 1976.

Judd, Denis. *Empire: The British Imperial Experience from 1765 to the Present.* New York: Basic Books, 1996.

Judis, John B. *The Folly of Empire: What George Bush Could Learn from Theodore Roosevelt and Woodrow Wilson.* New York: Scribner, 2004.

Jumper, Sharon. "Powell, Wisdom, and the White Man's Burden." *Daily Kos,* January 7, 2006. http://www.dailykos.com (accessed January 27, 2006).

Juneja, Renu. "The Native and the Nabob: Representations of the Indian Experience in Eighteenth-Century English Literature." *Journal of Commonwealth Literature* 27 (1992): 183–200.

Kaplan, Robert D. *Imperial Grunts: The American Military on the Ground.* New York: Random House, 2005.

Karnow, Stanley. *In Our Image: America's Empire in the Philippines.* New York: Ballantine Books, 1990.

Keating, Peter. *Kipling the Poet.* London: Secker and Warburg, 1994.

———. *The Working Classes in Victorian Fiction.* London: Routledge and Kegan Paul, 1971.

Kee, Robert. *The Green Flag*. Vol. 1. *The Most Distressful Country*. London: Penguin, 1989.

——. *The Green Flag*. Vol. 2. *The Bold Fenian Men*. London: Penguin, 1989.

Keegan, Timothy. *Colonial South Africa and the Origins of the Racial Order*. Leicester: Leicester University Press, 1996.

Keep, Christopher. "Technology and Information: Accelerating Developments." In *A Companion to the Victorian Novel*, edited by Patrick Brantlinger and William B. Thesing, 137–54. Oxford: Blackwell, 2002.

Kerr, Donal. *A Nation of Beggars? Priests, People, and Politics in Famine Ireland*. Oxford: Oxford University Press, 1994.

Kessler, Richard J. *Rebellion and Repression in the Philippines*. New Haven: Yale University Press, 1989.

Kevles, Daniel J. *In the Name of Eugenics: Genetics and the Uses of Human Heredity*. Cambridge: Harvard University Press, 1995.

Kikau, R. "Family Accepts Clan's Apology." *Fiji Times,* November 14, 2003.

Kinealy, Christine. *The Great Irish Famine: Impact, Ideology and Rebellion*. Houndmills: Palgrave, 2002.

Kingsley, Charles. *The Roman and the Teuton: A Series of Lectures Delivered before the University of Cambridge*. London: Macmillan, 1890.

Kipling, Rudyard. *Complete Verse*. New York: Doubleday, 1989.

——. *Kim*. New York: Modern Library, 2004.

——. *The Letters of Rudyard Kipling*. Vol. 1, *1872–89*. Edited by Thomas Pinney. London: Macmillan, 1990.

——. *The Letters of Rudyard Kipling*. Vol. 2, *1890–99*. Edited by Thomas Pinney. London: Macmillan, 1990.

——. *Plain Tales from the Hills*. Oxford: Oxford University Press, 1987.

——. *Something of Myself*. Edited by Thomas Pinney. Cambridge: Cambridge University Press, 1990.

——. *Writings on Writing*. Cambridge: Cambridge University Press, 1996.

Kirch, P. V. *On the Road of the Winds: An Archaeological History of the Pacific Islands before European Contact*. Berkeley: University of California Press, 2000.

Kitson, Peter J. *Romantic Literature, Race, and Colonial Encounter*. New York: Palgrave Macmillan, 2007.

Kittler, Friedrich. "Dracula's Legacy." In *Literature, Media, Information Systems,* edited by John Johnston, 50–84. Amsterdam: Overseas Publishers Association, 1997.

——. *Gramophone, Film, Typewriter*. Stanford: Stanford University Press, 1999.

Klaf, Franklin, and William Brown. "Necrophilia: Brief Review and Case Report." *Psychoanalytic Quarterly* 29, no. 143 (1958): 159.

Knauft, B. M. *South Coast New Guinea Cultures: History, Comparison, Dialectic*. Cambridge: Cambridge University Press, 1993.

Knox, Robert. *The Races of Men: A Fragment*. 1850. Miami: Mnemosyne, 1969.

Koven, Seth. *Slumming: Sexual and Social Politics in Victorian London*. Princeton: Princeton University Press, 2004.

Krebs, Paula. *Gender, Race, and the Writing of Empire: Public Discourse and the Boer War*. Cambridge: Cambridge University Press, 1999.

Kroker, Arthur, and Michael A. Weinstein. *Data Trash: The Theory of the Virtual Class.* New York: St. Martin's Press, 1994.

Krugman, Paul. "White Man's Burden." In *The Great Unraveling: Losing Our Way in the New Century,* 388–90. New York: W. W. Norton, 2004.

Kuchta, Todd. *Semi-Detached Empire: Suburbia and the Colonization of Britain, 1880 to the Present.* Charlottesville: University of Virginia Press, 2010.

Kucich, John. *Imperial Masochism: British Fiction, Fantasy, and Social Class.* Princeton: Princeton University Press, 2007.

Kuklick, Henrika. "Contested Monuments: The Politics of Archeology in Southern Africa." In *Colonial Situations: Essays on the Contextualization of Ethnographic Knowledge,* edited by George Stocking, 135–69. Madison: University of Wisconsin Press, 1991.

Labouchère, Henry. "The Brown Man's Burden." *Literary Digest* 18, no. 8 (February 25, 1899): 219.

Lacan, Jacques. *Écrits: A Selection.* New York: W. W. Norton, 1977.

Lamb, Jonathan, Vanessa Smith, and Nicholas Thomas, eds. *Exploration and Exchange: A South Seas Anthology, 1680–1900.* Chicago: University of Chicago Press, 2000.

Lazarus, Neil. "Introducing Postcolonial Studies." In *The Cambridge Companion to Postcolonial Literary Studies,* edited by Neil Lazarus, 1–16. Cambridge: Cambridge University Press, 2004.

Leach, Edmund. "Long Pig, Tall Story." *New Society,* August 30, 1979, 467.

Leask, Nigel. *British Romantic Writers and the East: Anxieties of Empire.* Cambridge: Cambridge University Press, 1992.

Lefever, Ernest. *America's Imperial Burden: Is the Past Prologue?* Boulder: Westview Press, 1999.

Lennon, Joseph. *Irish Orientalism: A Literary and Intellectual History.* Syracuse: Syracuse University Press, 2004.

Lens, Sidney. *The Forging of the American Empire.* Chicago: Haymarket Books, 2003.

Lester, Alan. "George Augustus Robinson and Imperial Networks." In *Reading Robinson: Companion Essays to Friendly Mission,* edited by Anna Johnston and Mitchell Rolls, 27–43. Hobart: Quintus Publishing, University of Tasmania, 2008.

Lestringant, Frank. *Cannibals: The Discovery and Representation of the Cannibal from Columbus to Jules Verne.* Berkeley: University of California Press, 1997.

Lévi-Strauss, Claude. *Tristes Tropiques.* New York: Atheneum, 1974.

Lewis, I. M. *Religion in Context: Cults and Charisma.* Cambridge: Cambridge University Press, 1986.

Lindenbaum, Shirley. "Thinking about Cannibalism." *Annual Review of Anthropology* 33 (2004): 475–98.

Linton, Eliza Lynn. "The Wild Women." *Nineteenth Century* 30 (1891): 79–88.

Linton, Ralph. *Ethnology of Polynesia and Micronesia.* Chicago: Field Museum of Natural History, 1926.

Lippmann, Walter. *Public Opinion.* 1922. New York: Free Press, 1965.

Lloyd, David. *Nationalism and Minor Literature: James Clarence Mangan and the Emergence of Irish Cultural Nationalism.* Berkeley: University of California Press, 1987.

Locke, John. *Two Treatises of Government.* London: J. M. Dent, 1991.

Lodge, Henry Cabot, and Charles F. Redmond, eds. *Selections from the Correspondence of Theodore Roosevelt and Henry Cabot Lodge, 1884–1918.* 2 vols. New York: Da Capo Press, 1971.

Loeb, Kurt. *White Man's Burden.* Toronto: Lugus Productions, 1992.

Loomba, Ania. *Colonialism/Postcolonialism.* London: Routledge, 1998.

Lorimer, Douglas. *Colour, Class and the Victorians: English Attitudes to the Negro in the Mid-Nineteenth Century.* New York: Holmes and Meier, 1978.

Love, Eric T. *Race over Empire: Racism and U.S. Imperialism, 1865–1900.* Chapel Hill: University of North Carolina Press, 2004.

Lovett, Richard. *The History of the London Missionary Society, 1795–1895.* 2 vols. London: H. Frowde, 1899.

Lowe, Lisa. *Critical Terrains: French and British Orientalisms.* Ithaca: Cornell University Press, 1991.

Ludlow, J. M., and Lloyd Jones. *Progress of the Working Class, 1832–1867.* 1867. Clifton, N.J.: Augustus M. Kelley, 1973.

Macaulay, Thomas Babington. "Lord Clive." In *Poetry and Prose.* Edited by G. M. Young, 306–73. Cambridge: Harvard University Press, 1970.

MacDougall, Hugh A. *Racial Myth in English History: Trojans, Teutons, and Anglo-Saxons.* Hanover: University Press of New England, 1982.

MacKenzie, John M. *Propaganda and Empire: The Manipulation of British Public Opinion, 1880–1960.* Manchester: Manchester University Press, 1984.

MacLean, Gerald. *Looking East: English Writing and the Ottoman Empire before 1800.* Houndmills: Palgrave Macmillan, 2007.

MacMaster, Neil. *Racism in Europe, 1870–2000.* New York: Palgrave, 2001.

Magnus, Philip. *Gladstone: A Biography.* New York: E. P. Dutton, 1964.

Magubane, Bernard M. *Race and the Construction of the Dispensable Other.* Pretoria: University of South Africa Press, 2007.

Magubane, Zine. *Bringing the Empire Home: Race, Class, and Gender in Britain and Colonial South Africa.* Chicago: University of Chicago Press, 2004.

Malchow, Howard. *Gothic Images of Race in Nineteenth-Century Britain.* Stanford: Stanford University Press, 1996.

Malik, Kenan. *The Meaning of Race: Race, History, and Culture in Western Society.* New York: New York University Press, 1996.

Mallett, Philip. *Rudyard Kipling: A Literary Life.* New York: Palgrave Macmillan, 2003.

Mally, Shawn. "'Time Hath No Power against Identity': Historical Continuity and Archaeological Adventure in H. Rider Haggard's *She.*" *English Literature in Transition, 1880–1920* 40, no. 3 (1997): 281.

Maning, Frederick Edward ("A Pakeha Maori"). *Old New Zealand: A Tale of the Good Old Times....* Christchurch, New Zealand: Whitcombe and Tombes, 1906.

Manne, Robert, ed. *Whitewash: On Keith Windschuttle's Fabrication of Aboriginal History.* Melbourne: Black, 2003.

Mannoni, Laurent. *The Great Art of Light and Shadow: Archaeology of the Cinema.* Exeter: University of Exeter Press, 2000.

Marcuse, Herbert. *One-Dimensional Man.* Boston: Beacon Press, 1964.

Maretu. *Cannibals and Converts: Radical Change in the Cook Islands.* Suva: University of the South Pacific, 1983.

Marks, George P. *The Black Press Views American Imperialism (1898–1900)*. New York: Arno Press, 1971.

Marriott, John. *The Other Empire: Metropolis, India and Progress in the Colonial Imagination*. Manchester: Manchester University Press, 2003.

Marsden, Ben, and Crosbie Smith. *Engineering Empires: A Cultural History of Technology in Nineteenth-Century Britain*. New York: Palgrave Macmillan, 2005.

Marsh, Joss, and Kamilla Elliott. "The Victorian Novel in Film and on Television." In *A Companion to the Victorian Novel*, edited by Patrick Brantlinger and William B. Thesing, 458–77. Oxford: Blackwell, 2002.

Marsh, Richard. *The Beetle*. Edited by Julian Wolfreys. Peterborough, Ont.: Broadview, 2004.

Marx, Karl, and Frederick Engels. "Manifesto of the Communist Party." In *The Marx-Engels Reader,* edited by Robert Tucker, 469–500. New York: Norton, 1978.

———. *Ireland and the Irish Question*. New York: International Publishers, 1972.

———. *On Colonialism*. New York: International Publishers, 1972.

Mayhew, Henry. *London Labour and the London Poor.* 4 vols. New York: Dover, 1968.

McBratney, John. *Imperial Subjects, Imperial Space: Rudyard Kipling's Fiction of the Native-Born*. Columbus: Ohio State University Press, 2002.

McCarthy, Thomas. *Race, Empire, and the Idea of Human Development*. Cambridge: Cambridge University Press, 2009.

McClintock, Anne. *Imperial Leather: Race, Gender, and Sexuality in the Colonial Contest*. New York: Routledge, 1995.

McClure, John. *Kipling and Conrad: The Colonial Fiction*. Cambridge: Harvard University Press, 1981.

McGregor, Russell. *Imagined Destinies: Aboriginal Australians and the Doomed Race Theory, 1880–1939*. Melbourne: Melbourne University Press, 1997.

McLean, Steven. *The Early Fiction of H. G. Wells: Fantasies of Science Fiction*. New York: Palgrave Macmillan, 2009.

Mellor, Anne K. "Frankenstein, Racial Science, and the Yellow Peril." *Nineteenth-Century Contexts* 23 (2001): 1–28.

Melman, Billie. *Women's Orients: English Women and the Middle East, 1718–1918*. Ann Arbor: University of Michigan Press, 1992.

Melville, Henry. *The Present State of Australia, Including New South Wales, Western Australia, South Australia, Victoria and New Zealand....* London: G. Willis, 1851.

Menke, Richard. *Telegraphic Realism: Victorian Fiction and Other Information Systems*. Stanford: Stanford University Press, 2008.

Metcalf, Thomas. *The Aftermath of Revolt: India, 1857–1870*. Princeton: Princeton University Press, 1964.

Meyer, Susan. *Imperialism at Home: Race and Victorian Women's Fiction*. Ithaca: Cornell University Press, 1996.

Miller, Richard W. "Social and Political Theory: Class, State, Revolution." In *The Cambridge Companion to Marx,* edited by Terrell Carver, 55–105. Cambridge: Cambridge University Press, 1991.

Miller, Stuart Creighton. *"Benevolent Assimilation": The American Conquest of the Philippines, 1899–1903*. New Haven: Yale University Press, 1982.

Mitford, Bertram. *The King's Assegai*. London: Chatto and Windus, 1894.

Monsman, Gerald. "Who Is Ayesha? An Allegory of Isis Unveiled." In *She: Explorations into a Romance,* edited by Tania Zulli, 15–35. Rome: Aracne, 2009.

Moore, Thomas. *Poetical Works.* London: Oxford University Press, 1929.

Morel, E. D. *The Black Man's Burden.* New York: B. W. Huebsch, 1920.

Morgan, H. Wayne. *William McKinley and His America.* Syracuse: Syracuse University Press, 1963.

Morgan, John. *The Life and Adventures of William Buckley: Thirty-two Years a Wanderer amongst the Aborigines of the Unexplored Country Round Port Philip.* Canberra: Australian National University Press, 1980.

Morgan, Kenneth, ed. *The Oxford History of Britain.* Rev. ed. Oxford: Oxford University Press, 1999.

Morrell, W. P. *Britain in the Pacific Islands.* Oxford: Oxford University Press, 1960.

Morus, Iwan Rhys. "The Electric Ariel: Telegraphy and Commercial Culture in Early Victorian England." *Victorian Studies* 39 (1996): 339–78.

Nagai, Kaori. *Empire of Analogies: Kipling, India and Ireland.* Cork: Cork University Press, 2006.

Nash, Geoffrey P. *From Empire to Orient: Travellers to the Middle East 1830–1926.* London: I. B. Tauris, 2005.

Nichols, John, ed. *Against the Beast: A Documentary History of American Opposition to Empire.* New York: Nation Books, 2004.

Nord, Deborah Epstein. "The Social Explorer as Anthropologist: Victorian Travellers among the Urban Poor." In *Visions of the Modern City: Essays in History, Art, and Literature,* edited by William Sharpe and Leonard Wallock, 122–34. Baltimore: Johns Hopkins University Press, 1987.

Nussbaum, Felicity. *The Limits of the Human: Fictions of Anomaly in the Long Eighteenth Century.* Cambridge: Cambridge University Press, 2003.

Nutting, Anthony. *Gordon of Khartoum: Martyr and Misfit.* New York: Clarkson N. Potter, 1966.

Obeyesekere, Gananath. *Cannibal Talk: The Man-Eating Myth and Human Sacrifice in the South Pacific.* Berkeley: University of California Press, 2005.

Orel, Harold, ed. *Critical Essays on Rudyard Kipling.* Boston: G. K. Hall, 1989.

——. *A Kipling Chronology.* Boston: G. K. Hall, 1990.

Osborne, Lawrence. "Does Man Eat Man? Inside the Great Cannibalism Controversy." *Lingua Franca* 7, no. 4 (1997): 28–38.

Owenson, Sydney (Lady Morgan). *The Wild Irish Girl: Two Irish National Tales.* Edited by James M. Smith. Boston: Houghton Mifflin, 2005.

Pagliaro, Harold E., ed. *Racism in the Eighteenth Century: Studies in Eighteenth-Century Culture.* Cleveland: Case Western Reserve University Press, 1973.

Panikkar, K. M. *Asia and Western Dominance: A Survey of the Vasco da Gama Epoch of Asian History, 1498–1945.* London: George Allen and Unwin, 1953.

Parry, Ann. *The Poetry of Rudyard Kipling.* Buckingham: Open University Press, 1992.

Patton, William. *The White Man's Burden.* London: Epworth Press, 1939.

Paul, Robert A. "Freud's Anthropology: A Reading of the 'Cultural Books.'" In *The Cambridge Companion to Freud,* edited by Jerome Neu, 267–86. Cambridge: Cambridge University Press, 1991.

Pearson, Richard. "Archaeology and Gothic Desire: Vitality beyond the Grave in H. Rider Haggard's Ancient Egypt." In *Victorian Gothic,* edited by Ruth Robbins and Julian Wolfreys, 218–44. New York: Palgrave, 2000.

Peating, Gary. "Race and Empire in Nineteenth-Century British Intellectual Life: James Fitzjames Stephen, James Anthony Froude, Ireland, and India." *Éire-Ireland* 42, nos. 1, 2 (Spring–Summer 2007): 157–79.

Pick, Daniel. *Faces of Degeneration: A European Disorder, c. 1848–c. 1918.* Cambridge: Cambridge University Press, 1989.

Pickering, Michael. "Consuming Doubts: What Some People Ate? Or What Some People Swallowed?" In *The Anthropology of Cannibalism,* edited by L. R. Goldman, 51–74. Westport, Conn.: Bergin and Garvey, 1999.

———. *Stereotyping: The Politics of Representation.* New York: Palgrave, 2001.

Pieterse, Jan Nederveen. *Empire and Emancipation: Power and Liberation on a World Scale.* London: Pluto Press, 1989.

———. *White on Black: Images of Africa and Blacks in Western Popular Culture.* New Haven: Yale University Press, 1992.

Pike, Luke Owen. *The English and Their Origin: A Prologue to Authentic English History.* London: Longmans, Green, 1866.

Plomley, N. J. B. Introduction to *Friendly Mission: The Tasmanian Journals and Papers of George Augustus Robinson, 1829–1834,* edited by Norman J. B. Plomley, 1–8. Hobart: Quintus Publishing, 2008.

Plowright, John. *The Routledge Dictionary of Modern British History.* London: Routledge, 2006.

Poliakov, Leon. "Racism from the Enlightenment to the Age of Imperialism." In *Racism and Colonialism,* edited by Robert Ross, 55–64. The Hague: N. Nijhoff, 1982.

Pomeroy, William J. *American Neo-colonialism: Its Emergence in the Philippines and Asia.* New York: International Publishers, 1970.

Porter, Andrew. "Introduction: Britain and the Empire in the Nineteenth Century." In *The Nineteenth Century.* Vol. 3 of *Oxford History of the British Empire.* Oxford: Oxford University Press, 1999.

Price, Richard. *Making Empire: Colonial Encounters and the Creation of Imperial Rule in Nineteenth-Century Africa.* Cambridge: Cambridge University Press, 2008.

Punter, David. *The Literature of Terror: A History of Gothic Fictions from 1765 to the Present Day.* London: Longman, 1980.

Pybus, Cassandra. "A Self-made Man." In *Reading Robinson: Companion Essays to Friendly Mission,* edited by Anna Johnston and Mitchell Rolls, 97–109. Hobart: Quintus Publishing, University of Tasmania, 2008.

Ragussis, Michael. *Figures of Conversion: "The Jewish Question" and English National Identity.* Durham: Duke University Press, 1995.

Randall, Donald. *Kipling's Imperial Boy: Adolescence and Cultural Hybridity.* New York: Palgrave, 2000.

Rattansi, Ali. *Racism: A Very Short Introduction.* Oxford: Oxford University Press, 2007.

Reade, Charles. *A Simpleton: A Story of the Day.* 1873. London: Chatto and Windus, n.d.

Renan, Ernest. *The Poetry of the Celtic Races, and Other Studies.* Translated by William Hutchison. London: Walter Scott, 1896.

Reynolds, Henry. *The Fate of a Free People.* Ringwood, Victoria: Penguin Australia, 1995.

———. "George Augustus Robinson in Van Diemen's Land: Race, Status and Religion." In *Reading Robinson: Companion Essays to Friendly Mission,* edited by Anna Johnston and Mitchell Rolls, 161–69. Hobart: Quintus Publishing, University of Tasmania, 2008.

———. *An Indelible Stain? The Question of Genocide in Australia's History.* Ringwood, Victoria: Viking Penguin, 2001.

———. *The Law of the Land.* Ringwood, Victoria: Penguin Australia, 1992.

———. *Nowhere People: How International Race Thinking Shaped Australia's Identity.* New York: Viking, 2005.

Rice, Edward. *Captain Sir Richard Francis Burton.* New York: Charles Scribner's, 1990.

Rich, Paul B. *Race and Empire in British Politics.* Cambridge: Cambridge University Press, 1986.

Richards, Thomas. *The Imperial Archive: Knowledge and the Fantasy of Empire.* London: Verso, 1993.

Richmond, Charles. "Disraeli's Education." In *The Self-fashioning of Disraeli, 1818–1851,* edited by Charles Richmond and Paul Smith, 16–41. Cambridge: Cambridge University Press, 1998.

Richmond, Charles, and Paul Smith, eds. *The Self-fashioning of Disraeli, 1818–1851.* Cambridge: Cambridge University Press, 1998.

Riley, B. F. *The White Man's Burden: A Discussion of the Interracial Question with Special Reference to the Responsibility of the White Race to the Negro Problem.* 1910. New York: Negro Universities Press, 1969.

Robbins, Keith. *Nineteenth-Century Britain: Integration and Diversity.* Oxford: Clarendon Press, 1988.

Robinson, Albert G. *The Philippines: The War and the People.* New York: McClure, Phillips, 1901.

Robinson, George Augustus. *Friendly Mission: The Tasmanian Journals and Papers of George Augustus Robinson, 1829–1834.* Edited by Norman J. B. Plomley. Hobart: Quintus Publishing, 2008.

Robinson, Ronald, and John Gallagher, with Alice Denny. *Africa and the Victorians.* New York: St. Martin's, 1961.

Robson, Lloyd. *A History of Tasmania.* Vol. 1. *Van Diemen's Land from the Earliest Times to 1855.* Melbourne: Oxford University Press, 1983.

Roediger, David R. *The Wages of Whiteness: Race and the Making of the American Working Class.* London: Verso, 1991.

Roosevelt, Theodore. *Letters and Speeches.* Edited by Louis Auchinloss. New York: Library of America, 2004.

———. *Presidential Addresses and State Papers.* 2 vols. New York: Review of Reviews, n.d.

Roth, Cecil. *Benjamin Disraeli, Earl of Beaconsfield.* New York, 1952.

Roth, H. Ling. *The Aborigines of Tasmania.* 1890. Halifax: F. King, 1899.

Roth, Russell. *Muddy Glory: America's "Indian Wars" in the Philippines, 1899–1935.* W. Hanover, Mass.: Christopher Publishing House, 1981.

Rushdie, Salman. *Imaginary Homelands: Essays and Criticism, 1981–1991.* London: Penguin, 1992.

Ruskin, John. *The Genius of John Ruskin: Selections from His Writings.* Edited by John Rosenberg. Boston: Houghton Mifflin, 1963.

Ryan, Lyndall. *The Aboriginal Tasmanians.* Vancouver: University of British Columbia Press, 1981.

Saab, Ann Pottinger. "Disraeli, Judaism, and the Eastern Question." *International History Review* 10, no. 4 (November 1988): 559–78.

Sahlins, Marshall. "Artificially Maintained Controversies: Global Warming and Fijian Cannibalism." *Anthropology Today* 19, no. 3 (June 2003): 3–6, and 19, no. 6 (December 2003): 21–23.

———. *Islands of History.* Chicago: University of Chicago Press, 1985.

Said, Edward. *Covering Islam.* New York: Pantheon Books, 1981.

———. *Culture and Imperialism.* New York: Alfred A. Knopf, 1993.

———. *Orientalism.* New York: Random House, 1978.

St. John, Spenser. *The Life of Sir James Brooke, Rajah of Sarawak.* Edinburgh: William Blackwood and Sons, 1879.

Samson, Jane. "Ethnology and Theology: Nineteenth-Century Mission Dilemmas in the South Pacific." In *Christian Missions and the Enlightenment,* edited by Brian Stanley, 99–122. Grand Rapids: W. B. Eerdmans, 2001.

———. *Race and Empire.* Harlow, U.K.: Pearson Education, 2005.

Sanday, Peggy R. *Divine Hunger: Cannibalism as a Cultural System.* Cambridge: Cambridge University Press, 1986.

Scarr, Deryck. *Fiji: A Short History.* Sydney: George Allen and Unwin, 1984.

Schaffer, Kay. *In the Wake of First Contact: The Eliza Fraser Stories.* Cambridge: Cambridge University Press, 1995.

Schütz, A. J. Introduction to *The Diaries and Correspondence of David Cargill.* Edited by A. J. Schütz, 1–9. Canberra: Australian National University Press, 1977.

Sconce, Jeffrey. *Haunted Media: Electronic Presence from Telegraphy to Television.* Durham: Duke University Press, 2000.

Scott, Sir Walter. *The Lay of the Last Minstrel: A Poem.* London: Longman, Hurst, Rees, and Orme, 1805.

Seeman, Berthold. *Viti: An Account of a Government Mission to the Vitian or Fijian Islands, 1860–1861.* New York: Barnes and Noble, 1973.

Semmel, Bernard. *Democracy versus Empire: The Jamaica Riots of 1865 and the Governor Eyre Controversy.* Garden City: Doubleday Anchor, 1965.

Senf, Carol A. *Science and Social Science in Bram Stoker's Fiction.* Westport: Greenwood, 2002.

Shannon, Richard T. *Gladstone and the Bulgarian Agitation, 1876.* London: Thomas Nelson and Sons, 1963.

Shaw, R. D. "Three-Day Visitors: The Samo Response to Colonialism in Western Province, Papua New Guinea." In *Colonial New Guinea: Anthropological Perspectives,* edited by N. M. McPherson, 171–93. Pittsburgh: University of Pittsburgh Press, 2001.

Shelley, Mary. *Frankenstein*. New York: Norton, 1996.

Sherry, Norman. *Conrad's Eastern World*. Cambridge: Cambridge University Press, 1966.

Slotkin, Richard. *Gunfighter Nation: The Myth of the Frontier in Twentieth-Century America*. Norman: University of Oklahoma Press, 1998.

Smiles, Samuel. *Self-Help*. 1859. Sphere, London: 1968.

Smith, Francis B. *The Making of the Second Reform Bill*. Cambridge: Cambridge University Press, 1966.

Smith, Paul. Introduction to *The Self-fashioning of Disraeli, 1818–1851*, edited by Charles Richmond and Paul Smith, 1–15. Cambridge: Cambridge University Press, 1998.

Smith, Ruth. *White Man's Burden: A Personal Statement*. New York: Vanguard Press, 1946.

Spivak, Gayatri Chakravorty. "Can the Subaltern Speak?" In *Marxism and the Interpretation of Culture,* edited by Cary Nelson and Lawrence Grossberg, 271–313. Urbana: University of Illinois Press, 1988.

——. "Three Women's Texts and a Critique of Imperialism." In *"Race," Writing, and Difference,* edited by Henry Louis Gates Jr., 262–80. Chicago: University of Chicago Press, 1986.

Sprinker, Michael, ed. *Edward Said: A Critical Reader*. Oxford: Oxford University Press, 1992.

Stallybrass, Peter, and Allon White. *The Politics and Poetics of Transgression*. Ithaca: Cornell University Press, 1986.

Stanley, Peter W. *A Nation in the Making: The Philippines and the United States, 1899–1921*. Cambridge: Harvard University Press, 1974.

Stanner, W. E. H. *White Man Got No Dreaming: Essays, 1938–1973*. Canberra: Australian National University Press, 1979.

Stedman Jones, Gareth. *Outcast London: A Study in the Relationship between Classes in Victorian London*. Oxford: Clarendon Press, 1971.

Stepan, Nancy. *The Idea of Race in Science: Great Britain, 1800–1960*. Hamden, Conn.: Archon Books, 1982.

Stevenson, Robert Louis. *South Sea Tales*. Edited by Roslyn Jolly. Oxford: Oxford World Classics, 1996.

Stocking, George. *Victorian Anthropology*. New York: Free Press, 1987.

Stockwell, Sarah, ed. *The British Empire: Themes and Perspectives*. Oxford: Blackwell, 2008.

Stoker, Bram. *Dracula*. Edited by Nina Auerbach and David J. Skal. New York: Norton, 1997.

——. *The Jewel of Seven Stars*. London: Penguin, 2008.

Storey, Moorfield, and Marcial P. Lichauco. *The Conquest of the Philippines by the United States, 1898–1925*. New York: G. P. Putnam, 1926.

Strachey, Lytton. *Eminent Victorians*. London: Bloomsbury, 1988.

Sullivan, Zoreh. *Narratives of Empire: The Fictions of Rudyard Kipling*. Cambridge: Cambridge University Press, 1993.

Sussman, Herbert. *Victorians and the Machine: The Literary Response to Technology.* Cambridge: Harvard University Press, 1968.

Suvin, Darko. *Victorian Science Fiction in the UK: The Discourses of Knowledge and of Power.* Boston: G. K. Hall, 1983.

Ta'unga. *The Works of Ta'unga: Records of a Polynesian Traveller in the South Seas, 1833–1896.* Canberra: Australian National University Press, 1968.

Taylor, Philip Meadows. *Confessions of a Thug.* Oxford: Oxford University Press, 1998.

Tennyson, Alfred. *The Poems of Tennyson.* Edited by Christopher Ricks. London: Longman, 1969.

Thackeray, William Makepeace. *The Irish Sketchbook, 1842.* Belfast: Blackstaff Press, 1985.

Theroux, Paul. *White Man's Burden: A Play in Two Acts.* London: Hamish Hamilton, 1987.

Thomas, Nicholas. *Out of Time: History and Evolution in Anthropological Discourse.* Cambridge: Cambridge University Press, 1989.

Thorp, Daniel. "Going Native in New Zealand and America: Comparing Pakeha Maori and White Indians." *Journal of Imperial and Commonwealth History* 31, no. 3 (September 2003): 1–23.

Thurschwell, Pamela. *Literature, Technology and Magical Thinking, 1880–1920.* Cambridge: Cambridge University Press, 2001.

Tidrick, Kathryn. *Empire and the English Character.* London: I. B. Tauris, 1990.

——. *Heart-Beguiling Araby.* Cambridge: Cambridge University Press, 1981.

Tippett, Alan R. *Aspects of Pacific Ethnohistory.* South Pasadena: William Carey Library, 1973.

Todorov, Tzvetan. *The Conquest of America: The Question of the Other.* New York: Harper Collins, 1984.

Tracy, Roger Sherman. *The White Man's Burden: A Satirical Forecast.* Boston: Gorham Press, 1915.

Travers, Peter. "White Man's Burden." *Rolling Stone,* December 14, 1995, 92.

Trevelyan, G. M. "The White Peril." *Nineteenth Century* 50 (December 1901): 1043–55.

Trilling, Lionel. *Matthew Arnold.* 1939. Cleveland: Meridian Books, 1963.

Trollope, Anthony. *Castle Richmond.* Oxford: Oxford University Press, 1989.

Trumpener, Katie. *Bardic Nationalism: The Romantic Novel and the British Empire.* Princeton: Princeton University Press, 1997.

[Tucker, James.] *Adventures of an Outlaw: The Memoirs of Ralph Rashleigh, A Penal Exile in Australia, 1825–1844.* 1845. New York: Jonathan Cape and Harrison Smith, 1929.

Turner, Rev. George. *Samoa a Hundred Years Ago, and Long Before.* London: Macmillan, 1884.

Twain, Mark. *Mark Twain's Weapons of Satire: Anti-imperialist Writings on the Philippine-American War.* Edited by Jim Zwick. Syracuse: Syracuse University Press, 1992.

Tylor, Edward Burnett. *Primitive Culture.* 1871. 2 vols. New York: Harper and Row, 1970.

Valls, Andrew, ed. *Race and Racism in Modern Philosophy.* Ithaca: Cornell University Press, 2005.

Vereté, Mayir. "The Idea of the Restoration of the Jews in English Protestant Thought." In *From Palmerston to Balfour: Collected Essays of Mayir Vereté,* edited by Norman Rose, 78–140. London: Routledge, 1992.

Vincent, John. *Disraeli.* Oxford: Oxford University Press, 1990.

Viswanathan, Gauri. *Outside the Fold: Conversion, Modernity, and Belief.* Princeton: Princeton University Press, 1998.

Wallis, Mary. *Life in Feejee, or Five Years among the Cannibals.* Boston: William Heath, 1851.

Walmsley, Hugh. *The Ruined Cities of Zululand.* London: Chapman and Hall, 1869.

Waterhouse, Rev. Joseph. *The King and People of Fiji: Containing a Life of Thakombau; with Notices of the Fijians, Their Manners, Customs, and Superstitions, Previous to the Great Religious Reformation in 1854.* London: Wesleyan Conference Office, 1865.

Watt, Ian. *Conrad in the Nineteenth Century.* Berkeley: University of California Press, 1979.

Watts, Phillips. *The Wild Tribes of London.* London: Ward and Lock, 1855.

Weir, Christine. "Fiji and the Fijians: Two Modes of Missionary Discourse." *Journal of Religious History* 22, no. 2 (1998): 152–67.

Welch, Richard E., Jr. *Response to Imperialism: The United States and the Philippine-American War, 1899–1902.* Chapel Hill: University of North Carolina Press, 1979.

Wells, H. G. *Anticipations of the Reaction of Mechanical and Scientific Progress on Human Life and Thought.* New York: Harper, 1902.

——. *The Complete Short Stories.* New York: St. Martin's Press, 1987.

——. *The First Men in the Moon.* Edited by Leon Stover. Jefferson, N.C.: McFarland, 1998.

——. *The Time Machine: An Invention.* Peterborough, Ont.: Broadview, 2001.

——. *The War of the Worlds.* Peterborough, Ont.: Broadview, 2003.

——. *When the Sleeper Wakes.* New York: Modern Library, 2003.

Welsh, Alexander. *George Eliot and Blackmail.* Cambridge: Harvard University Press, 1985.

West, Shearer, ed. *The Victorians and Race.* Brookfield, Vt.: Ashgate, 1996.

Wheatcroft, Andrew. *The Ottomans.* London: Viking Penguin, 1993.

Wheatcroft, Geoffrey. "A White Man's Burden: Rudyard Kipling's Pathos and Pre-science." *Harper's Magazine* 305, no. 1828 (September 2002): 81–84.

Wheeler, Roxann. *The Complexion of Race: Categories of Difference in Eighteenth-Century British Culture.* Philadelphia: University of Pennsylvania Press, 2000.

White, Tim D. *Prehistoric Cannibalism at Mancos.* Princeton: Princeton University Press, 1992.

Wicke, Jennifer. "Vampiric Typewriting: *Dracula* and Its Media." *English Literary History* 59 (1992): 467–93.

Wilkins, William H. *The Romance of Isabel Burton.* London: Hutchinson, 1898.

Williams, Rev. John. *A Narrative of Missionary Enterprises in the South Sea Islands....* London: Snow, 1838.

Williams, Rev. Thomas. *Fiji and the Fijians.* Part 1. *The Islands and Their Inhabitants.* New York: D. Appleton, 1859.

Williams, Raymond. "Welsh Culture." In *Resources of Hope,* 99–104. London: Verso, 1989.

Wilmot, Alexander. *Monomotapa (Rhodesia): Its Monuments, and Its History from the Most Ancient Times to the Present Century.* 1896. New York: Negro University Press, 1969.

Wilson, Angus. *The Strange Ride of Rudyard Kipling: His Life and Works.* London: Secker and Warburg, 1977.

Wilson, Edmund. "The Kipling That Nobody Read." In *The Wound and the Bow: Seven Studies in Literature,* 86–147. New York: Oxford University Press, 1947.

Wilson, Kathleen. *The Island Race: Englishness, Empire and Gender in the Eighteenth Century.* London: Routledge, 2003.

Windschuttle, Keith. *The Fabrication of Aboriginal History.* Vol. 1. *Van Diemen's Land, 1803–1947.* Sydney: Macleay Press, 2002.

Winstone, H. V. F. *Lady Anne Blunt: A Biography.* London: Barzan Publishing, 2003.

Winthrop-Young, Geoffrey. "Undead Networks: Information Processing and Media Boundary Conflicts in *Dracula.*" In *Literature and Science,* edited by Donald Bruce and Anthony Purdy, 107–29. Atlanta: Rodopi, 1994.

Winthrop-Young, Geoffrey, and Michael Wutz. Translator's Introduction to Friedrich Kittler, *Gramophone, Film, Typewriter,* xi–xli. Stanford: Stanford University Press, 1999.

Wohl, Anthony S. *The Eternal Slum: Housing and Social Policy in Victorian London.* London: Edward Arnold, 1977.

Wolff, Leon. *Little Brown Brother: How the United States Purchased and Pacified the Philippine Islands at the Century's Turn.* Garden City, N.Y.: Doubleday, 1961.

Wood, Marcus. *Slavery, Empathy, and Pornography.* Oxford: Oxford University Press, 2003.

Wortham, John David. *The Genesis of British Egyptology, 1549–1906.* Norman: University of Oklahoma Press, 1971.

Wright, Thomas. *Our New Masters.* New York: A. M. Kelley, 1969.

Wylie, Dan. *Savage Delight: White Myths of Shaka.* Pietermaritzburg: University of Natal Press, 2000.

Yeats, William Butler. "The Celtic Element in Literature." In *Essays and Introductions,* 173–88. New York: Collier Books, 1968.

———. *The Celtic Twilight, and a Selection of Early Poems.* New York: Signet Classics, 1962.

Young, Robert. *Colonial Desire: Hybridity in Theory, Culture, and Race.* New York: Routledge, 1995.

Zulli, Tania, ed. *She: Explorations into a Romance.* Rome: Aracne, 2009.

Zwick, Jim. "Anti-imperialism." http://www.boondocksnet.com.

INDEX

147, 151, 170–171, 175, 195–196, 199–201, 212–213, 224. *See also* Vampirism
Capécia, Mayotte, 17–18
Čapek, Karl, 202
Cargill, Rev. David, 36–37
Caribs, 31, 130
Carlyle, Thomas, 9, 97, 108, 119, 126, 128, 131, 140, 142, 146, 153, 192
Carnegie, Andrew, 207
Carter, Howard, 160
Caucasian race, 6, 91, 100, 106, 114, 115, 144
Celticism, Celtic race, 22, 84, 117, 134, 135, 136–156. *See also* Celtic revivals; Irish
Celtic revivals, 144–145, 150–156
Champollion, Jean-François, 162
Charnock, Job, 72
Chartism, 111, 142
Chimpanzees, 2, 30, 112, 116. *See also* Apes
China, 76, 82, 116, 125
Chinese, 125, 190, 207
Christianity, 8, 19, 20, 21, 30, 34, 38, 40, 41, 43, 47, 48, 52, 54, 65, 66, 72, 103, 104, 106, 107, 121, 128, 130, 140, 181, 209–210. *See also* Bible; Missionaries; Protestantism; Roman Catholicism
Church Missionary Society, 67
Civilizing mission, 2, 7–8, 18–19, 52, 53, 54, 65, 74, 79, 80, 85, 114, 130, 139–140, 168, 188, 203–222. *See also* Missionaries
Civil War. *See* American Civil War
Class, 11, 16, 21, 22, 68, 73, 78, 111–135, 187–196
Clive, Robert, 73
Coleridge, Samuel Taylor, 5–6
Colonialism. *See* Imperialism
Congo, 67–68
Conrad, Joseph, 1, 30, 67–68, 73, 79, 80–81, 84–85, 171
Cook, Captain James, 31, 32, 33, 36
Craniology, 55, 57, 58, 60, 116, 117
Crèvecouer, Hector St. John, 69
Crimean War, 88, 129
Criminology, 129
Cromer, Lord, 8–9, 182
Cuba, 206, 209, 214

Darwin, Charles, 2, 5, 20, 21, 31, 46, 48–49, 54, 55, 78, 79, 84, 114, 116, 117, 118, 127–129, 132–133, 139, 194
Davies, Rev. John, 35–36

Davis, Thomas, 150, 152
Defoe, Daniel, 2–4, 14, 17, 18, 70–71
Degeneration, 2, 5–6, 22, 23, 67, 79–80, 113, 127–135, 166, 168, 181, 187–188, 193, 199, 201–202, 212. *See also* Evolution; Going native
De Quincey, Thomas, 6, 93, 181
Dewey, Admiral, 207
Dicey, A. V., 221
Dickens, Charles, 9, 66, 78, 84, 126, 193, 196, 223
Dilke, Charles, 80, 119
Dillon, Peter, 32–33
Disraeli, Benjamin, 21, 87–108, 112, 114, 131, 144, 196, 213
Disraeli, Isaac, 89, 90
Dixon, Thomas, 217
Doyle, Sir Arthur, 180
Dry, Sir Richard, 58
Dryden, John, 3
Du Bois, W. E. B., 215–216
Duffy, Charles Gavan, 153
Dutch empire, 11, 16, 82
Dyaks, 74–75

Eastern Association, 108
East India Company, 74–75
Ebers, Georg, 160
Edwards, Amelia, 160, 172
Egypt, 9, 22, 84, 88, 92, 106, 108, 160–166, 168, 171–179, 180–182, 191–192, 196, 210, 211
Egypt Exploration Society, 160
Egyptology, 160, 163, 172, 176, 180
Eliot, George, 23, 84, 186, 194
Eliot, T. S., 202, 205
Emigration, 1, 10, 23, 71, 131, 132, 185, 205, 207
Endicott, William, 32, 33
Engels, Friedrich, 111, 131, 138, 149, 192–193, 195
Enlightenment, 3–5, 94, 117, 213
Entropy, 187–188
Ethnological Society, 115
Eugenics, 22, 80, 128–131, 139, 186–187, 190–191, 193
Evolution, 5, 20, 22, 31, 55, 57, 78, 79, 84–85, 112, 114–118, 124, 127–135, 182–202. *See also* Degeneration; Eugenics; Social Darwinism
Eyre, Edward, 9, 21, 112, 115

www.ingramcontent.com/pod-product-compliance
Ingram Content Group UK Ltd.
Pitfield, Milton Keynes, MK11 3LW, UK
UKHW041038130325
456188UK00002B/87